DATE DUE

APR 1 3 1994	

International Organizations, Constitutional Law, and Human Rights

International Organizations, Constitutional Law, and Human Rights

John S. Gibson

New York
Westport, Connecticut
London

Library of Congress Cataloging-in-Publication Data

Gibson, John S.
　　International organizations, constitutional law, and human rights /
John S. Gibson.
　　　p.　cm.
　　Includes bibliographical references and index.
　　ISBN 0–275–93359–8 (alk. paper)
　　1. International organization.　2. Human rights.　I. Title.
JX1954.G53　　　1991
341.2—dc20　　　90–24508

British Library Cataloguing in Publication Data is available.

Library of Congress Catalog Card Number: 90–24508
ISBN: 0–275–93359–8

First published in 1991

Praeger Publishers, One Madison Avenue, New York, NY 10010
An imprint of Greenwood Publishing Group, Inc.

Printed in the United States of America

The paper used in this book complies with the
Permanent Paper Standard issued by the National
Information Standards Organization (Z39.48–1984).

10 9 8 7 6 5 4 3 2 1

For Ede, with love

CONTENTS

PREFACE

With each passing year, international organizations such as the United Nations and the World Health Organization become more essential to serving the vital requirements of states and state goals of security and well-being for their central interests, especially their people. Organizations at one level serve the needs of their members and at a higher level "harmonize the action of nations" in the pursuit of common goals in the finely crafted words of Article 1 of the U.N. Charter and constitution. Beyond, organizations have been given authority by their members to function as independent legal actors in the pursuit of shared security and shared and progressive well-being as set forth in the goals of the organizations in their constitutions. We still reside on this small planet in a interactive system of sovereign states. Increasingly, however, the state, whether large or small, powerful or weak, is confronted with problems and challenges and with requirements for its goals of security and well-being that are incapable of solution by proud sovereign policy.

Down through the ages, political communities—now states—have had to shape rules and then organizations to facilitate the necessary relations and transactions between and among each other in a positive manner to enhance cooperation and on the other side of the coin to prevent collisions, confrontation, and conflict. There have always been states that see in confrontation and conflict the desirable option for enhanced security and well-being, however defined. But the march has been toward more effective international laws and organizations to reduce options for confrontation and conflict and, in a more positive sense, to enhance through law any organization the pursuit of security and well-being. That march has made remarkable progress since the end of World War II and, in spite of sideshows and detours, it remains a vital progression toward international constitutional law for shared security and well-being for states and people. This book seeks to record that progression and its meaning for our times and beyond.

International organizations are established by international treaties, the prime source of international law. The founding treaties, such as the Charter of the United Nations, are also international constitutions that provide for a legal order to confirm and advance the goals their authors have articulated in the organization's constitution.[1] A treaty may be a covenant (League of Nations), statute (International Court of Justice), convention (United Nations Conventions on Human Rights), or a charter (United Nations), among other authoritative and legal terms. It may also be a constitution, such as the founding treaty for the International Labor Organization; the Food and Agricultural Organization; the United Nations Scientific, Educational, and Cultural Organization; or the World Health Organization. A treaty by whatever name also becomes a constitution if and when it is clear that the founding states intend it to be an international organization both to serve the interests of its members and to be an independent legal authority with powers of its own. The law of the organization is thus international constitutional law, which is the core of our present study.[2]

As we survey the landscape of international relations since the end of World War II in 1945, the world we know today was only a vague shadow on the horizon when the U.N. Charter was signed in San Francisco on June 26, 1945. That was a day that knew of no forthcoming cold war, the nuclear era, the forthcoming explosion of new states from the ashes of colonialism, or the decentralization of the economics of the international marketplace. Contemporary global villains such as acid rain and AIDS penetrating the sovereign domains of states and ignorant of boundaries or passports were unknown. Since that day in 1945, however, international organizations grounded in the idealism of statesmen and philosophers of the past as well as earlier organizations have generated new international law and, indeed, new international organizations as well and have presented us in our times with structures and tools for global shared security and well-being.

But the reality of our times is the challenge to utilize those structures and tools in the further progression of international constitutional law in the face of people, groups, and states who have an agenda of the pursuit of security and well-being on their own terms. The reach of international constitutional law is short if there are those who seek to advance a law of their own, if that is the correct term. The so-called realist points to international wars and violence as a repudiation of international law. But there is crime and violence in all of our nations that repudiate national, state, and local law. Violence and crime at any national or international level must be confronted not by cynical and benign acceptance of its reality but rather to reverse their incidence through mobilization of will and construction of law toward shared security and shared and progressive well-being.

We emphasize this imperative in the second part of our study in the selection of international human rights law as a significant component of the more broad international constitutional law. Generated by international organizations and especially the United Nations, international human rights law seeks to advance shared and progressive well-being for people everywhere in the protection and enhancement of their human rights and fundamental freedoms. Progression toward solid human rights law and means of state compliance to that law has been extraordinarily impressive since 1945. But this takes place in a world and in nations still plagued by the violence of international and civil war and other patterns of violence such as that which surrounds traffic in drugs. The historic confrontation between the pursuit of security, however defined, and the need for human and national well-being, too often gives harsh priority to the former over the latter, especially in the domain of protection of human rights. But this reality has only encouraged those in and out of governments to advance protection through international human rights law and the means to make that law effective. Such is the task before us and the goal of our study.

We turn first in Part 1 of our study to the historic processes of political communities relating to each other and then developing patterns of mutual reliance essential for their requirements for security and well-being. Progression of the law of the sea and of diplomacy provide modest case studies of the march from political independence to relating and relations and then to international law to provide stability and predictibility to necessary relations and transactions. The cycle of invention and discovery and new events leads to the necessity of law and organization, and that cycle never ends.

We observe in Chapter 2 how these historic patterns take a more concrete form in the evolution and progression toward maturity of organizations down to the era of the United Nations in 1945. We then proceed in Chapter 3 to examine the U.N. era to the early 1990s in the context of international constitutional law and organizing for shared security and shared and progressive well-being during the changing tides of international history in the second half of the twentieth century.

In Chapter 4, we draw upon the U.N. Charter, the constitutions of other international organizations, and important international treaties to document the prime goals of the totality of international constitutional law, shared security, and shared and progressive well-being. These goals are not derived from the studies of scholars but rather from the specific words of constitutions and treaties used as primary resources for confirming these goals. We then employ the same methodology to define organizations' means to goals through friendly relations, exchanges of resources, valued conditions, commitments to pursue the goals, and then transactions and exchanges in the international marketplace. Finally, we derive from the organizations' goals of shared security and well-being the essential goals of states of their own security and well-being and how those goals and their requirements are determined.

In Chapter 5, we study the spectrum from high state authority over its goals and policies, to supra-organization authority and state delegation to some organizations to determine shared security and shared and progressive well-being for states delegating such authority. Two positions between these high state determination of its security and well-being and supra-organization authority are partnership between state and organization and high organization authority. We provide abundant rationales and examples of these four positions from state to supra-authority but also observe that the trend has been and continues to be an erosion of high state authority.

This is, of course, the heart of our study. In September 1961, the same month he met his tragic death on duty with the United Nations, Secretary General Dag Hammarskjold presented his annual report to the General Assembly. His introduction concentrated on the dualism of high state authority as viewed by some nations, and partnership and especially high organization authority, which clearly was his preference.

The first concept can refer to history and to the traditions of national policies of the past. The second can point to the needs of the present and of the future in a world of ever closer international interdependence where nations have at their disposal armaments of hitherto unknown destructive strength. The first [high state authority] is firmly anchored in the time-honored philosophy of sovereign national states in armed competition of which the most that may be expected in the international field is that they achieve a peaceful coexistence. The second one [organization authority] envisages possibilities of intergovernmental action overriding such a philosophy, and opens the road toward more developed and increasingly effective forms of constructive international cooperation.

He then called on members "to make their choice and decide the direction in which they wish the Organization to develop." He amplified on this dualism in his introduction—thirty years ago.

Finally, in Chapter 5, we derive from organizations' goals of shared security and well-being the basic goals of security and well-being for their central interests by states, however they may define those goals. Partnership, high organization authority, and certainly supra-organization authority require a blending between and among states in moving from their unilateral goals of security and well-being to higher levels of shared security and well-being. The development of the European Community from its beginnings in 1958 to its new supra-organization authority by January 1, 1993, is a clear case in point.

Part 2 is an in-depth case study of bringing together the themes and progression of international constitutional law in Part 1 in a study of international human rights law. We return to the historical evolution of patterns and needs of mutuality as we trace in Chapter 6 human rights from origins in religions and philosophy to norms of "rights" over thousands of years. We then see the basic standards articulated for the first time in the 1948 U.N. Universal Declaration of Human Rights. Based on the U.N. Charter's encouragement of the "progressive development of international law and its codification" in Article 13 and the authority of the Economic and Social Council to "prepare draft conventions for submission to the General Assembly," we appraise the norms and standards moving on into international human rights law with the two U.N. Covenants on Human Rights of 1966.

Chapter 7 studies the role of the state as the key participant in international organization and law. The structure and processes for policy in international organizations are examined, with special emphasis on U.S. government agencies and policy formulation in the area of international human rights. We then move on to the mission of the state at the location of the international organization, and then to the U.S. mission to international organizations in Geneva for participation in the U.N. Commission on Human Rights. Finally, the delegation of the state to the assembly of members of the organization is appraised, as is the U.S. delegation to the Commission on Human Rights.

Chapter 8 concludes the study with the major attributes of the organization on the basis of state policy and participation. The assembly we study is the fifty-three–member Commission on Human Rights, how it evolved, and how it functions in fairly new areas of international law, such as international legislation and procedural law. In the progression toward high organization authority and thus international constitutional law, we find that an assembly is authorized to develop new treaties, which then generate new international law and treaty bodies or organizations themselves to gain compliance by states ratifying treaties to the provisions to which they commit themselves, the ever growing body of international treaty law in human rights.[3]

Administration of international organizations is then studied with particular emphasis on the U.N. Centre for Human Rights, where the international administrative law for human rights implements commission decisions. The history of the centre proceeds from the early offices in the U.N. secretariat to the contemporary centre in Geneva, which is organized to service and administer many responsibilities delegated to it, especially the management of the annual six week session of the commission. We study in depth the rapidly evolving area of international due process law for those alleged to be victims of violations of human rights by states, and then we study modes of compliance and international judicial review. Again we explore the contention between the claim of high state authority over human rights law against the claim of high organization authority to ensure protection of rights to enhance shared and progressive human well-being. The chapter concludes with a brief survey of productivity, or outputs, of organizations, the beneficiaries of that productivity, and then the annual cycle and loops as states and organizations move on to the next year.

It is the author's hope that scholars and students will draw upon the chapters in Part 2 to develop their own case studies of many other organizations, including their history, role of the state, and role of the organization as set forth in Chapters 6, 7, and 8. Groups of human rights organizations, such as those under the European and Inter-American Conventions on Human Rights, would provide valuable comparative analysis of international legislations, administration, due process and compliance in international human rights law. Economic organizations, such as the General Agreement on Tariffs and Trade, the International

Monetary Fund, and the World Bank, would stand as important studies on their own and also in comparison to human rights organizations in the areas of state compliance. Comparative studies of intergovernmental agencies, such as the World Health Organization in providing services toward enhanced shared and progressive well-being and the International Atomic Energy Agency and the International Civil Aviation Organization in regulatory activity and high organization authority, would provide valuable insights into what organizations actually can and cannot do at any level of authority. This study was undertaken with the goal of broadening interest in and adding more depth to understanding international organizations and also to serve as a tool for students—in particular to engage in comparative and innovative studies about international organizations, their goals, and means to goals. In this vein, it was designed to emphasize Brooks Adams' reflection that "they know enough who know how to learn."

Students of today will live in an increasingly complex world of tomorrow and with the continuing need for international organizations that must progressively deal with an ever interdependent world of nations. Gaining a better knowledge of international organizations will help students of today to better serve their citizen obligations tomorrow; they will recognize the need for more and better international institutions that can serve states in ways states increasingly cannot provide for themselves. Of great importance is the extensive variety of nongovernmental institutions, which offer many means of participation by citizens from all walks of life. This is particularly the case with human rights nongovernmental organizations.

There is a strong strain of idealism in this book, which reflects the author's training, teaching, writing, and working in the real world of international organizations. But without ideals, reality can be quite brutal. All international organizations have in their constitutional charters an abundance of ideals. As we work in these institutions, we can observe representatives of states and international civil servants realistically pursuing the ideals. The Great Creator of any faith placed stars in the heavens for an obvious reason. In the words of perhaps one of the greatest international civil servants, Sir Brian Urquhart, who managed the Nobel-prize winning U.N. peacekeeping organization for so many years, "The United Nations may not get you into heaven, but it certainly can save you from hell."

This is a study of the progression of international law, international constitutional law, and especially international human rights law—with emphasis on the past forty-five years. We are abundantly aware of many places on our small planet that are afflicted by violations and deprivations of the human physical and moral being and of the reality that essential civil, political, economic, social, and cultural rights in the law of the two principal U.N. conventions are only ideals for so many of our fellow humans. Tribal mayhem in the Republic of South Africa, religious and ethnic violence in Sri Lanka, forty-two nations with an average income of less than $200 a year, death by starvation in the Sudan, and the crisis affecting so many in the Middle East, especially as a result of the

Gulf War, are realities as we write these words. The remedy lies in large part in leadership by the advantaged nations to bring about—through international organizations and law—an end to threats and uses of force and an increase of measures of economic and social justice for greater equity among all human kind.

On the other side of the coin is the vast enhancement of human rights realized in the Soviet Union, the formerly socialist Eastern European states, and in southern Africa, especially in the Republic of South Africa and the new nation of Namibia. Two quotes by President Mikhail Gorbachev headline the momentous changes from decadent communism to basic freedoms for hundreds of millions behind the fallen "iron curtain." "It is time to recognize that the world today does not consist of two mutually exclusive civilizations . . . it is one common civilization in which human values and freedom of choice have primacy." And, "respect for the peoples' national, state, spiritual and cultural identity is an indispensible condition for . . . a new period of peace."

In the Republic of South Africa, President F. W. de Klerk took office in September 1990 and launched a process of reforms that steadily corrodes the monstrous national policy of apartheid. Within six months, he released top officials of the African National Congress (ANC), allowed freedom of speech and assembly for all, legitimized the ANC, the Pan-Africanist Congress, and the South African Communist Party, and freed the 71-year-old Nelson Mandela, the ANC leader who was jailed for twenty-eight years. In so doing, he declared that reconciliation had arrived.[4] Only a few years ago, human repression behind the iron curtain and gross deprivations and violations of human rights for over 30 million South Africans were horror stories of denial of national and international law protecting human rights.

Again, we return to the words and vision of Secretary General Hammarskjold, who almost thirty years ago issued both a warning and a prediction.

It is my firm conviction that any result bought at the price of a compromise with the principles and ideals of the Organization [United Nations] either by yielding to force, by disregard of justice, by neglect of common interests or by contempt for human rights is bought at too high a price. This is so because a compromise with its principles and purposes weakens the Organization in a way representing a definite loss for the future that cannot be balanced by any immediate advantage achieved. . . . It is impossible for anyone to say where the international community is heading and how the United Nations will change in the further course of the evolution of international politics. But it can safely be said that international cooperation will become increasingly essential for the maintenance of peace, progress, and international justice. . . . Therefore [Members] will find it increasingly necessary to maintain its strength as an instrument for the world community in their effort to reduce areas of major conflict . . . and to resolve problems . . . in a spirit reflecting the overriding common interest.[5]

This is the goal of shared security and shared and progressive well-being. The U.N.'s success in taking collective measures against Iraq in the 1991 war in the

Persian Gulf has hopefully introduced what President George Bush determined to be a "new world order" in his address to Congress on October 11, 1990. The new world order was the fifth in the articulation of goals by the President as he hailed the "new partnership of nations." He proposed the new order in his address to the General Assembly of the United Nations on October 1, 1990, in expanding on the concept of partnership of nations based on "international and regional organizations," citing "democracy and human rights" as "values enshrined in the United Nations Charter," calling for a "new compact" to "bring the United Nations into the 21st century" and declaring that the "United Nations is now fulfilling its promise as the world's parliament of peace." He further defined the new world order in his address to Congress on March 6, 1991, when he observed that the United Nations "freed from cold war stalemate is poised to fulfill the historic vision of its founders" in a world in which "freedom and respect for human rights find a home among all nations." The U.N. achievement, he added, was a "victory for unprecedented international cooperation and diplomacy . . . a victory for the rule of law and what is right." The chapters that follow in this book parallel this idealism but offer the challenge to move idealism toward the reality of global peace and security under the U.N. international organizations and law.

Writing about any area of international relations and law in the late 1980s and early 1990s presents an enormous challenge to any author, given the rapid pace of global events, the implosion of the socialist states, and the conflict and residues of the Gulf War. The problems and complexities of human and national relations soar into the 1990s. But this decade was declared by the General Assembly on November 17, 1989, as the United Nations Decade of International Law. This is a challenge to all of us to look forward to the year 2000 as a confirmation of the ideals of the U.N. Charter and the constitutions of all intergovernmental international organizations.

I am most grateful to my colleague in the Tufts International Relations Program, Claire Martin, for her dedicated and professional preparation of the manuscript of this book. To John Pace, Secretary of the United Nations Commission on Human Rights, I convey praise for his extraordinary professional achievements as well as for his friendship. To my wife, Edythe R. Gibson, I dedicate this book with few but precious words.

NOTES

1. The Statute of the International Court of Justice in Article 34.3 refers to founding constitutions as "the constituent instrument of a public international organization," and the authoritative Vienna Convention on the Law of Treaties in Article 5 refers to them as the "constituent instrument of an international organization."

2. Titles of studies that have contributed to the theory and practice of international constitutional law and to which we later refer include the following: Benjamin Cohen, *The United Nations: Development, Growth, and Possibilities* (Cambridge: Harvard Uni-

versity Press, 1961) (the idea of the U.N. Charter as a constitution to be liberally interpreted); Louis B. Sohn's pioneering study, *Cases on United Nations Law*, 2d.ed. (New
York: Brooklyn Foundation Press, 1967); Frederic L. Kirgis, Jr., *International Orga-
nizations in Their Legal Setting* (St. Paul: West Publishing Co., 1977); the many con-
tributions of my late esteemed colleague Leo Gross, including ''Development of
International Law by the United Nations'' in *Essays on International Organization and
Law* (Dobbs Ferry, N.Y.: Transnational Publishers, 1984); D. W. Bowett, *The Law of
International Institutions* (London: Stevens & Sons, 1984); and R. St. J. Macdonald,
''The Charter of the United Nations and the Development of Fundamental Principles of
International Law,'' in Bin Cheng and E. D. Brown, eds., *Contemporary Problems of
International Law* (London: Stephens & Sons, 1988), p. 196 ff.

3. Titles of pioneering studies in human rights law include Paul Sieghart, *The Inter-
national Law of Human Rights* (Oxford: Clarendon Press, 1983); Theodor Meron, *Human
Rights in International Law* (Oxford: Clarendon Press, 1984); and Meron's *Human Rights
Law Making in the United Nations: A Critique of Instruments and Processes* (Oxford:
Clarendon Press, 1986).

4. *New York Times*, November 15, 1989, December 1, 1989, and February 2, 1990.

5. Introduction to the Annual Report of the Secretary-General on the Work of the
Organization, June 15, 1959–June 15, 1960.

Part 1
International Organizations:
Evolution and Mission

Political communities have always sought to preserve their identity and uniqueness. They have also found it imperative in time and place to relate in varying degrees with other political communities for their common good. Sovereignty is still a powerful force today as shown in the manifestation of desire for political independence and territorial integrity in the wording of Article 2 of the U.N. Charter. The condition of sovereignty, however, is difficult to sustain when security and well-being require increasingly enhanced measures of dependence on other states, often within the domain of international law and organization. This is the essential theme of Part 1 of our study on the evolution of international organizations and how states construct and expand their mission of "harmonizing the action of nations in the attainment of [the] common ends" of shared security and progressive well-being, as stated in Article 1 of the U.N. Charter.

1

THE PROCESSES OF HISTORY AND PATTERNS OF MUTUALITY

From the very beginning of the trek of humans from the forests, woods, river-banks, and fields to gather in very small communal settlements for their mutual security and well-being, the process of formation of political entities or polities has been the subject of great interest and intensive study. What brings people together for common security and well-being? Who is permitted to join others in the political community or polity and who is not? How did patterns of concentric circles of polities develop with larger polities ruling over others?

The inclination of polities to govern their own affairs and make determinations of security and well-being has always been confronted by the necessity in time and place to yield some measure of self-governance to rules and organizations for a number of polities, invariably for mutual security and well-being. The framework for mutuality, or shared security and well-being, has evolved from very primitive understandings and arrangements to the highly complex international organizations of today. But whether in ancient times or the 1990s, the issue is the same—what is the extent to which polities desire or are forced to advance from their sovereign capacity to determine their own goals of security and well-being and to enter some kind of joint enterprise with one or more polities for mutual or shared security and well-being? The cost is some yielding of authority by rulers to make sovereign decisions, but the benefit may be the enhancement of achieving more security and well-being.

History is infused with contention between the political organization's aspiration for self-governance on the one hand and voluntarily entering into a broader framework for sharing and mutuality. For the most part, history records that war and conquest have been the forces to bring some polities under the control of the victor in warfare. We often view history as marked more by conflict than by cooperation in changing patterns of state independence and dependence.

However, as we shall soon observe, polities have, throughout history, embraced cooperation and mutuality for shared security and well-being as well, not only for self-interest but also in rejection of force as a mode of relationship between and among polities.

In this chapter we turn first to some early historical processes demonstrating patterns of cooperation and conflict between and among polities, when the ancient and medieval world moved toward the landmark year of 1648 and the modern state emerged following the Thirty Years' War. We then explore patterns of cooperation in the evolution of the laws of the sea and of diplomacy, which brought forth shared security and well-being between and among states as patterns of mutuality that laid the foundations in theory and practice of modern international organizations.

THE BEGINNINGS

Socrates observes in Plato's immortal *Republic* that "a state arises . . . out of the needs of mankind. No one is self-sufficient but all of us have many wants. Can any other origin of the state be imagined?" There can be no other, replies his friend, Adiemantus. The political community of Plato's city-state—and later the nation-state or state today—had their origins in a time when two or more family units banded together because they realized that "self-sufficiency" could not meet their "wants" and "needs" for mutual protection and welfare. Security and well-being remain the dual and interrelated goals of all states today in their relations and transactions with other states and actors in the international system of states, or the international marketplace.

In appraising the origins and expansion of the state, Socrates finds that as humans need the political community to gain their wants, the community itself must have required supplies from other states. Neither the individual nor the state is therefore self-sufficient. He notes that a state where "nothing need be imported is well nigh impossible." Therefore, what people of the state produce "must be not only enough for themselves, but in such quantity and quality as to accommodate those from whom their wants are supplies." As the people within their state "will need a marketplace" for purpose of exchange, importers and exporters must conduct relations and exchanges in the broader marketplace of city-states.

Socrates then proceeds to describe how the exchange system within and between and among states advances the well-being of the people to levels of increasingly conspicuous consumption. Production and exchanges involving "sofas and table . . . dainties and perfumes, and incense and courtesans and cakes" bring demands for well-being for the populace to the point that the original dimensions of the state are no longer satisfactory for state goals.

Then, we must enlarge our borders; for the original healthy state in no longer sufficient . . . the country which was enough to support the original inhabitants will be too small now and not enough. . . . Then, a slice of our neighbors' land [note that neighbor is plural] will be wanted by us for pasture and tillage, and they will want a slice of ours if, like ourselves, they exceed the limit of necessity, and give themselves up to the unlimited accumulation of wealth. That, Socrates [observed Glaucon] will be inevitable. "And so [said Socrates] we shall go to war, Glaucon, shall we not?" "Most certainly," he replied.

State "necessities" of resources and conditions for security and well-being are attained through mutually beneficial transactions, such as trade with "importers and exporters." However, states may "exceed the limits of necessity" if and when their leadership determines that resources and conditions within the state are not sufficient in "quantity and quality" and mutually accepted transactions cannot gain those conditions. And so they use threats or force to seek what they deem necessary, not being satisfied with the "limits of necessity," however defined.[1]

Lagash and Umma were two ancient communities in Mesopotamia that developed slowly but independently of each other as they competed for more land for their expanding populations. They drained marshes to gain solid land and, in so doing, began to claim the same marshlands for development. This competition lead to threats and then armed conflict, loss of life, and destruction of land.

The top leader of each of these communities was faced with the decision to continue the fighting until his community gained supremacy or to negotiate a commitment toward a condition of sharing the valued resource, land, and peaceful relations. The leaders were influenced by pro and con demands of domestic sources of policy within each city. They considered the costs and benefits of an agreement with the other city or a continuation of belligerency as a condition. Both finally decided they should talk. Then they negotiated a treaty that was a commitment to share land and to abide by conditions of peace and friendly relations. This commitment was enshrined in a treaty in 3100 B.C. and it exists for our reading and analysis today. It is perhaps the oldest artifact of a bilateral negotiation leading to a commitment for mutually beneficial conditions of shared security and well-being. The punishment of the community breaching this commitment was the wrath of the gods who were guarantors of the treaty.[2]

The salutary condition of sharing and peace continued until Ur, another community, began to drain marshes in the area shared by Lagash and Umma. This gradually upset the equilibrium and order established by Lagash and Umma and presented the leaders of these two communities with several options. They could join forces to attack Ur, or each could join Ur in an alliance against their old enemy. A third option was to invite Ur into the agreement to share resources, commit each to friendly relations, and establish a procedure to guarantee these conditions for the future. The two leaders chose the order-building maintenance option and Ur agreed to negotiations for a commitment of sharing and peaceful relations. The three communities then established a committee of three representing each community to oversee the agreement of the new regime. The committee engaged a learned scribe to administer the agreement, to manage its provision, and to give notice if there were any violations of the agreement. Thus emerged laws, bureaucracy, and a modest organization for maintaining the established order.

Our vast global exchange system—the international marketplace—has its origins in the real world of early political communities and in the political philosophy of Plato. Lagash and Umma went to war because conflict passed the bounds of confrontation and earlier of competition and cooperation. But both agreed to shared security and well-being when conflict proved to be counterproductive to their needs for security and well-being. Socrates, on the other hand, takes his political communities or city-states from cooperation and competition in mutual exchanges to confrontation and conflict when they choose to exceed the "limits of necessity." We know nothing, however, about how they resolved conflict and established an authority for shared security and well-being.[3] The international marketplace then and now gives witness to units seeking their own goals whatever may come and order-building and maintenance for shared security and well-being. The contention continues, but at what price for "stability and well-being"—conditions mentioned often in the U.N. Charter and constitutions of other international organizations.

Patterns of interactions of cooperation and conflict marked the evolution of the international marketplace in the 3,000 years before the beginning of the Christian era. The river valleys of the Tigris and Euphrates, the Nile, the Indus, the Ganges, and the Yellow or Huang Ho River were marked with settlements of people who came together for communal security and well-being. Treaties of peace and friendship produced alliances and regimes such as that of Lagash, Umma, and Ur. These alliances and regimes evolved into larger polities and later into small then greater empires. Rules were developed for exchanges and transactions for the security and well-being of polities of all kinds and sizes. Where rules and organization did not meet security and well-being of some polities, recourse to threats and uses of force followed, as did control by some over others. The political landscape constantly changed because top leaders in particular shaped for their polities determinations of security and well-being that were incompatible with others.

The many and varied polities of the Near East began to shape the structure and substance of the international marketplace we know today. The development of the venerable Egyptian empire and its dynasties, the rise and fall of many polities where Turkey, Syria, Iraq, and Jordan are located today, the polities of the Hebrews, and the slow but steady move of civilizing processes toward the eastern Mediterranean and southeastern Europe further molded the patterns of relations between and among polities of all kinds.

The Persian threat to the Greek city-states in the late sixth and early fifth centuries led to Greek victory and then the establishment of the Delian League under the leadership of Athens. Comprised largely of maritime Ionian city-states around the rim of the Aegean Sea and its islands, the league was a confederation of polities seeking self-defense against a possible revival of a Persian attack. It had a council to administer its affairs and a treasury located in the temple of Apollo on the island of Delos. The league continued under strong Athenian leadership well after the Persian threat had subsided and its treasury was transferred to Athens after the death of Persian King Xerxes in 465 B.C. The league ended with the Spartan defeat of Athens in 404 B.C. at the end of Peloponnesian War. It was revived in the fourth century but Philip II of Macedon brought the league to its final end in 338 B.C.

The Delian League is probably the first collective defense organization of polities against a common threat and is analogous in principle to the North Atlantic Treaty Organization (NATO) of today. It brought polities together for shared security but really came under the domination of Athens once the main reason for the league, the Persian threat, had ended. The league's council administered its affairs and members had an equal vote in its early years. Members were fairly assessed to meet league expenses and states contributed many resources, such as ships and arms, to the leagues's common cause of shared security for its members. In his famous *History of the Peloponnesian War*, the Greek historian Thucydides describes the league and its history in detail. We study it today as the first major international organization drawing to its center resources, decision-making authority, and commitments by its members to achieve a goal of security each could not gain on its own.

We can study many major political entities as organizations, such as the Roman Republic and later the Roman Empire down to its demise in the West in A.D. 476. The early growth and development of the Church of Rome as an organization makes an interesting study, especially in its construction on the broken foundations and the symbols of the Roman Empire. Charlemagne, crowned in A.D. 800, added to the organizational structure of Europe, followed by the so-called Holy Roman Empire. How was power drawn to the center of these organizations and how was it maintained and administered? How and why did Islam as an organization spread so fast in the seventh and eighth centuries? How and why did schisms and processes of decentralization sever the unity of these organizations? What explains the fragmentation of Europe after the ninth century and how did new polities such as England and France arise? Historians have not served us well in viewing ancient and medieval institutions as organizations with power and authority moving to and from centers of decision-making power. There is much to learn today in studying these institutions as organizations and how patterns and trends of centralization and decentralization do so much to determine the dynamics of the international marketplace.

In the realm of evolving rules and laws for marketplace transactions, polities of all kinds, whether small city-states or vast empires, developed rules necessary for their relations, security, and well-being. In the law of the sea and the law of diplomacy, we can detect the evolution of rules that then shaped the structure and web of exchange mechanisms in the international marketplace.

HISTORICAL PATTERNS OF MUTUALITY: LAW OF THE SEA AND OF DIPLOMACY

These two vast and historical dimensions of international law and organizations demonstrate the gradual but ever expanding processes of political communities embracing mutuality and rules for shared security and well-being in preference to the use of force as the prime means for unilaterally seeking to advance security and well-being.

The Law of the Sea

The civilization of the river valleys looked to rivers and the seas as essential routes of transportation to buy, sell, and barter in the early international marketplace and toward the end of gaining resources needed and wanted for security and well-being. Customs evolved for rights and privileges of boats of one polity in the jurisdiction of others, for ships passing through the waters of others, for rights and duties in times of war such as protection of wounded sailors and prisoners, and for the rights of neutrals or nonbelligerents. These customs over hundreds of years became "law" because they were observed and considered by seafaring polities to be essential to their reciprocal relations of mutual and shared security and well-being.

All trading nations, such as Phoenicia, Egypt, Rhodes, Crete, Greece, and later Rome, came into basic agreements and commitments over such issues as jurisdiction on land, in ports, and at sea as customs became encrusted into agreed-upon rules or laws. Where confrontation and conflict took place, judges in the maritime states were called upon to decide between two contending positions of states and they drew upon established custom in making their judgments.

The evolving laws were confirmed in writing into judges' decisions and codes such as the Rhodian Sea Law, the French Laws of Oleron, the English Black Book of the Admiralty, and the Spanish Consulates of the Sea. Monarchs ordered their merchant fleets and navies to conform to these laws, which all had remarkable similarity. Thus the sources of the law of the sea included custom based on usage and then judges' decisions based on that custom. Codes of sea law followed and then ordinances and commands of monarchs. A vast array of rules for relations, exchanges, and transactions in peace and in war emerged, which gave cohesion to the international marketplace in transportation on the seas, rivers, and in the ports of the maritime states. In the absence of such rules, transportation by water would be utter chaos, with huge loss of life, ships, and property. Seafaring states would have been unable to pursue goals of security and well-being in such a condition of global disorder.

A major issue through the centuries has been the rights of ships on the high seas, beyond the jurisdiction of the maritime state. By custom, mutual interest, and later a powerful endorsement by Rome, the seas beyond state jurisdictions (several miles out to sea) were considered open to all ships so that each polity could enjoy the basic freedom of the sea. Pirates cared nothing for this right and thus became universal outlaws, punishable by any state capturing them. During peace and war ships on the high seas were plundered from time to time. However, on the basis of reciprocity and state interests, the seas continued to be considered open pathways for all.

With the advent of the discoveries at the end of the fifteenth century, Pope Alexander VI decreed in 1493 that the non-Christian world should come under the jurisdiction of Spain and Portugal, and the Pope's edict was confirmed in the Treaty of Tordesilles of 1494. Spain and Portugal acted as though the seas included in the Pope's magnanimous declaration were theirs to control. However, the rising sea powers of the Netherlands, England, and then France began to contest this theory. The father of international law, Hugo Grotius, employed his Dutch legal talents to defend a Dutch admiral's seizure of a Portuguese ship in the Indian Ocean, presumably under the jurisdiction of Portugal. His justification for the seizure, *Mare Liberum* (free or open seas) of 1609, is not only a stirring defense of freedom on the sea (and thus benefiting Dutch ships) but also the first major treatise on the sources and precepts of international law. Irrespective of the many violations of that freedom over the ages, the doctrine of the freedom of the high seas became the law.

Who owns what is under the sea? Hugo Grotius provides this parable. "The Sea is certainly common to all persons," declares the slave, and the fisherman agrees. The slave then continues, "Well, what is found in the common sea is common property." "Not so," says the fisherman. "What my net and hooks have taken in is absolutely my own." This parable is applicable today, almost 400 years later, over the issue of who owns the vast and immensely wealthy minerals of the seabed.

The evolution of the laws of the seas has led to the near universal law of the sea treaty, which was signed in Jamaica in December 1982 after almost twenty-five years of negotiations. The treaty is a broad commitment to codify the existing customary law of the sea accumulated over 5,000 years and to create new international sea law as well. Again, it is another example of commitment by states to reaffirm and establish conditions that facilitate indispensable relations among states and their respective goals of security and well-being. The law of the sea treaty is gradually bringing together and into place the international legal authority for the seas. The treaty establishes new international institutions, including the International Sea Bed Authority, with an assembly, council, and secretariat; the Enterprise, which will be responsible for sea bed operations, including the mining and distribution of mineral resources; and the Chamber of the International Tribunal for the Law of the Sea.

The Law of Diplomacy

Diplomacy is a set of transactions between and among state officials and especially top leadership to seek exchanges of resources, conditions, and commitments for the goals of state security and well-being. We must assume top leaders and officials paved the way for the trading or resource exchange of which Plato speaks and the order-building of the treaty of peace between Lagash and Umma. Any treaty such as theirs of some 5,000 years ago was preceded by the give and take of diplomatic negotiation to reach words that express mutuality of the parties. The commitment established conditions for friendly relations and fruitful exchanges in the marketplace of polities, now nation-states.

Diplomacy and diplomats, however, are not always concerned with agreements and commitments toward shared security and well-being by any means. Diplomats and diplomacy seek to advance the security and well-being of the state and to seek resources and conditions that often are sought by other states as well. These bilateral and multilateral quests are usually competitive due to different perceptions of national security and well-being, competition for resources and allies, and competition for conditions that often vary from state to state, especially among the major powers. Diplomats often seek advantages for their states over others and when advantage leads to quests for superiority and domination, diplomacy may be a process leading to threats and uses of force and then controls. Such was the pattern of Hitler's diplomacy in the 1930s.

Processes and outcomes of diplomacy permeate the evolution of the international marketplace and are found in all the primary resources of history. Given the tensions and conflict marking Israeli-Lebanese relations in the 1980s, it is interesting to note in 1 Kings 5 in the Old Testament negotiation and then a treaty and commitment between King Solomon and King Hiram of Tyre. That agreement led to a condition of stability after war and an exchange of an abundance of Solomon's wheat and oil in exchange for cedars of Lebanon for the construction of Solomon's temple in Jerusalem.

Diplomacy evolved in all areas of the world as polities came into contact with each other and required processes and language of communication and agreement. The term *diploma* comes from the Greek *diplaisos*, meaning double. A *diplos* is two folds of a piece of paper and the folded paper, or diploma, was used by the Romans first as a passport and then as a medium for an imperial grant of privileges. The term was revived in the Middle Ages as the Crusaders penetrated the Near East and brought back to Europe much of the Roman world that continued in the East but had disappeared in the West, including Roman law. The diploma became the symbol of privileges and immunities of the state agents or diplomats of the early Renaissance.

During the so-called dark ages in Europe, Islam had its golden age in terms of education, culture, medicine, literature, and in many areas of philosophy. Diplomacy became well advanced under the Prophet Mohammed, who established houses for foreign guests and agents, who were given many immunities and privileges because they were envoys from other states. Mohammed expected his own envoys to receive the same treatment.

Mohammed's successor or Caliph, Omar (581–644), developed procedures for negotiation, arbitration, conciliation, and other approaches to peaceful settlement of disputes. These diplomatic usages were also brought back to Europe by the Crusaders and traders as well as much of the Islamic learning in science and philosophy. Bodies of the rediscovered Roman law and Islamic medical science flowed into Italy and then into other parts of Western Europe. Trade in goods and other valued resources rapidly expanded as the Italian city-states, especially Venice and Genoa, became ports of call and centers for transmission of goods and services overland to Western Europe.

All of this expansion of relations and communications between and among polities necessitated increased forms and processes of interpolity diplomacy. To this time, diplomatic relations and communications were conducted on an ad hoc basis by top leaders or their agents who traveled back and forth in the conduct of the state's business and guests. Venice sent two merchants with official credentials to London in 1496 to conduct trade relations; they were instructed to remain in the English capital city as repetitive overland travel was too dangerous and time-consuming. This was the first permanent mission or embassy. Within 100 years, almost all polities had permanent missions or embassies in the capital cities of others if there were mutual recognition and accreditation of diplomats. Diplomatic privileges and immunities became the bedrock of diplomatic law as the fine craft and laws of diplomacy became well honed, respected, and considered essential to the reciprocities and transactions of polities in the international marketplace.

The laws of diplomacy were further codified at the Congress of Vienna in 1815 at the end of the Napoleonic Wars when diplomats in all major nations entered the ranks of the state's public service or the foreign service. The nineteenth century was marked by the classic diplomacy of diplomats meeting behind closed doors, engaging in private negotiations in the French language, and observing strict rules of protocol. They knew their craft well. They constantly sought to avoid taking state policy beyond diplomacy and into threats and uses of force to achieve desired goals. They were largely responsible for order-maintenance in the nineteenth century.

Diplomacy entered a new era in 1917 when both President Wilson and Bolshevik leader Lenin called for two diametrically opposite world conditions, one for democracy and one for socialism. Wilson called for ''open diplomacy'' in the first of his Fourteen Points of January 8, 1918. He was convinced that if diplomacy were out in the open for all to see, private negotiations and agreements would be laid aside in favor of democratic processes of state relations. The open or parliamentary diplomacy of the League of Nations has been carried on in the United Nations and most other international organizations in the post-World War II era. Summit diplomacy of top leaders, cultural diplomacy of traveling orchestras and musical groups, and technical diplomacy in the areas of science and technology are all attributes of public diplomatic relations since 1920.

The laws of diplomacy were codified in Vienna in 1961 in treaties subscribed to by almost all of the world's nations, thus establishing an international legal regime for diplomacy that few states would care to violate. The laws of diplomacy permeate all international organizations where diplomacy is practiced in all its facets, private and public. A key provision in the U.N. Charter emphasizes the importance of diplomacy as negotiation for accommodation and order. Article 33 reads as follows:

The parties to any dispute, the continuance of which is likely to endanger the maintenance of international peace and security, shall first of all, seek a solution by negotiation, enquiry, mediation, conciliation, arbitration, judicial settlement, resort to regional agencies or arrangements, or other peaceful means of their own choice.

This brief overview of the law of the sea and the law of diplomacy demonstrates that with the early and increasing relations between and among polities, those polities had to devise rules for relations and transactions mainly to protect their security and well-being and to advance those dual goals. The rules and laws did not appear from on high but rather were conceived and grew as state contrivances for state goals. The evolution of the laws, however, created a web of commitments that were agreed to by existing states and new states as well and thus became established rules of order for the international marketplace.

The Cycle of Invention/Discovery/Necessity

The cycle of invention and discovery makes rules for relations and transactions a necessity. Invention and discovery are the parents of necessity and the necessity itself leads to further inventions and discoveries. The invention of the wheel and the discovery of fire led to the necessity of using the wheel and the containment of fire. The necessities led to further discoveries and inventions as the cycle continued. The invention of the car led to the necessity of rules for the road and the invention of the Soviet *Sputnik* in 1957 led to the necessity for rules for vehicles in outer space. Those rules led to further cycles of invention and discovery and the process continues, producing new legal authorities for the international marketplace. We must add to the fashionable cycle of invention and necessity another component, "events." The medieval plagues drained the energy of states and other political communities. Events of today, such as the transnational villains of radioactivity, AIDS, and global warming, bring forth responses in the forms of international organizations and laws as we see in the next chapter.

Discovery and invention for Western civilization greatly accelerated the evolution of the marketplace when the Crusades began late in the eleventh century. Discovery and invention led to necessity of trade and ocean commerce. The web of permanent diplomatic missions wired most states together in a network of relations, communications, transactions, and commitments. A second major landmark in the expansion of the marketplace was the discovery of new lands and continents in the fourteenth and fifteenth centuries. Voyages across the seas led to the necessity of better sea navigation and thus the invention of the astrolabe and mariner's compass. They, in turn, led to further discoveries and inventions as the cycle continues. The third and major transformation of the marketplace came with the agricultural and industrial revolutions in England and then in other states that chose to follow the English model of industrialization. Today, these are the industrialized democracies. Most other states either did not choose to emulate the model of industrialization or were kept in a position of bondage by the colonial powers, also the industrial democracies. Some underwent major structural changes and became the producers while most remained supplier of primary materials and consumers of industrialized goods and services. This division of states was more or less in place by the 1880s and 1890s and became the international economic order that still exists in the marketplace.

England's insular position and its dependency on others for most of its food resources led the British landlords to seek better ways to produce food. In the fourteenth century they began to fence in wastelands to make enclosures for more efficient production of grains and for raising sheep. Common lands were then enclosed, which led peasants such as Wat Tyler to revolt at this deprivation of land. This was the famous Peasant's Revolt of 1381, which marked a major effort toward land reform and toward an acceleration of agricultural development.

Great advances in horticultural knowledge, crop rotation, livestock breeding, and the establishment of a board of agriculture in England in the 1780s brought about a major transformation in the production of foodstuffs. The cycle of invention, discovery, and necessity continued with new machines, such as the sugar mill and the cotton gin, weaving looms, and new sources of energy such as steam and, later, electricity. Urban growth took place as men and women migrated to cities from rural areas to gain employment and also because the agricultural revolution greatly reduced the numbers of people needed to work the farms. Further discoveries and inventions, such as steelmaking and rail transportation, transformed England and those other states following the English pattern of agricultural transformation and industrialization. England's preeminence in the international marketplace was unchallenged until the 1880s, when German industrialization produced major competition to England in quests for security and well-being.[4]

All of this brought forth many and varied transactions between and among the industrial states and then those states and the primary producing states. The need for new rules in the marketplace for trade and finance, for dealing with colonialism (which shifted into high gear in the mid 1880s), for giving some order to the transnational impact of new inventions such as the telegraph, and for other state needs for their goals of security and well-being led to the necessity of new institutions to facilitate and harmonize the interest of states in an ever-increasing interdependent system of states.

Throughout the ages that led to the emergence of the modern international organization in the nineteenth century, war and conquest were also endemic to the state system along with cooperation and mutuality. Our study naturally emphasizes the significance and attributes of cooperation but recognizes that confrontation and conflict are also realities in international life and relations. Force, even for the idealist, may be necessary for self-defense and the pursuit of national self-determination and independence. There is not always a clear line between force used in offense and force used in defense. But we reject force for domination and hail the steady but unmistakable role of international organizations and international law in reducing uses of force and relations of conflict as options for a militant definition of state security and well-being.

Organizations' goals of shared and progressive well-being are more widely accepted by member states, especially by those that have a high level of dependency on others and inadequate resources and conditions to supply well-being services for their populace in areas such as education and health. The more generously endowed states, such as the industrial democracies, are much better equipped to provide well-being resources and services to their populace, and they make substantial contributions to organizations that try to elevate the quality of life in other nations and reduce their dependency on other states and institutions in the international marketplace. Such is the case for the industrial democracies seeking means to reduce the more than 1 trillion dollar indebtedness of many developing nations. Shared security through international organizations is more difficult because "shared" means basic consensus on what security actually means. Most nations jealously guard their sovereign right to determine their own security from external threats or uses of force. While they have alliances on a regional basis, they never in history have delegated much authority to universal organizations such as the United Nations to shape firm policy for shared, universal security. These are all issues and prospects for the future that we explore later in our study. For the present, we now turn to the emergence of international organizations and their growth to maturity and beyond.

NOTES

1. Unfortunately, Plato's philosophy does not deal with placing limits on a city-state's determination of its requirement for necessity as does the U.N. Charter.

2. Arthur Nussbaum, *A Concise History of the Law of Nations* (New York: Macmillan Co., 1947).

3. Article 26 of the U.N. Charter called for "the establishment and maintenance of international peace and security" or "order-building and maintenance." Modern history has witnessed four order-building or establishment years after great wars (1648, 1815, 1919, and 1945). Order maintenance authorities or organizations include the Quadruple Alliance after 1815, the League of Nations, and United Nations.

4. W. Arthur Lewis observes in his seminal *The Evolution of the International Economic Order* (Princeton: Princeton University Press, 1978) that the contemporary international economic order of the manufacturing industrial democracies and the primary resource producing nations fell into place about 100 years ago. Agricultural revolution in England and later in most Western states paved the growth of industry because food surpluses led to urbanization where industrialization took place. This did not happen in most other nations and areas of the world.

2

INTERNATIONAL ORGANIZATIONS: THE FIRST HUNDRED YEARS

The emergence of the Rhine River Commission—and shortly thereafter other river commissions—marks the beginnings of an ever expanding network of organized approaches by states to harmonize their interests and goals in specific areas of international relations. These were areas where they chose cooperation because they could not perform as well in sovereign pursuit of their goals of security and well-being. They opted for cooperation rather than confrontation and possible conflict, although any state policy as it emerged was the product of debate within the state—especially between ministries of foreign affairs and war—as to whether cooperation or confrontation would best achieve state goals. This debate is historic, continuous, contemporary, and one often neglected by scholars who explore products of states' policies rather than contentions within as to what is best to pursue national security and well-being.

In the early years of the evolution of international organizations as evidenced by the birth of river commissions, nations bordering on the commercial waterways chose to devise and then to join a cooperative enterprise to facilitate harmony in river traffic in preference to a unilateral policy of confrontation and thus possible conflict. Drawing upon the historic cooperation and accommodation on the seas and in diplomacy, states proceeded from the successful functioning of the river commissions to devise increasingly more complex international organizations. Governance of states have always taken note of what advances their goals of security and well-being, and as they began to observe early patterns of cooperation and accommodation, they were prepared to move on to new and untested areas of harmonizing state interests. They were confronted by continuous innovations, discoveries, inventions, and thus necessities for mutuality in state pursuit of security and well-being in response to inadequacy of state capability unilaterally to pursue its own goals.

In the mid-nineteenth century, the invention/discovery/necessity spiral led to imperatives for collaborative arrangements and institutions and thus diplomacy that shaped constitutional charters for a wide variety of international organizations. The evolutionary process included appointing international civil servants who manage the organizations and offices or bureaus as physical manifestations of the permanence of the fledgling institution. The constitutional charters provided for periodic meetings of states choosing to be members so that they could shape policy for their shared security and well-being within the context of the specific goals of the organizations set forth in their charters. That process continues.

The authors of the founding constitutions of the emerging international organizations attained agreement on the specific wording of the charters through extensive diplomatic negotiations. They realized in varying degrees that they were creating a living and breathing document that would serve as the legal foundation for a new institution. The wording of the charter would be reviewed and interpreted to provide grounds for policy and future orientation of the organization. To amplify, we take a passage from an important decision of the U.S. Supreme Court with respect to a founding charter that constitutes an organization.

[W]hen we are dealing with words that also are a constituent act, like the Constitution of the United States, we must realize that they have called into life a being the development of which could not have been foreseen completely by the most gifted of its begetters. It was enough for them to realize or to hope that they had created an organism [for the continuous growth and creativity].[1]

We thus see an organic growth of both organizations and expansive interpretations of their constitutional charters to respond to the interdependence and increased volume and complexity of exchanges and transactions between and among growing numbers of states and other international actors.

THE RHINE COMMISSION: COMMITMENT TO
FACILITATE RELATIONS AND ORDERLY TRANSACTIONS

The some 700 miles of the Rhine River and its hundreds of connective links of tributaries and canals has for many hundreds of years served as a route for tribes and later political communities exchanging resources in evolving patterns of trade. River traffic was fairly uncontested until James Watt's invention of the steam engine in 1769 led to the adaptation of steam energy to water transportation and later the steam locomotive. Robert Fulton's construction of the Clermont in 1807, the most prominent of the early steamships, launched a new mode of water transportation to accelerate the pace of the industrial revolution. Steamships abounded but chaos soon developed as states claimed jurisdiction over shipping in their territorial water, leading to confusion and confrontation of rights, privileges, fees, and rules of the road. Invention was leading to the necessity of order-building with rules and agreement to abide by. This was particularly a necessity for the Rhine, which soon became a thriving highway for trade and commerce, linking the Atlantic and North Sea to the heart of Europe and joining producers and consumers in many nations.

The diplomats at the Congress of Vienna in 1815 established the principle of free navigation on the Rhine, which called for removal of any restrictions on traffic by nations bordering on the river. A conference at Mainz in 1831 devised a convention to reaffirm the commitment to free navigation. It also established the Central Commission for Navigation of the Rhine, which was expanded in the Mannheim Convention of 1868 to enlarge the body of rules for the ever-growing river traffic. It was the first significant international collaborative enterprise to facilitate relations and for advancing shared well-being and equal treatment for all nations traveling on the Rhine, large or small.

The Rhine Commission was originally composed of France, the Netherlands, and five German states, but it soon grew in size and in importance in providing conditions for order and rules for navigation that members thought essential to their own security and well-being. It was broadened in 1919 to become the Central Rhine Commission with headquarters in Strasbourg. Many other similar river commissions were modeled on the Rhine Commission, especially the European Commission of the Danube established in the Treaty of Paris of 1856 at the end of the Crimean War. In the language of Article 1 of the U.N. Charter, the purposes of the Rhine Commission were to enhance "friendly relations among nations based on equal rights . . . [and] to achieve international cooperation in solving international problems of an economic . . . character." The reverse of these purposes would be manifested by unfriendly relations, rights of the more powerful, and lack of cooperation in a vital area of economic relationships. In brief, the commission and its long era of service have greatly enhanced the well-being of states navigating on the river trade routes and thus their shared well-being as well.

FROM COMMISSION TO ORGANIZATION

The establishment of the International Committee of the Red Cross in 1863 and the International Telegraph Union (ITU) in 1865 marked the origins of what then was called a bureau and now is called an organization, which has a staff to administer the goals and policies set forth in its founding constitution. The International Committee (ICRC) was not and is not an international organization but rather is a committee of Swiss citizens and a nonpublic or private sector organization with extensive international responsibilities. The ITU (now the International Telecommunications Union) is the first genuinely international organization and serves today the cutting edge of global and space communications. The ICRC draws upon the U.N. Charter's purpose in Article 1 in advancing "international cooperation in solving problems of an . . . humanitarian character" while the ITU promotes cooperation "in solving problems of an economic and social . . . character."

The International Committee of the Red Cross

Henri Dunant, a young Geneva businessman, witnessed the horrors of wounded and suffering soldiers on the battlefield of Solferino in 1859. He was astounded that there was no international organization or law that had any concern for the wounded, prisoners of war, or human devastation of any kind during a war and the tragedy of the aftermath of war. Returning to Geneva, he took initiatives to form what became the International Committee of the Red Cross in 1863, which continues today as the principal authority for the administration of international humanitarian law. The first Geneva Convention of 1864 brought twenty-six nations together to commit themselves to a covenant ensuring humanitarian conditions of treatment of any wounded or disabled soldier on or off the battlefield, irrespective of the nationality of the person. The cause is humanitarian and the national identity of the victim and even the cause of warfare itself are no barriers to the concerns for the well-being of those afflicted by warfare. This was confirmed in the covenant of 1864 and all succeeding treaties with the administration of humanitarian assistance by the ICRC and the neutral status of Switzerland in international law. That neutrality extends to all ICRC personnel, ambulances, hospitals, and any person or thing bearing the red cross of humanitarian concern and protection.

The committee's work was buttressed by the Hague Conventions of 1899 and 1907. Convened through the initiatives of Czar Nicholas II of Russia, the first conference, attended by twenty-six states, failed to gain agreement on arms reduction. It did succeed, however, in developing conventions and commitments on the laws of warfare, including prohibitions on the dropping of projectiles from balloons, use of asphyxiating gases and expanding "dumdum" bullets, and harm to prisoners of war. The second conference, instigated by Czar Nicholas and President Theodore Roosevelt, was attended by forty-four states. It produced agreement on a number of new laws of war on land and sea, protection of peoples and territory occupied by a belligerent after the termination of war, and the legal rights of neutral states in a time of war.

The Hague conferences were the first major parliamentary gatherings of states where negotiations and agreements on commitments or conventions led to the improvement of harsh conditions in the international marketplace. They served as a precedent for the creation of the assembly of the League of Nations and that of the United Nations and the assemblies of many other international organizations employing parliamentary processes for advancing shared security and progressive well-being. The conferences and their conventions were also a major source of law for the 1945 and 1946 trials of German and Japanese war criminals.

The laws of war were further codified in 1949 with the four Geneva Conventions codifying the laws of war on land and sea, prisoners of war, and territory occupied by a belligerent after a war. These conventions, in turn, were supplemented with the Geneva Protocols of 1977, which deal with areas of war untouched by earlier laws, including fighters for national liberation movements, guerrilla warfare, and other patterns of belligerency. As the first recipient of the Nobel Prize for Peace in 1901, Henri Dunant is a shining example of what one person's vision and initiatives can do for "solving international problems" of a "humanitarian character."

The International Telecommunications Union

The sending of messages over distances has fascinated humans for thousands of years. It was not, however, until the advent of electricity in the seventeenth and especially eighteenth centuries that inventors approached the concept of transmission of words and messages by electricity. As with most inventions that evolve over long stretches of time with inventors building on the ideas and developments of others, telegraphy took time to become a concrete process for communication. Telegraphy finally evolved in Europe with Ampere's telegraph machine of 1820 and Morse's telegraph in America in 1837. Morse developed his famous code and clicked off the historic words in 1844 in a message from Washington to Baltimore, "What hath God wrought?" Before long, messages based on the Morse code were darting across national boundaries, soon leading to an unregulated chaos of a multitude of languages, no standardization, and states seeking to protect their own interests by making the transnational process all the more confusing.

In 1849 Prussia and Austria advanced mutual well-being by signing a treaty committing them to a degree of order in telegraphic communications. They joined forces in constructing telegraph lines along the railroad lines linking them and agreed that they should alternate the days when their messages would be transmitted. Prussia had priority on even-numbered days and Austria on the odd days. Government messages had priority over all other messages. Other bilateral treaties were negotiated by Prussia and Austria with other German states and in 1850 an Austro-German Telegraph Union was formed.

A Western European Telegraph Union was formed in 1855, which was linked up with the Austro-German Union in 1858. Cooperation and sharing was thus advanced for the transmission and receiving of messages, standards for communications, erecting lines and wires across state borders, and reporting breakdowns in the system. These successes led to the desire of other states to enter the system. A major conference was held in Paris in 1865, with twenty states agreeing to a convention and organization for common rules, rates, standards, and processes for development. The ensuing International Telegraph Union was expanded again in 1868 with the creation of a central office, secretariat, and a director general. This is the first international bureau, staffed by what has become an international civil service, and performing services and administering rules for member states. Private communications companies were given the right to accede to the convention in the first major union of the public and private sectors in the international marketplace.

With the invention of radio, the necessity arose again for cooperation and orderly transactions across state lines. An International Radiotelegraph Union was formed after World War I. It joined forces with the Telegraph Union in 1932 at a Madrid conference to form the present International Telecommunications Union (ITU). The cycle of discovery/invention/necessity continues as the ITU's regulative and allocative authority reaches further and further into outer space.

With vastly increased mail communications between and among states and resulting state controls over mail passing through their territory, chaos and confusion led to the necessity of an organization and rules to provide orderly state transactions. State mail authorities moved governments to meet at Bern, Switzerland, in 1874, where the Universal Postal Union was established. The Union, paralleling the ITU with a permanent office or bureau, an international secretariat headed by a director general, and a convention or commitment to administer the laws of transnational postal communication, moved quickly to give order to chaos. It established cooperation and rules for freedom of transit in the flow of mail across state boundaries, common scales and weights and accompanying charges and fees, policies for insured letters, money orders, parcels, and other problem areas of mail communications and exchanges. The entire world is the sole jurisdiction of this organization, which has made the unfettered and swift flow of the mails an important feature of progressive order in the marketplace.

INTERNATIONAL ORGANIZATION FOR SOCIAL WELL-BEING

Article 1 of the U.N. Charter on organizations' purposes cites the need to solve international problems of a social character. Social in this context means human well-being, and for about 150 years nations have pursued international cooperation to deal with problems of health. Disease and epidemics know no borders and do not carry passports. They are among many uninvited guests that sweep across national boundaries to damage human well-being, and no sovereign state by itself can solve the international problem of transnational intruders.

London was afflicted with the Great Plague in 1665, which caused the deaths of thousands of people and crippling sickness to many more. Daniel Defoe's *Journal of the Plague Year*, written in 1722, described for hundreds of thousands of people the impact and curse of the plague. This work led to the establishment by England and many other states strict rules against infested imports as well as quarantine laws protecting trading nations from the plague. However, with the advent of the industrial revolution and greatly accelerated trade between these nations, they also found that these national laws and quarantines were substantially damaging and obstructive to the flow of trade. This is a classic example of what we continue to see today in contentions within the state on what constitutes well-being. Should the national regulations continue to protect people from harmful imports of disease? Or should national well-being be furthered by an international and cooperative approach to reduce the damage of the uninvited transnational guest? In this case, patterns of cooperation and later organization and rules won over separate and national policies seeking to immunize the nation from external contamination.

Alexandra in 1831 and Constantinople in 1839 established mechanisms at their ports to inspect departing cargos for contamination. As major ports of departure of goods for Europe, this was a heralded step toward international concern and cooperation. Cholera joined the ranks of uninvited diseases in Europe in 1830 and soon penetrated the European states in epidemic proportions. The Ottoman Empire established the *Counseil superieur de sante* in 1838, which was comprised of principal maritime nations as well as the Ottoman Empire to contain as far as possible the spread of cholera and other diseases from Constantinople to other ports. Other enterprises were soon established as the beginnings of modest international cooperation for shared well-being. France convened the first International Sanitary Conference in 1851 to deal with cholera and other diseases of transnational significance. Ten conferences followed before 1900 to share information on preventive medicine, identify sources of disease transmission, and develop cooperative approaches to confine disease and epidemics.[2]

Another 1903 conference in Paris paved the way for the Rome conference of 1907, which established the International Office of Public Health. Located in Paris, the office became a clearing house for information on epidemics, circulated periodic reports on global health and disease conditions, established groups of experts to study health issues, and sought cooperation with public health bureaucracies of member states. The office and members developed a series of international sanitary conventions dealing with cholera, the plague, typhus, smallpox, and yellow fever. In the western hemisphere, twenty-one American republics gathered under the new Pan-American Union, established in 1890, to form the Pan-American Sanitary Bureau. The bureau staff engaged in research, provided information to be shared with all American republics on disease conditions, and explored approaches and developed initiatives toward containing epidemics. The bureau convened many conferences to further its work and became a regional office of the World Health Organization in 1949.

The League of Nations' major human well-being activity was the League's Health Section, organized in 1923.[3] It complemented the work of other health organizations in providing and sharing information to contain epidemics, developing international biological standards, and engaging in research on a wide variety of diseases. The section provided services to a number of national public health bureaucracies, worked on epidemic controls in Greece and China, and developed a worldwide epidemic intelligence network. Located in Geneva, the office established a number of regional bureaus and was thus the first international organization to decentralize its activities and services.

United Nations Relief and Rehabilitation Agency provided many international health services after its founding in 1943, especially to deal with intense problems at the end of World War II. Most of the work and activities of all of these organizations flowed into the World Health Organization, which was founded in 1946.

IDEALISM AND ORIGINS OF INTERNATIONAL ORGANIZATIONS: THE LEAGUE OF NATIONS AND OTHERS

Throughout modern history, one's vision of the ideal as the guiding principle for organizing people and states has led to international machinery for seeking to translate the ideal into reality. After all, Plato always articulated the lofty ideal of the republic and governance by philosopher kings and held that aspiration to the ideal was far better than blind acceptance of reality. The ideals of Confucius, St. Thomas Aquinas, Dante, and many others have been translated into statecraft and are very much part of our philosophical heritage. The ideals and blueprints for organizations of states of William Penn, Saint-Simon, Goethe, Kant, and others has flowed into the intellectual idealism of international relations.[4]

Marx posited a model for global organization based on the supremacy of the proletariat rather than states, which would eventually "wither away." This remains an ideal today for the true believer in Marxism-Leninism, although the empires of communism in the Soviet Union and the Peoples Republic of China have veered far from the philosophical premises and prescriptions of Marx. Woodrow Wilson proclaimed on April 2, 1917, that World War I was one to make the world safe for democracy. Two weeks later to the day, Vladimir Lenin called for the worldwide socialist revolution. The contention continues today between those visions of ideals that are grounded in quite different foundations of reality irrespective of the abatement of the Cold War.[5]

Wilson's idealism, of course, inspired and led to the establishment of the League of Nations. His speeches, state papers, and especially his articulation of "Fourteen Points" as the basis for settlement of World War I are infused with his ideals *for* the state system. It would be based on national self-determination of people and nations, open and public diplomacy, democratic processes in resolving disputes, and the new global organization—the League of Nations—having a concert of power to deter nations' threats of force against each other and to take collective action against aggression. The Covenant of the League of Nations expresses an abundance of idealism in its Preamble and also in Articles 10, 11, and 16, with respect to the league's pursuit of shared security for its members. Wilson came closer than any other national leader in witnessing his ideals being translated into a founding constitution, structure, and processes of an international organization, especially one that was the first, near-universal, multipurpose institution for shared security and well-being of its members.

For a variety of reasons, leadership in the U.S. Senate decided against the United States joining the League of Nations and this led to the withdrawal of the United States from participating in the machinery for the post–World War I marketplace. Given its power and prestige, this clearly was a loss for the ideals and potential of the league. It was a message to those who wanted to change the league's organization and rules for the marketplace that the United States would not be a participant in upholding the post-war organization for order-building and maintenance. Nevertheless, Wilson's idealism and prescriptions flowed into that marketplace, including the principle of national self-determination, arenas and processes of public diplomacy, and democratic concepts such as one vote for each nation in the League Assembly (and then the U.N. Assembly and most other international organizations). Wilson's ideal of enforcement power being mobilized by the league or a "concert of power" that takes—in the language of Article 11 of the covenant—"any action that may be deemed wise and effectual to safeguard the peace of nations" remained an ideal for the league. This was because the first sentence of Article 11 assumed that an attack by one state on another would be an attack on all members and the reality of international relations then and now does not reflect that ideal. It may take time but this fundamental ideal of Wilson and the wording of the covenant—and the U.N. Charter as well in the area of collective security—is gradually moving toward reality.

The League of Nations in Geneva became a vibrant center for diplomacy, not only as an arena where statesmen could meet to advance the goals of the organization but also as a neutral ground for the conduct of all kinds of bilateral and multilateral transactions between and among states. Diplomats knew that at the league headquarters, diplomacy could take place on an international turf rather than to and from foreign ministries and embassies of governments. There were far more ways of gaining cooperation and friendly relations let alone commitments at the league than anyone knows because it afforded states the opportunity to engage in quiet and private diplomacy—although in a new organization hailed for its public forums and parliamentary diplomacy in its Assembly and other organs. All of this is engraved in the fourth purpose of the United Nations in Article 1: "to be a center for harmonizing the actions of nations in the attainment of these common ends," the purposes that precede this fourth paragraph.

The theme of idealism was woven into the founding constitutions of many other international organizations. The International Labor Organization (ILO), the first specialized agency under the United Nations, was created at the Paris Peace Conference in 1919 and was an integral part of the League of Nations until it became an independent agency in 1946. In the preamble to the 1919 ILO constitution we find that "universal and lasting peace can be established only if it is based on social justice . . . whereas conditions of labor exist involving such injustice, hardship, and privation to large numbers of people as to produce unrest so great that the peace and harmony of the world are imperiled."

The equating of the ideal, usually of peace, with the purpose of the organization is found in many other organizations. The constitution of the United Nations Educational, Scientific, and Cultural Organization (UNESCO) of November 16, 1945, begins with this statement: "since wars begin in the minds of men, it is in the minds of men that the defenses of peace must be constructed." The constitution of the World Health Organization (WHO) of July 22, 1946, begins with the third paragraph of the preamble declaring that "the health of all peoples is fundamental to the attainment of peace and security and is dependent upon the fullest cooperation of individuals and states." The charter of the International Trade Organization (ITO) of March 24, 1948, opens by "recognizing the determination of the U.N. Charter's objectives in its Article 55 for the attainment of higher standards of living, full employment, and conditions of economic and social progress." Members of the ITO thus pledge themselves to further these objectives toward an "expanding world economy." The ITO never came into existence but part of its charter became the General Agreement of Tariffs and Trade (GATT) of 1948. The constitution of the International Civil Aviation Organization (ICAO) declares that "it is desirable to avoid friction and to promote cooperation between people and nations [in civil aviation] upon which the peace of the world depends."

Many other examples could be cited linking goals of international organizations to the ideals of peace and shared security and well-being. Many of the provisions in the U.N. Charter, for instance, incorporate so much of the venerable philosophers' prescriptions for the elimination of warfare and uses of force. Michael Howard traces the genesis of such provisions as sovereign equality of nations (Article 2, paragraph 1), inviolability of territorial integrity and political independence (Article 2, paragraph 4), the independence and neutrality of international civil servants (Article 100), and rights to self determination (Preamble and Article 2, paragraph 2) among many others.[6] It is important to note, however, that ideals and idealism are most fully and eloquently expressed at the end of wars and thus in the constitutions of international organizations at that time, especially after 1919 and then 1945. Organizations' authors represent victorious nations and vow in the constitutions to strive toward shared security and well-being so as to avoid future conflagrations. They generally are unified in purpose as they were in the war they fought. With the defeat of the common enemy and then the emergence of differences between and among them on definitions of and requirements for security and well-being, they compete with and confront each other within and outside of the organizations they created. The reality of state differences in goals and requirements for goals does not, however, diminish the pursuit of the ideal.

COOPERATION AND SHARED WELL-BEING
THROUGH COMMITMENTS

Treaties are commitments to establish conditions set forth in the purposes and principles of any organization as set forth in the first articles of the constitution of the organization such as the United Nations Charter. The third sentence in the Charter's Preamble calls on the global organization "to establish conditions under which justice and respect for the obligations arising from treaties and other courses of law can be maintained."

The International Labor Organization (ILO) was the first major organization to improve and advance a specific area of human and national well-being through parliamentary processes, a sizable central office, and the development of conventions as commitments by its members to improve well-being conditions within their states. The ILO continues today as a most significant organization with processes and rules to elevate standards for laboring people throughout the world.

During the processes of industrialization in the nineteenth century, interests of the working man and woman were usually quite secondary to the interests of owners of institutions of production and employers as well. Legislation in the industrial states favored the employer for the most part and shunned government intervention in assisting the conditions or rights of workers in conformity with the doctrine of laissez-faire, which opposed regulative or allocative national policy. Marx denounced this doctrine; he equated the exploitation of workers by owners and employers with state leadership. Marx called on the proletariat, whom he assumed had transnational interests and loyalty, to forgo loyalty to the state and its bourgeois capitalists.

The status of labor began to improve in the second half of the nineteenth century due to trade union organization, progressive judicial decisions, and enlightened legislation in many of the industrial states, and also through strikes, protests and often violence. Improvement certainly was not even or steady in all these states. Trade union members and leaders of the industrial states began to communicate to study the feasibility of organizing across state lines for their collective well-being much as they began to organize within their respective states.

In 1900, an International Association for Labor Legislation was formed in Basel, Switzerland. Labor leaders gathered from many nations and explored the possibility of establishing an international organization having the authority to pass legislation to shape treaties binding on their states that improve labor conditions within states and across state lines. Their labors led to a conference in 1906 that produced two conventions, one placing limits on night work by women and the other demanding the elimination of phosphorus in the manufacture of matches.

Only a few states ratified these conventions. However, an important process was launched in 1906, which remains essential to organization theory and practice today. An organization of leaders—here in the private sector, later in the public sector—meet in assembly to discuss, negotiate, and agree on a convention or treaty as a legal commitment seeking improvement in conditions—here, in the workingplace. The treaty is then submitted to state members of the organization and to nonmembers as well for adoption and ratification. The legal norms then are incorporated into the municipal or national law of the states ratifying the treaty and accepting the commitments.

During World War I, laboring people in all belligerent nations worked long and hard hours for the national war effort. For years they made few claims on management or their government for improvement of working conditions, higher wages, and rights of collective bargaining with management. As the war drew to an end, however, labor leaders in the victorious states were ready to go to the barricades not only for improvement of conditions within their states but also to advance their transnational collective interests. A number of labor leaders of the Allied nations demanded representation at the peace conference for the purpose of building into any organization or machinery for the post-war international order mechanisms for the improvement of labor conditions and social justice, which they equated with peace.

A conference of labor leaders met in January 1919 in Bern, Switzerland, and called for an international labor parliament in which labor itself would have one half of each state's representation. However, led by Samuel Gompers, president of the American Federation of Labor (AFL), the labor leaders associated themselves with leaders of their governments to negotiate a new International Labor Organization. The ILO was, as we have noted, written into Part 13 of the Treaty of Versailles and placed under the authority of the League of Nations in the Covenant's Article 24. Paragraph *a* of Article 23 of the Covenant states that the members of the league

will endeavor to secure and maintain fair and humane conditions of labor for men, women, and children, both in their own countries and in all countries to which their commercial industrial relations extend, and for that purpose will establish and maintain the necessary international organizations.

The ILO carried on the concept set forth in the 1906 conference of discussing, negotiating, and concluding conventions, which would then flow into the municipal of treaty ratifying states. It had a totally new structure for member-state representation, with each state having four representatives, two from the government and one each from labor and management.

The new ILO had the immediate support of all major trade unions in the industrial democracies, largely because union leadership in these states were deeply involved in developing the new organization. Unions under the influence of communism at that time shunned the ILO, due in part to the international community's castigation of the Soviet Union. The ILO nevertheless represented an authentic labor movement of participating members and led to a reduction of appeal of the Marxist-Leninist ideal of unity of the proletariat working people as a transnational collectivity. The working man, with few exceptions, remained loyal to his or her state and found international solidarity in the ILO. The idealism of Lenin noted earlier and his clarion call for a world socialist revolution based on the common interests of the working person everywhere simply did not produce his desired results. The Lenin idealism, unlike that of Wilson, did not flow into the purposes, structure, or processes of international organization.

It is interesting to note that the ILO was principally the result of leadership from the private sector and the trade union movement rather than from major initiatives of governments or management. Origins of many international organizations may be traced to domestic sources of policy within the state acting on state leadership. These private sector sources of policy are underestimated and understudied in generating national support and in making demands on leadership to move toward cooperation, organization, and concerted policy in the international marketplace.

NOTES

1. *Missouri v. Holland*, United States Supreme Court, 1920, 252 U.S. 416.

2. Two important treaties were the 1892 Sanitary Convention with provisions for maritime quarantines to prevent the spread of cholera and a convention in 1897 for cooperation in reducing the incidence of the plague.

3. Under Article 23 of the Covenant of the League of Nations, "Social Responsibilities," the members of the league "will endeavor to take steps in matters of international concern for the prevention and control of disease."

4. Perhaps the most significant contribution to the literature of idealism is Michael Howard's *War and the Liberal Conscience* (New Brunswick, N.J.: Rutgers University Press, 1986). Idealists with a liberal conscience include Cruce, More, Locke, Montesquieu, St. Pierre, Kant, Bentham, and many others. The liberal conscience holds that war is irrational, right reason should prevail, and that these values should be consolidated in international organizations. Some of the original works of the liberal conscience are on display at the U.N. Museum in Geneva, including Erasmus' *Querela Pacis*, 1517; Grotius' *War and Peace*, 1657; Duc de Sully's *Grand Design*, 1664; William Penn's *Essay Toward Present and Future Peace of Europe*; Rousseau's *Perpetual Peace*, 1761; and Kant's *Project for Perpetual Peace*.

5. A seminal study of the dualism of idealism and realism in Edward Hallet Carr's *The Twenty Years Crisis, 1919–1939: An Introduction to the Study of International Relations,* (London: Macmillan, 1939). U.S. foreign policy and especially Wilsonism is critiqued by George Kennan in his *American Diplomacy, 1900–1950* (Chicago: University of Chicago Press, 1951).

6. Howard, *War and the Liberal Conscience*.

3

THE UNITED NATIONS ERA: 1945 TO TODAY AND TOMORROW

The Charter of the United Nations was signed on June 26, 1945, and was constituted as an independent legal authority on October 24, 1945, when sufficient ratifications of the founding constitution were received. We must view the global organization not only as the institution with six organs established by the U.N. Charter, but as a much broader "United Nations system" with a wide variety of other international organizations either organically associated with the United Nations as specialized agencies or independent legal authorities such as the World Bank, which are closely associated with the United Nations and other organizations. The legal foundations for specialized agencies are provided for in the U.N. Charter, especially in Articles 57, 63, and 64, and other organizations are affiliated with the global organization in agreement or practice in various ways.

The United Nations and the other international organizations with constitutional roots in their founding charters are international legal authorities as actors in the international marketplace. Today we have an abundance of international constitutional law that is the legal basis for the operation and conduct of international policy by these institutions comprised of member states. The members thus have delegated in the founding constitutions of series of powers to be exercised by the organizations and also legal status as set forth in specific provisions. That delegation of authority continued under resolutions and decisions of the organizations through the years by vote of their members. The management of these organizations by international civil servants constitutes what may be called international administrative law and international legislation, the body of resolutions and decisions that pour out of the organizations with each passing year.[1]

Article 1 of the U.N. Charter is the bedrock statement of the "purposes of the United Nations."

Article 1

The Purposes of the United Nations are:

1. To maintain international peace and security and to that end: to take effective collective measures for the prevention and removal of threats to the peace, and for the suppression of acts of aggression or other breaches of the peace, and to bring about by peaceful means, and in conformity with the principles of justice and international law, adjustment or settlement of international disputes or situations which might lead to a breach of the peace;

2. To develop friendly relations among nations based on respect for the principle of equal rights and self-determination of peoples, and to take other appropriate measures to strengthen universal peace;

3. To achieve international cooperation in solving international problems of an economic, social, cultural, or humanitarian character, and in promoting and encouraging respect for human rights and for fundamental freedoms for all without distinction as to race, sex, language or religion; and

4. To be a center for harmonizing the actions of nations in the attainment of these common ends.

Article 1 appropriately delineates six clusters of organizations. The first grouping is derived from paragraph 1, the goal of international peace and security. The second is equal rights and self-determination of peoples in paragraph 2, beyond, of course, the indispensable goal of friendly relations. The third cluster, economic organizations, the fourth on social and cultural organizations, and the fifth on humanitarian and human rights institutions all stem from paragraph 3. A sixth cluster includes organizations that combine some of these categories. The vibrant charge to member states in paragraph 4 is to move on with the business of the world.

The men and women who constituted the new organizations drew generously from the past to shape the structure of the future. The United States at last learned that its great power required great responsibilities. The authors of the United Nations explored in detail why the League of Nations did not gain support of its important members. Unlike the league, the United Nations is neither a part of any World War II peace settlement nor does it, again unlike the league, guarantee the post-war territorial status quo, enshrined in Article 10 of the league covenant. The authors learned that international protection of human rights requires international organization and policy, which were generally absent from pre-1945 international law. They now understood the need for rules dealing with economic relations that the global economic crisis of the late 1920s and early 1930s required. They realized the obligation of the international community to press forward with the dismantling of colonialism and to open the gates of national sovereignty to the oppressed in Africa, Asia, and the Middle East. History was a great teacher for the authors of the new international constitutions.

On the other hand, history could not enlighten those who signed the U.N. Charter on June 26, 1945, with respect to four striking new conditions in international relations that were not reflected in its wording. First, the cold war was only in the wings of the global stage in late June 1945, and the contention between the superpowers considerably eroded the concept of unanimity of voting on the Security Council as expressed in Article 27 of the U.N. Charter. Secondly, the advent of the atomic era and the first atomic detonation on July 16, 1946, only twenty days after the signing of the U.N. Charter, changed for all times the calculus of international peace and security. It also changed the meaning of having to await an "armed attack" before action in self-defense in Article 51.

Third, the June 1945 charter could not anticipate the transition from colonialism to independence for over 100 more states than the 51 original members in 1945—new international actors with new agendas and demands. Finally, the U.N. Charter and the new economic institutions established a year earlier, including the World Bank and International Monetary Fund (IMF), could never have anticipated the enormous structural changes in the international marketplace in the 1970s and the rise to international authority of the oil producing states and private sector actors such as corporations and banks.

In addition to these unprecedented conditions and events was the cycle of invention/discovery/necessity for further international collaboration. In addition to atomic energy, technology produced the Soviet *Sputnik*, which introduced man-made vehicles into outer space in October 1957. The extensive space law and treaties we have today under the aegis of the United Nations is the "necessity" that followed the invention of space vehicles. Another frontier for international relations is the technology that makes it possible to mine the ocean beds as well as inventions of optic fibers for revolution in communications and medical discoveries for curing disease, prolonging life, and contributing so much to human well-being. However, despite enormous changes in human life and activity since 1945, the United Nations and other organizations have adapted to change and continue to be indispensable for advancing shared security and progressive well-being on this small planet and infinite universe.

ORGANIZING FOR SHARED SECURITY

Article 1 of the U.N. Charter is quite specific in its statement of the prime goal of the global organization: maintenance of international peace and security. In a broad sweep, it sets forth means to that basic goal including a) collective measures for the prevention and removal of threats to the peace, and b) peaceful means for the settlement of international disputes. International organizing for shared security in the epoch since 1945 is exclusively vested in the United Nations although collective defense organization have evolved, such as the North Atlantic Treaty Organization (NATO), which is legally based on Article 51 of the U.N.

Charter providing for collective self-defense in the U.N. system. The goal of seeking the "maintenance of international peace and security" is stated twenty-six times in the Charter. The Security Council of the United Nations, composed of the five major powers as permanent members and eleven other states on a rotating basis, is delegated by member states "the primary responsibility for the maintenance of international peace and security" in Article 24. Article 25 states that U.N. members "agree to accept and carry out the decisions of the Security Council," which is a firm obligation in international law. The voting formula for the council agreed upon at the Yalta Conference of February 1945 by President Roosevelt, Prime Minister Churchill, and Marshall Stalin is that major decisions resulting in one negative vote or a veto precludes unanimity and thus a legal decision. The Security Council has responsibilities for peaceful settlement of disputes in Chapter 6 of the U.N. Charter and exclusive responsibility (in Chapter 7) for taking "action with respect to the peace and acts of aggression."

It is for other studies to explain how the United Nations has performed in over 40 years of pursuing its primary objective. Frequent lack of unanimity in Security Council voting reflects basically different interpretations of security by the permanent members and especially the United States and the Soviet Union. In other words, a unanimous vote in the Council is a unanimous agreement on the meaning of security on a specific issue. Given the different ways in which states define their security requirements, it should be clear how difficult it is to gain full agreement. Nevertheless, in a number of instances and especially in the late 1980s, more and more agreements have been reached as the two superpowers move closer together. Their great power means a greater responsibility to move away from confrontation and more toward cooperation and accommodation in the language of the U.N. Charter. Furthermore, constitutional interpretation of the Charter has enabled the United Nations to develop innovative approaches to maintaining international peace and security, especially through the structure and process of "peacekeeping." Article 10 has been interpreted through a General Assembly "Uniting for Peace" resolution in November 1950 to enable U.N. peacekeeping forces in a number of areas to serve as buffer units between contentious states. The concept of soldiers keeping peace rather than fighting is a revolutionary and successful idea on paper and in practice.

The machinery of the United Nations for pursuing its primary goal as set forth in Chapter 7 remains to be implemented in the manner intended by the organizations's authors. It has worked and worked well at times. However, as we have observed, the delineation of Chapter 7 took place at a time when the deep divisions of the cold war were not anticipated. The machinery worked in part when the organization took collective measures against the aggression by North Korea into South Korea in 1950. Security Council decisions in a number of instances have been widely observed and have ameliorated a number of disputes. But clearly the efficacy of the council depends on unanimity in voting and thus basic agreements in principle among the permanent members and especially superpowers.

A collective decision on the taking of measures for security really depends on the participants' agreement upon the meaning of the words "security" and "threat." Given the variables that determine each nation's security needs and threats, it is no simple matter to have a bottom line, common denominator definition. In the era since 1945, therefore, the variables determining a state's goal of security have been quite different for the United States and the Soviet Union. The toning down of the cold war in the mid-1980s brought the two superpowers closer together in a definition of mutual security to the extent that both sponsored a resolution in the General Assembly on November 3, 1989, calling for the United Nations to play a greater role in maintaining peace and fostering international cooperation. Both nations pledged to work together through the Security Council to "preserve peace and restore order" in the world.

The dramatic events in Eastern Europe in the fall of 1989 and the early December summit conference between Presidents Bush and Gorbachev redefined the entire range of security goals and requirements for the United States and the Soviet Union. The June 1990 summit brought the two superpowers closer together on a number of issues including arms agreements, enhanced trade relations, and the future of a unified Germany. This may well lead to a coalescence of security interests toward genuine shared security and consequently the Security Council swinging into action in the manner anticipated in the wording of the U.N. Charter of 1945.

This was evidenced in the August 1990 Middle East crisis with the invasion of Kuwait by Iraq on August 2. The Security Council, in a 13–0–2 vote on August 2, condemned the invasion, called for economic sanctions and a boycott against Iraq by the same vote on August 6, and unanimously declared the Iraqi annexation of Kuwait null and void in international law and called for immediate and unconditional withdrawal. This resolution was followed by ten more resolutions by the Council which included progressively harsher language, condemnation of Iraq for violations of human rights and international humanitarian law, and the implementation of sanctions. Iraq remained unmoved and thus the Council, on November 29, 1990, in Resolution 678, stated that "all necessary means" would be employed by the U.N. coalition of armed forces in the area if Iraq did not implement previous Council ordering that country to vacate Kuwait. These "means" which clearly implied use of force under Chapter VII of the Charter went into place on January 16, 1991, leading to the short but intense war in Kuwait and Iraq. The U.N. forces prevailed, followed by Council resolution on March 3, 1991, which confirmed Iraq's "agreement to comply fully with all of the resolutions" by the Council on this gross transgression of U.N. law. This resolution established the basis for interim settlement of the conflict and paved the way for diplomacy to restore stability to the area. A new era for organizing for security had, with all hope, truly begun.

ORGANIZING FOR SELF-DETERMINATION, DEVELOPMENT, AND MODERNIZATION

Article 1, paragraph 2 of the Charter calls for transactions and exchanges between and among friendly nations to be "based on respect for the principle of equal rights (of nations) and self-determination of peoples.'' Peoples living under the bondage of colonialism in 1945 found in this goal hope for independence and a place in the international legal system equal to that of any other nation, large or small, super-power or weak-power. The road to self-determination is amplified in Chapter 11 of the Charter on non–self-governing territories and in Chapter 12 on the international trusteeship system. International organizations of all kinds have played a progressively strong role in facilitating the transition from conditions of colonialism to independence of states and then political, economic, and human development toward higher levels of modernization of the new states and reductions in dependency on others. We study here the fortunes of the developing nations in Africa, the Middle East, Asia, and Latin America. We reject any concept such as "third world,'' which suggests categoric sameness other than the reality of rich differences between, among, and within these some 130 members of the international community. Most are afflicted with similar conditions of deprivation of the human and national well-being. Most have authoritarian governing elites who control the economic system and resources. Most have great urban poverty and the dogma of traditional and religious belief, which often is a barrier to development. Most are confronted with ever-rising rates of population. One fourth of the people who will live in the year 2000 have yet to be born. Ninety percent of the population growth up to the year 2000 will be in the developing states and 87 percent of the world's population will reside in these nations. They truly are the have-nots compared to the haves.[2]

However, in viewing these nations as a homogenous grouping, we too often fail to see the vast differences in territorial size as well as population. Great regional differences exist between Africa, Asia, Latin America, and the Middle East—differences in historical development and orientation toward other nations.

In the long era of imperialism and colonialism, there was no international cooperative concern for the plight of the colonial areas of the world save by private organizations and societies and church organizations as well. The colonial powers divided up much of Africa at the Berlin Conference in 1885 to ascertain who owned what and by 1910, much of the globe was colored colonial. But in only nine years, the mandate system emerged within the League of Nations Covenant. Its Article 22 provided innovative approaches for new organizations to oversee the colonial administration of territories that belonged to the defeated powers of World War I. The International Labor Organization (ILO) of 1919, which always had a concern for conditions of labor in all kinds of colonies, called for "economic and social advancements of the less developed regions of the world" in its "Declaration of the Aims and Purposes of the ILO" of 1944.

President Franklin D. Roosevelt said much and did much in his administration to advance the cause of national self-determination of colonial peoples, a term he learned from his presidential tutor, Woodrow Wilson. This leadership was a significant influence in incorporating into the language of the U.N. Charter the goal of self-determination in Article 1, paragraph 2. Article 55 as well promotes conditions of self-determination of peoples. Article 73 was a pioneering provision as a "Declaration Regarding Non–Self-Governing Territories," for territories "whose peoples have not yet attained a full measure of self-development." Its five provisions for the well-being of these inhabitants were a stimulus for progressive action by international organizations toward independence and development. Chapter 12 provides for the United Nations Trusteeship System, an extension and expansion of the League mandate organization.

The march to independence and sovereignty for former colonies after the end of World War II began with the Philippines in 1946 and India and Pakistan in 1947—although with massive and tragic loss of life in the conflict between Hindus and Moslems. Then came independence for Burma and Indonesia, which gained its freedom from the Netherlands with extensive United Nations involvement and diplomacy. Self-determination was on the march.

At the United Nations, the early years were full of cold war confrontations and, in fact, getting the new organizations underway. Self-determination was not at the forefront as is evidenced in the December 1948 Universal Declaration of Human Rights, which does not mention self-determination as a right and refers only to rights for "Member states themselves and among the peoples and territories under their jurisdiction." However, in the elaboration on the declaration in the two international legal covenants on human rights of 1966 (Civil and Political; Economic, Social, and Cultural), both treaties begin with the first right in Article 1: "all peoples have the right of self-determination. By virtue of that right they freely determine their political status and freely pursue their economic, social, and cultural development."

The change from 1948 to 1966 was historic in that so many colonial domains gained their independence and entered the United Nations to comprise about 72 percent of the total membership, or 87 of the 122 states. Upon gaining the majority of 1960, they mobilized to pass in the General Assembly the "Declaration on the Granting of Independence to Colonial Countries and Peoples." Ghana was the first black African nation in the twentieth century to gain independence in 1957. French President De Gaulle, upon assuming office in 1958, took measures to give independence to the vast majority of French colonies. The composition of states in the United Nations and related organizations now shifted to the new states and with one vote for one state as written in Article 18 of the Charter based on sovereign equality in Article 2, paragraph 1, the United Nations now faced new opportunities and challenges in moving the new states toward their "economic, social, and cultural development" in the wording of the Economic, Social, and Cultural Covenant.

Before the 1960s, international organizations were not too responsive to the development needs of newly independent states or trust territories of colonies. The International Bank for Reconstruction and Development basically considered its responsibilities to be for the industrial democracies. The International Monetary Fund (IMF) and the General Agreement on Tariffs and Trade (GATT) took the same position. President Truman launched a modest assistance program for the "improvement and growth of underdevelopment areas," and England and France launched some technical assistance programs as well. It was not until voting power in the General Assembly and the other organizations shifted to the developing states that the organizations began to support political, economic, and social development and modernization of former colonies.[3]

The United Nations Development Program was organized in 1965 to be the major U.N. source of financial support for development projects. It continues to be the central institution for working with a variety of other organizations on development of all kinds. Other organizations began to develop policies and programs for building national infrastructures, providing all kinds of services, and training and education for development. The World Health Organization (WHO), the International Labor Organization (ILO), the United Nations Educational, Scientific and Cultural Organization (UNESCO), the Food and Agricultural Organization (FAO), and later the International Fund for Agricultural Development all joined the United Nations programs for vast organizational activity in human and national development. In more recent years, the World Bank and the IMF have responded to global developmental needs and are the major organizations providing support for development and modernization.

It was at the United Nations, however, where the principal agency was established to advance development and modernization, the United Nations Conference on Trade and Development (UNCTAD). Dr. Raul Prebisch, an Argentine economist, was the founding father and first secretary-general of UNCTAD, which is under the aegis of the General Assembly. Prebisch held that the powerful international economic organizations such as the World Bank and GATT were oriented toward the need of the industrial democracies which, in turn, imposed a condition of dependency of the developing states on the developed nations. He viewed UNCTAD as largely serving the demands and requirements of development and the developing nations. UNCTAD got off to a slow start but the oil crisis of 1973 and 1974 led to the developing states making specific demands for a "new international economic order" in the Assembly on May 1, 1974, and then a Charter for Economic Rights and Responsibilities in the Assembly in December 1974.[4]

Basically the demands called for international mechanisms to provide price supports for developing states' sale and exports of primary resources—their main source of foreign exchange at prices dictated by the developed states in the international marketplace. They called for much more economic aid from the "haves," transfers of technology for a growth of industrialization from 7 percent to 25 percent of their national economies, preferential treatment for trade to protect their young and growing industries, and other demands. These demands of some 16 years ago led to global bargaining and political activity at the United Nations and in other organizations but have led to very modest results to date. The United Nations Industrial Development Organization is pressing for progressive industrialization and GATT has done and is doing much for advancing preferential trade for the developing nations. The International Trade Center in Geneva is providing important services in stimulating export and sales capability of the developing states, and UNCTAD itself has been a significant institution for development and modernization. Overarching problems of population growth and the almost 1.5 trillion dollars indebtedness of many developing states are among the other barriers. However, the march toward development and modernization after the gaining of independence can and must continue and only through the framework of international organizations. No state can develop, modernize, and become progressively more dependent on its own resources on its own. Only through organizations can the more fortunate states provide the resources, conditions, and commitments for bringing a greater measure of equity for all states.

ORGANIZING FOR ECONOMIC STABILITY AND SHARED WELL-BEING

"International cooperation in achieving international problems of an economic . . . character" in Article 1, paragraph 3, is another charge to the United Nations that also has been shared by many other organizations. The Economic and Social Council of the United Nations and its responsibilities in this area as set forth in Chapter 10 of the U.N. Charter has been and is as one of the six central organs of the United Nations primarily responsible for the pursuit of international economic and social cooperation detailed in Chapter 9. The council is joined by the regional economic commissions and specialized agencies of the United Nations in the pursuit of shared and progressive well-being for nations and peoples.

It was at the Bretton Woods Conference in July 1944, however, that the first initiatives were taken toward organizing for economic stability and well-being. The forty-four states at Bretton Woods rallied to the leadership of John Maynard Keynes, a top official in the British Treasury, and Harry D. White of the U.S. Department of the Treasury. Along with Winston Churchill, Keynes had warned in his *Economic Consequences of the Peace* that the punitive excessive economic and territorial penalties imposed on Germany by the victors of World War I would eventually lead to major disruptions in the interdependent global marketplace. Keynes drew upon the lessons of history and the causes of the international economic catastrophe of the late 1920s and 1930s to propose new organizations and policy for better management and coordination of the international marketplace in the forthcoming era of the United Nations.

At the beginnings of the modern era, states unilaterally sought well-being with intense competition, some confrontation, and occasional conflict, such as the War of Jenkins Ear of 1739–1741 over commercial rivalry between England and Spain. Trade and commercial policy were under the heavy hand of governments as evidenced by the British navigation laws and the East India Company of Boston tea party fame, the Dutch East India Company and the German merchants' Hanseatic League. Mercantilism or state pursuit of valued resources and maximizing exports far over imports—economic nationalism was the name of the game. Gradually, more liberal trade evolved, to some extent in response to England's recognizing the value of trade to fuel its own productivity in the emerging industrial revolution. Adam Smith in *The Wealth of Nations* of 1776 wrote of the "unseen hand" of supply and demand, as enhanced trade between and among nations would permit them to sell resources of their specialty for imports of resources of other states. Each nation had its own comparative advantage and thus the unseen hand and not governmental regulation would produce global exchanges benefiting all states and producing friendship, cooperation, and friendly competition. The name of the game was now liberal trade and laissez-faire—the reduction of governments' interventions in their economies.

Liberal trade and the flowering of industrialism greatly increased international transactions and exchanges as we have observed earlier in this chapter. Intense competition and confrontation did take place over spreading colonialism late in the nineteenth and early twentieth centuries. In *Imperialism, The Highest Stage of Capitalism* of 1916, Lenin argued that capitalist states' competition for resources and markets led to controls, confrontation, and then war in 1914. His prescription was within the framework of the predicted Bolshevik revolution with a transnational proletariat class later dominating the international marketplace. The revolution did take place in 1917 but the transnational proletarian class was only a myth and Soviet Russia went into economic isolation until the Gorbachev reforms of the late 1980s.

Post-World War I recovery of the industrial democracies was prosperous for almost ten years until cracks began to appear in 1928 and then the thundering crash of the stock market on Wall Street on October 24, 1929. Keynes knew and wrote of the reality of interdependence of the international marketplace, the global flow of capital seeking safe and secure havens, and economic dependencies in world trade and production. But that reality was not matched by any international organizations to facilitate relations and to coordinate through rules and managements trade relations, currency stability, and liquidity for national cash shortages. Furthermore, the key states clung to laissez-faire themselves and shunned economic regulations and regulatory machinery, relying on laissez-faire, free enterprise, and the "unseen hand" of supply and demand. With the collapse of the U.S. economy and subsequent bank and economic failures in Europe, the global depression set in. With it came heightened economic nationalism—new but old as well—and ensuing economic confrontation and collapse of friendly relations and trust, so essential for healthy economic relationships.

Perhaps the most disastrous action of economic nationalism in the name of unilateral national well-being was the U.S. Smoot Hawley Trade Act of 1930, which elevated the nation's tariff barriers to the highest point in U.S. history. The act produced quick retaliation by leading trading partners and led to a reduction of world trade by two-thirds between 1930 and 1936, as well as an enormous worldwide drop in production. Only World War II was to bring the world out of depression, although the industrial states of Europe and Japan suffered devastating damage. The United States, as the "arsenal of democracy" during the war, came out unscathed but required a revived global economy to absorb its productive capacity, which it could not consume on its own. Thus U.S. leadership at the 1944 Bretton Woods Conference led to the creation of the IMF, the International Bank for Reconstruction and Development (now the World Bank), and created momentum toward the new global trading authority, the GATT of 1948. In brief, the international marketplace now had the international institutions which, had they been in place in the 1920s and 1930s, might have through international cooperation avoided the unilateral actions of economic nationalism and confrontation.[5]

The IMF was established to provide mechanisms for orderly and stable currency exchanges between and among nations, to assist nations with liquidity during periods of capital short-fall, and to provide a fixed rate of exchange based on the gold standard and the U.S. dollar with gold pegged at $35 an ounce. The World Bank was first to supply financial aid for postwar reconstruction and economic development. Both were established as independent international legal authorities and the decision-making power was (and still is) vested in the leading industrial democracies through a structure of weighted voting (as distinguished from one vote for one nation in the United Nations and most other postwar international organizations).

The first purpose of the World Bank in its Article 1 of the 1945 "Articles of Agreement" is to facilitate "the investment of capital for productive purposes." The second goal is "to promote private foreign investment" and to supplement private enterprise "on suitable conditions for finance for productive enterprises by its own capital." The language for these institutions' founding constitutions and their practice over forty years underline their purpose of strengthening the global economy on the basis of principles of free enterprises and liberal trade. The socialist states did not participate in the Bretton Woods Conference because state planned and controlled economies were hardly congenial to the theory, international machinery, and practice of a dollar-centered, Western-oriented international economic system. By the late 1980s, however, eight socialist states were members—including the Peoples Republic of China, Hungary, and Rumania (the Soviet Union is knocking on the door).

Led by the United States, which needed overseas markets for its extensive overproduction of resources, the industrial democracies began planning for a postwar regime to guarantee trade as free as possible from high tariff barriers and other impediments to liberal trade. An International Trade Organization (ITO) was negotiated but never materialized because the U.S. Senate and many others felt it would usurp too much foreign commerce authority normally exercised by a sovereign state. In the meantime, principal trading nations were meeting in Geneva under the aegis of the United Nations Economic and Social Council to develop some basic rules for trading. They drew upon the proposed charter for the International Trade Organization to produce a General Agreement on Tariffs and Trade, which became the global institution for advancing liberal trade. Today, the Geneva-based GATT supervises over 80 percent of the almost 2 trillion dollars of world exchanges of resources required by states for their security and well-being.

Flowing from the creation of the GATT was the International Trade Center (ITC), established in 1964 as a joint authority of GATT and UNCTAD, which we appraise later in this chapter. The ITC is responsible for trade promotion, training, and services to enhance the developing states' capacity to export and sell resources to the industrial states and, indeed, to each other. The United Nations Industrial Development Organization (UNIDO), first an organ of the United Nations and now a specialized agency, was established to advance industrial development in the developing nations and to move them from emphasis on production of primary resources as the prime source for foreign exchange toward industrialization and thus greater diversification for their economies.

Joining these organizations are the regional economic commissions for Africa, Asia and the Pacific, Europe, Latin America and the Caribbean, and Western Asia, which focus on economic development, cooperation for regional economic well-being, and specific issues relating to each region. The Economic Commission for Europe, located in Geneva, is particularly interesting as its membership runs from the United States and Canada eastward to the Ural Mountains in the Soviet Union where "Asiatic" Russia begins. It has specific responsibilities for implementing the 1975 Helsinki Declaration on East-West relationships and the many follow-up conferences and policy recommendations that have ensued since 1975.

The Bretton Woods institutions codified an international economic order reflecting the industrial democracies' vision of security and well-being and the consolidation of an international economic order they, indeed, set in place in the 1980s. As we have seen, this order has been challenged by the developing nations' demands for a "new international economic order" to be developed through their commanding majorities in international organizations. Global bargaining was a significant attribute of the international marketplace in the 1960s and 1970s, although the industrial democracies held to their commanding authority in the international economic realm.

ORGANIZING FOR SOCIAL AND CULTURAL WELL-BEING

The wide-ranging activities of the Economic and Social Council of the United Nations have infused this goal of the United Nations with extensive activity and accomplishments for social and cultural well-being since 1945. Many organizational programs and projects of the council deal with social development, status of women, statistical information so valuable to member states, the U.N. Fund for Population Activities, Fund for Drug Abuse Control, the International Narcotics Control Board, as well as the Commission on Narcotics Drugs—all vivid examples of the extensive U.N. activities in advancing social and cultural well-being. Of major importance has been the United Nations Childrens' Fund

(UNICEF), which has made so many contributions to improving the quality of life for millions of every young human beings. We will examine other major programs such as the Commission on Human Rights and the High Commissioner for Refugees in the next section.

Also under the aegis of the Economic and Social Council are WHO, FAO and related agencies, and UNESCO. As we noted earlier in this chapter, a number of agencies and cooperative enterprises preceded the League of Nations in organization for advancing health well-being. Article 23 of the League Covenant called for "steps in matters of international concern for the prevention and control of disease." Then the post–World War II era health organization took a major stride ahead with the founding of WHO at the international health conference in New York and the signing of its constitution on July 22, 1946. The prime objective of WHO as set forth in Article 1 of its constitution of April 7, 1948, is simply phrased: "the attainment by all peoples of the highest possible level of health." The preamble to the constitution states that "health is a state of complete physical, mental, and social well-being and not merely the absence of disease or infirmity." Further, "the enjoyment of the highest attainable standard of health is one of the fundamental rights of every human being without distinction of race, religion, political belief, economic or social condition." The twenty-two functions of the organization set forth in Article 2 of its constitution provide an amazing array of programs, projects, and services, which, for the most part, have been pursued or achieved in the past four and a half decades. Of great significance has been the eradication of small pox from the face of the earth. AIDS, or Acquired Immune Deficiency Syndrome, which has reached epidemic proportions in dozens of nations, has become a major target for WHO operations. A Special Program on AIDS was established in 1987 to develop a global strategy to fight the disease through research on curative treatment and education on a vast scale. WHO has acquired an extensive and well-deserved reputation for its service to progressive and shared health well-being for hundreds of millions and especially for those in disadvantaged nations with totally inadequate resources to deal effectively with their adverse health conditions.

The constitution of the Food and Agricultural Organization (FAO) entered into force on October 16, 1945. The U.N. Conference on Food and Agriculture at Hot Springs, Virginia, in the spring of 1943, responded to President Roosevelt's call on January 6, 1941, for "freedom from want" as one of the four basic freedoms serving as prime goals for the allied cause in World War II. The roots of organization for enhancing global food resources go deeper. An International Institute of Agriculture was established in Rome in 1905 to provide information on agricultural statistics and market trends and to find means to protect farmers against price slumps and glutted markets. The League of Nations explored issues in the area of agriculture and nutrition but this activity clearly was on behalf of the league members and not for the hundreds of millions under colonial control. As with all postwar international organizations, the challenge and operations are truly global.

The preamble to the FAO constitution calls for "raising levels of nutrition and standards of living of the people under . . . jurisdiction of FAO members," securing improvements in efficiency of production and distribution of all food and agricultural products, and bettering the condition of rural populations. This contributes to an expanding world economy and ensures humanity's freedom from hunger and "want" for food. The FAO has earnestly pursued these objectives in its manifold activities since 1945 and has been joined by other international programs and organizations with more specific goals. The World Food Program was organized in 1961 to cope with emergency food needs, especially for nations and areas afflicted with chronic malnutrition and for children under age six with emergency food needs. An outcome of the 1974 World Food Conference was the World Food Council, which generates cooperation among agricultural ministers of states, coordinates international food programs and policies, appraises world food conditions and needs, and mobilizes support for effective and prompt delivery of food services. The Program and Council work closely with the FAO, and all share the same headquarters in Rome.

Another outcome of the 1974 conference was the establishment of the International Fund for Agricultural Development (IFAD), which was established in 1976 and also has its headquarters in Rome. The target for IFAD operations is the vast need of the developing nations for the introduction, expansion, and improvement of food productivity, with the focus on the poorest nations. Improving levels of nutrition is a co-equal goal with helping these nations rely less on others for food, gain enhanced self-reliance, and improve nutritional levels.

UNESCO is the third major organizational approach toward organizing for social and cultural well-being. The mission of UNESCO was and continues to be "cultural" international cooperation, as written in Article 1, paragraph 3 of the U.N. Charter, with education and science also under the umbrella of this goal for human and national well-being. As with most post–World War II organizations, UNESCO was preceded by an earlier approach to organizing for social and cultural well-being. The League of Nations established the Committee on Intellectual Cooperation in 1922 to enhance the living conditions of the "intellectual worker," to expand relations and contacts around the world of intellectuals in many areas, and to support league action for peace, especially through education. The committee, however, did not command sufficient financial support from the League Assembly to pursue its tasks. France, the strongest champion of organization for intellectual well-being, established the International Institute of Intellectual Cooperation in Paris in 1924, which served as the executive agency for the Institute. It gradually garnered assembly support as well as funding by private organizations, and established a number of functional committees that made important contributions to the goals of the committee. Of particular importance was the committee on textbook reform, which sought to reduce national chauvinism by encouraging textbook authors and governments not to use instructional resources as agents to accentuate national glory and to place blame on others for conflict and war. The work of the committee, the institute (and also another institute established in Rome) gained strong support by the late 1930s, especially through national committees of intellectual cooperation, which numbered over forty by 1939 and which served to link international efforts at cultural well-being to similar activities within states, and vice versa. World War II brought this broad endeavor to an official halt but the impetus for continuation survived and led to plans for the new post–World War II organization.

The London constitutional convention for UNESCO adopted the founding charter on November 16, 1945, and the constitution entered into force on November 4, 1946. The striking preamble to its constitution begins with the premise

that since wars begin in the minds of men, it is in the minds of men that the defenses of peace must be constructed; that ignorance of each other's ways and lives has been a common cause, throughout the history of mankind, of that suspicion and mistrust between the peoples of the world through which their differences have all too often broken into war.

Mutual understanding, open communications, reciprocal trust and confidence are distinctly UNESCO themes that were translated into the purposes of UNESCO in Article 1 of its constitution. They include using mass communication to advance the "mutual knowledge and understanding of peoples" and recommending international agreements "to promote the free flow of ideas of word and image." The next goal is "to give fresh impulse to popular education and to the spread of culture," especially "to prepare children of the world for responsibilities of freedom." A third broad purpose is to "maintain, increase, and diffuse knowledge" by all available means.

The record of UNESCO in the past forty-five years is impressive by any standard although the organization has been criticized for perhaps pursuing too ambitious a program and also for some administrative inefficiencies and leadership. It is also appropriate to review the goals of UNESCO to test some of their basic assumptions such as whether "wars begin in the minds of men." In the area of fundamental education and helping many millions at all age levels to gain some measure of literacy well-being, UNESCO is vital to progressive organizing for social and cultural well-being.

ORGANIZING FOR INTERNATIONAL PROTECTION OF HUMAN RIGHTS

Paragraph 3 of Article 1 of the U.N. Charter calls for solutions of international problems of a humanitarian character and for "promoting and encouraging respect for human rights and for fundamental freedoms for all without distinction as to race, sex, language, or religion." This is a legal obligation that implements the goal in the Charter's preamble: "to reaffirm faith in fundamental human rights, in the dignity and worth of the human person, in equal rights of men and women."[6] Organizing for international protection of human rights is a central obligation of the U.N. system and of other regional organizations because World War II clearly demonstrated that many nations did not protect human rights for those under their jurisdiction. Nazi Germany not only did not protect these rights but was found guilty as a matter of state legal policy to compile the worst record in modern history of devastating destruction of human rights, including the extermination of millions of people. It is no accident that the second mission of the United Nations in the preamble is in the domain of international protection of human rights.

A narrative on the evolution of human rights, their enhancement, and protection is in Chapter 6 of our study. Suffice it to say for the present that organizing nations for the national and international protection of human rights has been in the author's opinion the jewel in the crown of the U.N. system of international organizations. The provisions in the Charter led to the establishment of the U.N. Commission on Human Rights in 1946 and the historic Universal Declaration of Human Rights in December 1948. These foundations of organizations and standards and principles were channeled in turn into the two major United Nations Covenants on Human Rights, which entered into force in 1976. Other major U.N. covenants or treaties contributing to the ever-expanding body of international human rights laws include the crime of genocide, protection of and elimination of discrimination against women, elimination of all forms of discrimination, suppression and punishment of the crime of apartheid, the convention against discrimination in education, and protection of the rights of the child among others.

The many specialized agencies of the United Nations add to organization and law for protection and enhancement of human rights. Most of these agencies expand on the basic rights in the U.N. Covenant of Economic, Social, and Cultural Rights. The ILO, which preceded the establishment of the United Nations by over a quarter of a century finds further legal foundation in Articles 6, 7, and 8 of the covenant dealing with rights in the workplace. Article 11, paragraph 2 provides for the fundamental right of everyone to be free from hunger and this is implemented as best as conditions permit through the FAO, the IFAD, the World Food Program, and World Food Council. WHO strives to carry out the "right of everyone to the enjoyment of the highest attainable standard of physical and mental health" in Article 12 of the covenant. UNESCO is concerned with Article 13 and "the right of everyone to education." These are among the many examples of the interdependence between human rights law and organizations that pursue the maintenance of these rights.

At the regional level, law and organization for human rights have attained higher levels of authority and compliance. The 1950 European Human Rights Convention has specific rights backed by a Human Rights Commission and Court to which Convention members have delegated power to make decisions on states' violations of specific human rights and to order compliance to court orders that member states must implement in their municipal law. The African Charter of

Human and Peoples' Rights of 1981, which does not provide authority at the level of the European and Inter-American Conventions, does introduce the rights of "People," which furthers an important component of African customary law. Organizing for human rights protection took a major step in 1975 with the Helsinki Declaration of thirty-five states, including the Soviet Union and its Eastern European allies. The declaration's Section 7 is entitled "Respect for Human Rights and Fundamental Freedoms, including the Freedom of Thought, Conscience, Religion and Belief." The Declaration and its follow-up imple- mentation conferences, administered by the United Nations Economic Commis- sion for Europe, have made major contributions toward the Soviet Union's recognition that it cannot hide behind the doctrine of sovereignty in its treatment of those under its jurisdiction, and it has also been a striking advancement of human rights protection and enhancement in the socialist nations.

The U.N. mission to seek solutions to "international problems . . . of an hu- manitarian character" is particularly evident in the organization's concern and policy for the many millions of refugees or stateless persons who have and are wandering the landscape of this small planet. The League Assembly established the office of High Commissioner for Refugees in 1921, and Fridtjof Nansen of Norway was appointed to this position. He and his small staff first dealt with the flood of refugees from Soviet Russia and then the masses of Greeks and Armenians streaming out of Turkey in 1922. They provided some assistance to refugees from Nazi Germany from the mid-1930s until the beginning of World War II but never had adequate support from the league. A major contribution was the "Nansen Passport" which, upon recommendation by the High Com- missioner gave a refugee a certificate for crossing state borders in the search for new homes. The High Commissioner's operations continued on a modest basis into World War II when the United Nations Relief and Rehabilitation Organi- zation was established in 1943 to provide emergency relief for millions, especially through food programs, and also for some aid to millions of refugees and other displaced persons.

The first postwar organization to assist refugees without a nation was the International Refugee Organization, established by the General Assembly in 1947. It dealt with the flood of refugees in Eastern and Central Europe and was terminated in 1953 on the assumption the refugee problem was shortly coming to an end. In the meantime, a new office of High Commissioner and thus the United Nations High Commissioner for Refugees (UNHCR) was organized by the General Assembly in 1949 and went into business in 1951 as the terminal effort to find new homes for the nationally dispossessed. Its work was rooted in the United Nations Convention Relating to the Status of Refugees of 1951. However, the refugee problem did not fade away but only became more acute as the result of war and strife in Asia, especially the Indian subcontinent, and also as a response to continuing turmoil in Eastern Europe.

The 1967 Protocol Relating to the Status of Refugees recognized that the mass migrations of people fleeing persecution and seeking new homes rendered null and void the earlier assumption that the refugee problem would be temporary in nature. The 1967 Protocol defines a refugee as a person outside his country who has a "well founded fear of persecution on account of race, religion, nationality, membership in particular social group or political opinion" if he were to return to his country. The United States, which has taken in far more refugees than any other nation, incorporated this international legal definition of a refugee into United States law in its Refugee Act of 1980. The UNHCR, which is under the authority of the General Assembly, carries out worldwide operations from the office in Geneva in seeking to provide three major kinds of assistance to today's 14 million refugees. First, the UNHCR seeks to provide legal protection for refugees from any quarter seeking to harm them; second, extend material assistance to refugees in terms of food, shelter, and medical care; and third, to locate a new home. The home may be a voluntary arrangement to permit the refugee to return to his or her native state but only if the refugee and the UNHCR consider that there will be no persecution on return. Or, the refugee may be admitted to the nation to which he has fled or to another state for eventual naturalization as a citizen—the ideal goal.

In the 1980s, over 5 million refugees from Afghanistan found temporary homes in Pakistan and Iran, while millions of refugees continue to lead wretched lives in Africa and particularly East Africa. More than 1.5 million Indochinese refugees have come under the protection of the UNHCR as well as hundreds of thousands of people uprooted by wars in Central America. The work of the UNHCR becomes more widespread each year in seeking some semblance of human well-being for people without a state and a passport. It might be added, finally, that there are more than 1 million Palestinian refugees in the Middle East, tragically the victims of Israeli-Arab wars, who are under the umbrella of the United Nations Relief and Works Agency for Palestine Refugees in the Near East (UNRWA).

ORGANIZING FOR AN EXPANDING INTERDEPENDENT PLANET

A number of international organizations combine several of the purposes of the United Nations as set forth in Article 1 of the Charter in response to the ever-changing landscape of a constantly expanding interdependent planet. The Vienna-based International Atomic Energy Agency (IAEA) was established at its constitutional conference in October 1956 and entered into force on July 29, 1957. Article 2 of the IAEA's statute states that the objectives of the organization shall be to

seek to accelerate and enlarge the contribution of atomic energy to peace, health, and prosperity throughout the world. It shall ensure, so far as it is able, that assistance provided by it or at its request and under its supervision or control is not used in such a way as to further any military purpose.

Seven extensive functions are described in Article 3 as means toward the objective to promote and enhance peaceful uses of atomic energy and to take measures to avoid diversion of atomic energy into military channels. Its objectives include research on peaceful uses of atomic energy, advancement of peaceful uses of atomic energy, fostering of scientific exchange of technical information and exchange and training of scientists, establishment and administration of safeguards for preventing diversion of atomic energy into military purposes, establishment and adoption of standards for the protection of health, and acquiring facilities to carry out its statutory obligations. All of this is ''in accordance with the purposes and principles of the United Nations . . . and in conformity with the policies of the United Nations furthering the establishment of safe-guarded world-wide disarmament.''[7]

In looking backward from the origins of the IAEA in 1956 and 1957, we find a confrontation in 1946 between the United States and the Soviet Union on logistics and mechanisms for control over atomic weapons and eventual destruction of existing stocks.[8] With no agreement, the atomic race got underway, especially after the U.S. monopoly of the bomb was shattered by the Soviet entry as an atomic power in 1949. In December 1953 President Eisenhower called for international action and organization to enhance atomic energy for peace and steer it away from weapons. This eventually led to the creation of the IAEA in 1956.[9]

In looking beyond 1956 and 1957, the IAEA's operations have implemented its functions as cited above and it has been delegated by its members with increasing administrative and supervisory authority. Of particular note is the important role delegated to the IAEA in the 1968 Treaty on the Non-Proliferation of Nuclear Weapons in calling on each nonnuclear nation to enter into treaty with the IAEA to provide safeguards and accept inspection with respect to preventing atomic energy from being used for military purposes. As we shall see shortly, the IAEA has accepted increased authority as the only global agency to oversee international implications of atomic energy—for peace or war.

The International Civil Aviation Organization (ICAO) emerged from its Chicago constitutional convention in 1944 and launched operations on April 4, 1947. The dual purposes of the Montreal-based organization as stated in its convention is ''to avoid friction'' in international civil aviation and ''to promote that cooperation between nations and peoples upon which the peace of the world depends.'' The ICAO is quite specific about what obligations its extensive membership must adhere to with respect to international civil aviation. Its constitution contains many provisions to facilitate air navigation as well as international standards designed to facilitate security and well-being for air travel and to avoid conditions that might lead to extensive damage or loss of aircraft. If we return to the origins of the early river commissions in the nineteenth century, we find the same rationale for international organization to advance states' interests in transportation in the air as on the rivers of trade and commerce. The vast outpouring from the ICAO of regulatory measures, standards for international airports, communications, search and rescue, customs policies, and new international air conventions testify to the expanding responsibility and authority of the organization.

The World Meteorological Organization (WMO), successor to the International Meteorological Organization of 1873, joined the United Nations club of specialized agencies in March 1950. With headquarters in Geneva, the WMO's principal purposes include international cooperation in research, communication and information, standardization of meteorological operations of states, and enhancement of the application of meteorology as the science of the atmosphere to a wide range of human activities (including aviation, navigation, agriculture, and resource well-being such as foodstuffs and water). All organic activity on the earth is affected by conditions in the atmosphere, especially the weather, and the WMO is the only organization that has an international interest in maximizing human well-being, let alone security from atmospheric catastrophe. Given the rate of human pollution of the atmosphere, the tasks and services of the WMO become increasingly vital to human well-being, let alone survival, as we shall shortly observe.

The International Maritime Organization (IMO) was launched at its constitutional convention in Geneva on March 6, 1948, and entered into force within two weeks. The central purposes of the IMO as set forth in Article 1 of its constitution are as follows:

To provide machinery for cooperation among governments in the field of governmental regulation and practices in technical matters of all kinds affecting shipping engaged in international trade; to encourage the general adoption of the highest practicable standards in matters concerning maritime safety, efficiency of navigation and the prevention and control of maritime pollution from ships; and to deal with legal matters related to the purposes set out in this Article.

The committee structure of the IMO nicely presents the principal concerns and obligations of the organization. They include committees responsible for marine safety, maritime environment protection, technical cooperation and services for developing nations, and legal issues and preparation of draft conventions on international maritime issues and interests for consideration by its members and other nations. Along with rivers, aviation, and the atmosphere, the IMO seeks to facilitate relations and exchanges on the one hand and to prevent confrontation and conflict on the other, the core of why we have international organizations in the first place.

The World Intellectual Property Organization (WIPO), located in Geneva, traces its origins the International Union for the Protection of Industrial Property (patents and trademarks) of 1883, today the Paris Union, and the International Union for Protection of Literary and Artistic Works of 1886, today the Bern Union. WIPO, which administers both unions, is a specialized agency of the United Nations with delegated authority to administer worldwide registration and promotion of patents, copyrights, trademarks and other forms of intellectual property. The central purpose of the organization is to ensure that its some 120 members accord to other states the same intellectual property protection as they do to their own nationals.

As with most other international legal authorities, WIPO generates treaties that are amplifications of the purposes and functions of the founding constitution of WIPO of 1967. Examples include the 1978 Patent Cooperation Treaty, which regulates and simplifies the filing of international applications, the 1980 Trademark Registration Treaty for simplifying the registration of a trademark in more than one nation, and many others. Given the ease with which ideas and information flow around the world with no obedience to state sovereignty, WIPO has become an indispensable organization for legal protection of all kinds of intellectual property including recordings, works of art, broadcasts, inventions, and commercial names in addition to patents, trademarks, and copyrights.

Important suborgans of the United Nations have evolved in such a manner as to generate programs, policies, and new international agreements that have moved them toward a significant status of expanding international authority. Such has been the case with the United Nations Commission on Human Rights and the UNHCR, among other suborgans. Another is the United Nations Environment Program (UNEP), which now has its headquarters in Nairobi, Kenya. Environmental contamination has long been recognized as a transnational villain that does not recognize sovereign borders. In 1968, the United Nations Economic and Social Council recommended to the General Assembly that an international conference be convened to appraise the transnational implications of environmental conditions. Although it took three years to move this recommendation to a General Assembly 1971 resolution convening such a session, the United Nations Conference on the Human Environment did meet in Stockholm from June 5 to 16, 1972.[10]

The December 1971 General Assembly resolution calling for the conference stated that the sessions must "identify those aspects of [the human environment] that can only or best be solved through international cooperation and agreement." This is a most succinct statement of the absolute need for an international commitment by nations collectively to enhance a condition of well-being and at the same time to prohibit conditions adverse to human and national well-being. Such is the stuff of origins of international organizations.

The core proclamation of the Declaration of the United Nations Conference on the Human Environment states that "The protection and improvement of the human environment is a major issue which affects the well-being of people and economic development throughout the world; it is the urgent desire of the peoples of the whole world and the duty of all Governments." In December 1972 the U.N. General Assembly established the structure for international environmental cooperation with the UNEP, now located in Nairobi, Kenya. The administrative body of the UNEP is the Governing Council, which reports to the Economic and Social Council of the United Nations. The far-ranging activities of the UNEP since its inception in 1972 have generated extensive international cooperation and progressive treaties dealing with the manifold themes of environmental concern. A great challenge to the UNEP is the work of its World Commission on Environment and Development to minimize the impact of continuous economic growth, especially in the developing nations, on the fragile global environment.

ORGANIZATIONS TO CONFRONT ENEMIES OF HUMAN AND NATIONAL WELL-BEING

International organizations continue to respond to the ever-expanding international flow of hazardous resources and conditions that are the products of an ever changing global society. The need for international organizations thus becomes more powerful with each passing month and year, for only they can confront in any effective manner the uninvited guests and global villains that contaminate and destroy life and that cannot be harnessed by the sovereign state. The catalog of enemies to the noble goals of the United Nations and other international organizations includes drugs and terrorism and all kinds of pollution. Pollution is damaging in itself but it also produces global warming and deterioration of the ozone layer, which protects us from damaging ultraviolet rays of the sun. Atomic accidents and accompanying radioactivity, earthquakes, deforestation, drought, starvation, the population explosion, and the crippling disease of AIDS join with soil erosion, water shortages, hurricanes, and even the locust plague in Africa to inundate the earth and its waters as well as the air we breathe and the heavens above with the gravest threat to human well-being ever witnessed in history. Only a global nuclear holocaust poses a greater danger. The transnational villains are hard at work while the nuclear death threat, at least to the present, is under firm control.

Drugs and Terrorism

International organizations do not attempt to meet the global villains in any comprehensive manner but rather seek international cooperation, some regulation, and laws for each of them. The consumption of drugs such as cocaine, heroin, and their variants is an international epidemic of major proportions. The International Narcotics Control Board of the United Nations in its 1987 report states that the drug problem "continues not only to undermine the economic and social order, but also to imperil the social fabric, and even in some cases, the political stability and security of countries." Under the aegis of the U.N. Commission on Narcotic Drugs, new international conventions that expand on previous U.N. sponsored treaties seek strengthened means to capture and try drug traffickers. The United Nations Fund for Drug Abuse Control works with the FAO to advance crop substitution programs to replace the profitable growing of narcotic plants. The United Nations Industrial Development Program is concerned with conversion of narcotic stocks into pharmaceutical chemicals while the ILO has programs for the rehabilitation of addicts. The WHO's Expert Committee on Drug Dependence provides both education and services. Other organizations, including the IMO, the ICAO, and the Universal Postal Union, have experts and international task forces working on drug-related problems within the confines of the functional goals and operations of these organizations.

International terrorism has assumed proportions unprecedented in history and poses an enormous challenge to conditions of stability and order in the international marketplace. The United Nations International Convention Against Taking of Hostages, the IMO's Convention for the Suppression of Unlawful Acts Against the Safety of Maritime Navigation, and the ICAO's 1988 Protocol for the Suppression of Unlawful Acts Against Civil Aviation are among the more important attempts by international organizations and law to reduce the incidence of terrorism and the taking of hostages. As with all uses of force to achieve objectives, laws and organizations per se can do little to prevent the person intent on using any form of terrorism if the person believes the means advance the goals—whatever they may be—and if the person judges the act as more important than his or her life. The underlying causes of terrorism are many and varied. However, organizations and laws can contribute to enforcement and punishment and establish a global jurisdiction for international crimes so as to reduce the possibility that the terrorist can seek refuge and asylum in any one nation.

Global Pollution

The contamination produced by an ever-expanding global industrial economy creates conditions on the earth and in the atmosphere that continue to gravely damage the well-being of people and organic growth. Only increasingly effective international organizations fortified by regulatory law can cope with this plague that no nation can confront in any capable manner. Transnational global villains can be impeded only by transnational global organizations and laws.

Each year billions of pounds of hazardous wastes are spewed on and under the surface of the earth, 23 billion pounds in the United States alone in 1987. Most of this toxic waste comes from over forty years of production of nuclear weaponry at sixteen plants and research laboratories. It includes uranium, plutonium, cesium strontium, chromium, arsenic, and mercury substances. Of this contamination, some 10 billion pounds flow into streams and surface water. Another 3 billion pounds go into underground wells, almost 3 million pounds into land fills, and almost 3 million pounds into the air. Other surface pollutants include billions of tons of just plain nonbiodegradable trash, including plastic bags and styrofoam containers from the fast food industry. The Union Carbide pesticide plant in Bhopal, India, leaked forth tons of poisonous gas on December 3, 1984, killing almost 3,000 people and injuring—many permanently—some 270,000. Toxic drug spills filled the Rhine River in 1987 and phosphate-fed pollution caused an outbreak of oxygen-consuming algae, which killed fish along a 1,000-mile stretch of the Italian coast on the Adriatic Sea in the summer of 1988.

Massive oil spills are another transnational disaster. The Aramco Cadiz poured forth 1.6 million barrels of crude oil onto the shores of Brittany in 1978, followed by the explosion of an oil well into the Gulf of Mexico. In early 1989, the Exxon Valdez emitted 240,000 barrels of oil into Prince William Sound in Alaska, and many other lesser spills contribute to major contamination. How much longer the earth's surface and subsurface can absorb such wastes is a question increasingly asked.

Smog, acid rain, the global warming trend, and deterioration of the ozone layer are products of earthly wastes that present enormous challenges to the task of life-preservation on our small planet. Carbon dioxide is the principal culprit in contamination of the air. The causes are burning of coal for electricity, gasoline fumes, emissions from industrial smokestacks, and the burning of rain forests in such nations as Brazil. Evaporating fumes mix with sunlight, especially at higher earth temperatures, to produce ozone smog, which damages lungs and crops and trees. Any visitor to Los Angeles can talk with expertise about smog. Mexico City spews forth some 5 million tons of chemicals and suspended particles in the air each year as wastes from 3 million cars and 36,000 factories. Older people often must remain inside their houses and the schools were closed in January 1989 as it was not safe to have young people absorb all this filthy air. Other pollutants that produce ozone smog include carbon monoxide, sulfur dioxide, nitrogen dioxide, lead, and mercury. WHO reports that Mexico City, the largest city in the world with some 20 million people and growing, has ozone levels 60 percent higher than WHO standards for safe breathing.

Emissions of sulfur dioxide and nitrogen oxides primarily from coal burning electric power plants are transformed into acids in the atmosphere and then combine with rain to shower down contaminated water that kills aquatic life and forests. In the United States, the smokestacks of the Midwest and Southwest are the sources and the victims are the lakes and trees in northeastern United States and Canada. Industrial plants in northern Mexico and Arizona send acid rain to Idaho and Montana, and the scourge of acid rain is particularly intense in the western Soviet Union and Eastern Europe.

The next level in the atmosphere is the greenhouse band, which is an accumulation of gases that encircle our planet and serves as an insulating barrier that traps heat from the earth. The causal pollutants are familiar: carbon dioxide, carbon monoxide, sulfur dioxide, lead, and mercury. Over 20 million metric tons of these contaminants are released from cars, utilities, and industry into the atmosphere each year to construct a huge "greenhouse" that traps rising warmth from the earth. Elevation of temperatures on the earth can progressively melt glaciers, causing rising sea levels, and also bring about drought in inland areas of catastrophic proportions.

Then there is the progressive deterioration of the ozone layer, some thirty miles into the atmosphere. This is the protective shield that absorbs most of the ultraviolet rays from the sun that can cause skin cancer and can be damaging and even lethal to human and animal bodies. The ozone depleting culprits include the usual pollutants from fuel emissions but especially chlorofluorocarbons, which are chemicals used in refrigeration and for blowing and cleaning agents as well as aerosols. The depletion has been particularly evident over the Antarctic and Arctic poles, where the air is crystal clear and the ultraviolet radiation is not absorbed in the lower atmosphere.

Confrontation by International Organizations and Laws

UNEP, which was the principal achievement of the 1972 United Nations Conference on the Human Environment, was the first major international organizational response to the growing need—and demand—for concerted global action to confront the increasing contamination of, on, and above the earth. Environmental pollution was and still is a sovereign state obligation and for the most part the responsibility of local units of governance. Solid waste disposal in the United States, for instance, is under the authority of towns and cities. Most nations have only in recent years established bureaucracies at the national level to deal with these issues—such as the United States' Environmental Protection Agency and the Department of Energy. Increasing international organization for environmental contamination and international environmental law have and are bringing nations together to deal with conditions that simply cannot be addressed by sovereign states.

With respect to hazardous wastes, UNEP has brought some 100 nations together in March 1989 to produce the Basel Convention on the Control of Transboundary Movements of Hazardous Waste and Their Disposal. This treaty restricts shipments of hazardous wastes across borders, places controls on waste exporters, and provides assurances for environmentally safe discarding of wastes. The IMO has a Maritime Environment Protection Committee concerned with transnational effects of oil spills. The United Nations Energy Unit may also be strengthened to deal with this issue.

As far as pollution of the air is concerned, urban smog continues to be an urban if not national policy problem and there is also precious little international activity with respect to the transnational impact of acid rain. The United States and Canada have diplomatic discussions about acid rain but no hard and fast agreements. Of particular importance, however, is the Convention on the Long-Range Transboundary Air Pollution negotiated by the thirty-four members of the United Nations Economic Commission for Europe in 1983. It calls on signatories to develop policies and strategies for combating the discharge of air pollutants into the atmosphere and may serve as a model for more universal approaches to reducing the impact of acid rain.

The United Nations and the WMO have combined to bring nations together to attack the problem of global warming through the greenhouse effect. A conference at Geneva in November 1988 has led to further conferences and negotiations for a treaty with the aim to reduce fossil fuel emissions, especially carbon dioxide, by 20 percent by the year 2000. The United Nations Intergovernmental Panel on Climate Change is assessing trends in weather change, especially global warming. With respect to the thinning of the ozone layer, forty-two nations signed the Protocol on Substances That Deplete the Ozone Layer in Montreal in 1988. The convention calls on signatories progressively to reduce production of chlorofluorocarbons (CFCs) to 50 percent of the 1983 level of production by the year 2000. This treaty was the product of some ten years of diplomatic effort by UNEP and obviously met with resistance from producers of these contaminants. However, many industries are coming into compliance. In the United States, DuPont, which produces up to 25 percent of the anti-ozone chemicals, reports it will stop production by the year 2000. In March 1989, 124 nations met in a conference in London to address the global problem of ozone layer deterioration. All evidence points toward continued international organization and law in all areas of human-initiated planetary pollution.

Other transnational villains abound but there is an increase of international organizations and laws to deal with them. The disastrous explosion at the nuclear plant at Chernobyl in the Soviet Ukraine on April 26, 1986, spread atomic radiation over much of Europe and other parts of the world. This led to the initiative taken by the IAEA to negotiate two treaties, one dealing with early accident notification and the second with coordination of emergency assistance in the event of future accidents. The IAEA continues to formulate new international laws dealing with transnational radioactivity. The earthquake in Soviet Armenia of December 7, 1988, resulted in some 25,000 dead and at least a half million people homeless. Rescue efforts were slow and clumsy as there was little coordination of relief missions, gaps in information, and many barriers to assistance as well as endless red tape. This tragedy produced the International Convention on Free Movement of Communications Equipment of 1989 and many calls for a United Nations coordinated disaster network convention.

Deforestation by fires in Brazil, Indonesia, Colombia, and many other nations leads to destruction around the world of some fifty acres a minute. The fires produce 10 to 20 percent of man-made carbon dioxide, which contaminates our air as blazes consume trees to clear land for agriculture, ranching, and to build dams to produce hydroelectricity. Virgin forests the size of Maine were burned in Brazil in 1987. States claim a sovereign right to treat their land as they wish but the World Bank is providing loans to Brazil and other nations to save rain forests and to explore more options for electricity in energy poor nations.

Over 700 million people on earth suffer from chronic hunger and many more are afflicted with malnutrition. World cereal harvests fell some 4 percent in 1987 while import demands rose and the population increased. Hundreds of thousands died in the Sudan in 1987 and 1988 due to famine and civil war. Hunger, the uninvited guest, knows nothing of sovereignty but many international organizations respond in seeking to meet basic needs. They include the FAO, the World Food Program with about 40 percent of its resources directed to the area of greatest starvation, sub-Saharan Africa, the United Nations Program of Action for African Recovery, and the United Nations Development Program with some 25 percent of its resources directed to sub-Saharan Africa. Others include the International Fund for Agricultural Development, UNIDO, the World Food Council, and GATT.

Extensive organizational activity and cooperation also seek to confront the global villain AIDS, which now afflicts people in over 130 nations and is spreading in epidemic proportions in Latin America as it has in Africa. Reports to the General Assembly in 1988 indicated that from 5 to 10 million people are infected with HIV (Human Immune-deficiency Virus), most between the ages of twenty and twenty-nine—the most productive ages for human labor. AIDS is eating into economic production and development, especially in Africa, in addition to the enormous toll of life and human well-being. Research continues but disease-saving vaccines are years away. Nevertheless, WHO has mounted a ''Global AIDS Plan'' to coordinate international cooperation and a global strategy for assisting nations in prevention, control, and research. WHO's Special Program on AIDS also seeks to prevent transmission of HIV, to provide care for those already infected with the virus, and to unite national and international efforts to fight the disease. WHO is the flagship AIDS-prevention organization but has assistance from the United Nations Development Program, UNICEF, UNESCO in the area of AIDS education, World Bank studies and supports, and the ILO on AIDS transmission in the labor marketplace.

The accounting of international organization and law in seeking to deal with problems and conditions that adversely afflict human and national well-being could be extended much beyond our brief survey. The United Nations Fund for Population Activities seeks to deal as best it can with ever-expanding global population, today over 5 billion and another billion easily by the end of this century. The United Nations, through several agencies, confronts the plague of billions of locusts in Africa as well as desertification or the constant consumption by deserts of trees and green land. Drought, soil erosion, evaporation of wetlands, shortages of water for safe drinking and irrigation, horrendous effects of weather disasters such as the hurricanes that battered Bangladesh in December 1988, and other massive assaults on human and national well-being present international organization and law with cries for help and challenges to seek solutions of many and varied kinds. As President Kennedy said in his famous American University speech of June 10, 1963, ''in the final analysis, our most basic common link is that we all inhabit this small planet. We all breathe the same air. We all cherish our children's future. And we are all mortal.''[11]

The reasons international organizations began in the first place—to do for people and nations what they cannot do or do very well for themselves—continue to produce more and, it is hoped, effective institutional response to improving the global condition of security and well-being.[12]

We have traced in this chapter the evolution of contemporary international organizations from the early–nineteenth-century river commissions to the complex international legal edifices of the late twentieth century. The evolution continues into new and uncharted domains of human, national, and international behavior and activity. The foundations of international response to reciprocities of human and national relations are the international organizations, which constitute the ever-expanding growth of international constitutional law. The needs arise for mutual state dependence as we have observed, which in turn lead to diplomatic negotiations toward an international constitutional conference. The result is the constitution of a new international organization, grounded in international law.

THE INTERNATIONAL MARITIME ORGANIZATION: A CASE STUDY

The international constitutional law of the organizations we have appraised in this chapter may be examined by reviewing the constitution of one organization, the International Maritime Organization—IMO—as a case study that reflects for the most part the law of all other organizations. The convention or constitution of the IMO was signed in Geneva on March 6, 1948, at the conclusion of the United Nations Maritime Conference. It includes seventy-three articles in nineteen parts and contains annexes as well. Unlike most organization constitutions, the IMO has no preamble although this basic statement of purpose is legally not a part of the treaty of any organization. Following are the "parts" of the IMO constitution that closely parallel those of other organizations although each has its own specific organs to serve the purpose of the nature of the organization. The parts include Purposes, Functions, Membership, Organs, the Assembly, the Council, Maritime Safety Committee, Legal Committee, Marine Environment Protection Committee, Secretariat, Finances, Voting, Headquarters, Relationship with the United Nations, Legal Capacity, Privileges and Immunities, Amendments, Interpretation, Miscellaneous Provisions, and Entry into Force.

Organizations come into legal existence when states that are parties to the original convention sign the constitutional treaty, ratify that treaty in accordance with their own municipal or national law, and then submit their acceptance to the appropriate official or governing body as prescribed by provisions in the constitution. The IMO legally came into existence on March 17, 1958, when the required number of states ratified the 1948 convention as required by Articles 67 and 70.[13] The member state then passes "enabling" legislation, which provides authority for the state to participate in the organization.

Article 54 states that the "headquarters of the Organization shall be established in London." It then concludes a "headquarters agreement" with the United Kingdom that triggers the implementation of Article 60 of the convention.

The legal capacity, privileges and immunities to be accorded to, or in connection with the Organization, shall be derived from and governed by the General Convention on the Privileges and Immunities of the Specialized Agencies . . . [14]

States with missions to the IMO in London enter into a legal relationship with the organization under the Convention on Relations Between States and International Organizations of a Universal Character. The IMO is thus established with full status as an independent actor in international law. In the spring of 1958, the organization is a business in London following members' financial contributions to the IMO for its operational expenditures under Part 11 of the convention. Further, on the basis of its legal status, the IMO now enters into a treaty with the United Nations under Article 55 of its convention, which regulates its relationship with the United Nations as a specialized agency under Articles 57 and 63 of the U.N. Charter. Under Article 26 of the convention, the organization also has the authority to enter into treaty or agreements with other international organizations as prescribed in Part 14 of the convention, Relationship with the United Nations and other Organizations. These provisions assure that the IMO is an integral part of the total U.N. system and has the legal bases to cooperate and collaborate in common pursuits with other organizations, such as fighting marine pollution with UNEP.

Article 47 of the IMO convention and similar articles in other organizations' constitutions almost exactly repeat the wording of Article 100 of the U.N. Charter.

In the performance of their duties the Secretary General and the staff shall not seek or receive instructions from any Government or from any authority external to the Organization. They shall refrain from any action which might reflect on their position as international officials. Each member on its part undertakes to respect the exclusively international character of the responsibilities of the Secretary-General and the staff and not to seek to influence them in the discharge of their responsibilities.

A careful reading of this integral statement concerning the truly international nature of the secretariat of the organization emphasizes the international legal character and obligation of the organization and its staff. The secretary general and his associates, in other words, are committed to pursue the goals of the organization as compared to the member states and the pursuit of their goals.

As with many other international organizations, the constitution of the IMO authorizes it to generate new international conventions. The precedent for the organization serving as the source of new international law may be found in Article 10 of the 1919 constitution of the ILO, which provides that the secretariat, the International Labor Office, may bring before the conference on the organization or the assembly of states subjects for "the conclusion of international conventions." The ILO has produced more than 150 conventions as explicit proof that organizations themselves are creating new international law as well as serving as independent legal authorities in the international marketplace. On the basis of Article 3 of the IMO constitution, the organization to advance its purposes may "provide for the drafting of conventions, agreement, or other suitable instruments." The responsibility for producing new international law is that of the Legal Committee under Article 35, which is to prepare "drafts of international conventions" to be submitted to the executive body, the council, for implementation and then acceptance by member states. The IMO, along with other international organizations such as the International Civil Aviation Organization and the International Telecommunications Union, has assumed the authority to legislate new rules and standards which become mandatory on organization members unless the latter give notification that they are not bound by this progressive international law. Clearly international organizations should be added as prime sources of international law along with others including treaties, custom, and principles as set forth in the official listing in Article 38 of the Statute of the International Court of Justice.

Constitutions of most international organizations provide for avoidance of discrimination and unfair practices in their specific areas of responsibility. Article 1, paragraph b, of the IMO constitution calls for "removal of discriminatory action and unnecessary restrictions by Governments affecting shipping in international trade so as to promote the availability of shipping services to the commerce of the world" and to advance "freedom of shipping of all flags to take part in international trade." This emphasizes the cardinal purpose of international organizations to foster equity in international relations.

The constitutions of international organizations "make suitable arrangements for consultation and cooperation with nongovernmental international organizations" as stated in Article 58 of the IMO convention. Constitutions also provide for mechanisms to interpret provisions of the constitutions as set forth in Article 65 and 66 of the IMO convention, including reference to the "International Court of Justice for an advisory opinion in accordance with Article 96 of the Charter of the United Nations" if the assembly of the IMO cannot suitably interpret a provision. Authority for court interpretation is provided for in the constitutions of many international organizations. Articles 62 and 63 deal with the mechanics and logistics of amendment to the convention, which is also an important provision in the constitution of organizations. Finally, Article 16, paragraph 2 states that the assembly of the organization shall determine its own rules of procedure, which is a provision in almost all constitutions with respect to the specific organs of the organization such as the General Assembly, Security Council, and Economic and Social Council of the United Nations Charter in Articles 21, 30, and 72, respectively. Rules of procedure are particularly important in the development of international legislation in assemblies of organizations' members as we shall see in examining the operations of the Commission on Human Rights in Chapter 7.

Thus is the flow of international organizations in our era from the humble beginnings to growth, maturity, to the meeting of ever new needs for international organizations and laws, and the basic elements of international constitutional law. We now examine international organizations more thoroughly in terms of their goals, means to goals, and what they really seek to do in the international marketplace of states and other actors.

NOTES

1. The status of the United Nations (and thus other international governmental organizations) as an independent international legal authority was confirmed by the advisory opinion of the International Court of Justice in the case, "Reparation for Injuries Suffered in the Service of the United Nations" (the Count Bernadotte case), I.C.J. Rep. 174, 1949. The Court is "the principal judicial organ of the United Nations" in Article 92 of the U.N. Charter.

2. The industrial democracies account for about two thirds of global exports, 60 percent of production, and about 17 percent of the world's population. The same 125 developing states account for about 30 percent of exports, one fourth of global production, but around 75 percent of this planet's population.

3. This was not the case for organizations such as the World Bank that do not have a voting formula based on one nation, one vote.

4. The "new" order demanded by the developing nations thus represents a transformation of the present order described by W. Arthur Lewis in *The Evolution of the International Economic Order* (Princeton, N.J.: Princeton University Press, 1978). The demands for the "new" thus take place in the arenas of the United Nations and other international organizations.

5. The Bretton Woods institutions are the confirmation of lessons learned from the absence of international organizations of the 1920s and 1930s. They are a marvelous example of the truth of George Santayana's lesson that if we do not heed the lesson of the past, we are condemned to repeat its mistakes in the future.

6. The preamble of any constitution frames the comprehensive objectives of the national or international political system but is not binding as a legal commitment as is the body of the constitution.

7. The best collection of constitutions of international organizations and human rights conventions is in Louis B. Sohn's *International Organization and Integration* (Boston: Martinus Nijhoff Publishers, 1986). This invaluable collection of annotated primary resources is indispensible to research and scholarship in international constitutional law. A major collection of human rights resources is also to be found in Ian Brownlie's *Basic Documents on Human Rights*, 3d ed. (Oxford: Clarendon Press, 1991).

8. See the famous proposal put forth by the U.S. statesman, Bernard Baruch, for an international system of control and inspection of atomic energy for military purposes under the aegis of a proposed International Atomic Development Authority; Robert E. Riggs and Jack C. Plano, *The United Nations: International Organizations and World Politics* (Chicago: The Dorsey Press, 1988), pp. 155–56.

9. Although it obviously has close ties to the United Nations, the IAEA is not a U.N. specialized agency.

10. U.N.- sponsored conferences and conference diplomacy on specific, vital global issues have generated additional international laws and organizations to advance shared and progressive national and human well-being. Examples include conferences on population, Bucharest, 1974; food, Rome, 1974; women, Mexico City, 1975, and Nairobi, 1985; and others on water, desertification (erosion of green growth), and human settlements. These have produced global policy in areas of increasing concern affecting the human condition. Nongovernmental international organizations have made significant contributions to conference diplomacy.

11. Chief Seattle wrote a letter to President Franklin Pierce in 1855 in a calm diplomatic protest to the water and land acquisitions by the white man.

> The rivers are our brothers. They quench our thirst. They carry our canoes and feed our children. So you must give to the rivers the kindness you would give any brother. If we sell you our land, remember that the air is precious to us, that the air shares its spirit with all the life it supports. The wind that gave our grandfather his first breath also receives his last sigh. The wind also gives our children the spirit of life. So if we sell you our land, you must keep it apart and sacred, as a place where man can go to taste the wind that is sweetened by the meadow flowers. . . . This we know: the earth does not belong to man, man belongs to the earth. All things are connected like the blood that unites us all. Man did not weave the web of life, he is merely a strand in it. Whatever he does to the web, he does to himself. (*The Cape Naturalist*, Winter, 1988–1989).

12. There are many major studies of global conditions that require international organization and response. Two particularly important works are those by Lester R. Brown, et al., *State of the World, 1989* (New York: W. W. Norton & Company, 1989) and A Report by the World Resources Institute, J. Alan Brewster, Director, and The International Institute for Environment and Development in Collaboration with the UNEP, *World Resources, 1988–1989* (New York: Basic Books, 1988). Brown's work is an annual study dealing with global conditions in a "world without borders" and is the Worldwatch Institute Report on "progress toward a sustainable society." *World Resources* is a comprehensive report on many topics explored in this chapter and is produced by the World Resources Institute and the International Institute for Environment and Development and in collaboration with the United Nations Environment Program.

13. Conventions of all international organizations are to be found in the official *United Nations Treaty Series*.

14. See the General Convention on Privileges and Immunities of Specialized Agencies approved by the General Assembly of the United Nations, November 21, 1947, which governs legal capacity, privileges, and immunities.

4

INTERNATIONAL ORGANIZATIONS: GOALS AND MEANS TO GOALS

Authors of the United Nations and other international organizations' constitutions invariably articulate goals or purposes for the organizations in preambles and then in the first and second articles they moved on to specify the machinery or means to pursue the goals. We follow this approach in our study of international organizations in order to reflect as accurately as possible in our analysis the structure of the real world of international organizations. In so doing, we draw upon the precise wording in organizations' constitutions of how they develop goals and means to goals in facilitating relations between and among states and in serving as legal actors on behalf of their members.

Our analysis of the U.N. Charter and provisions in other organizations in the U.N. system concludes that the two basic goals for organizations in the system are shared or collective security and shared and progressive well-being for nations and peoples. We draw upon the U.N. Charter for definitions of security and well-being and on constitutional provisions in other organizations' constitutions for elaboration of these goals. We rely on the U.N. Charter for specific means to goals including friendly relations between and among states, assisting nations to gain through exchanges and transactions the resources they require, and establishing conditions through commitments for their pursuits of their goals. The organizations thus seek to help state quests for goals of security and well-being. The Charter then refers to means for collective action by states to enhance cooperation and healthy competition and to reduce and avoid as much as possible confrontation and certainly conflict.

This leads us to the basic conclusion that the United Nations and international organizations in its system represent the further evolution of the constant search by people and their political communities to pursue shared security and well-being in a collective manner—as they cannot achieve these essential goals by themselves. We gained insights from Plato and the historical evolution of political collectivity that the family and then families gathered in political communities to meet basic needs they could not provide without the collectivity. Much later these communities, now states, likewise moved to higher levels of shared behavior within the context of the elemental and then increasingly complex international organization. We observed in Plato the family and then political community as a marketplace for some orderly exchange of resources through exchanges and transactions required for security and well-being. The basic function of international organizations is to provide for order in the exchanges and transactions between and among nations and also to serve as authority on its own for advancing shared security and well-being when states delegate authority to the organizations for these ends.

The structure of goals and means to goals is basic to about all constitutions and covenants in the U.N. system. The preamble to the U.N. Charter begins with four goals or "determinations" by the authors of the Charter and then states "and for these ends" four eloquent means to the ends of "international machinery." Article 1, paragraph 4, is particularly important in its statement that the global organization is "to be the center for harmonizing the actions of nations in the attainment of these common ends" (purposes in Article 1, paragraphs 1 through 3). Some articles, such as 55 and 73, set forth specific goals that are followed by means to ends—"achievement of purposes" in Article 56 and "to this end" in Article 73.

The two principal U.N. covenants on human rights, civil and political, and economic, social, and cultural, embrace the construction of goals and means to goals. For instance, Article 12 in the Economic, Social, and Cultural Covenant states that the parties to the covenant "recognize the right of everyone to the enjoyment of the highest attainable standard of physical and mental health." This is immediately followed by means or "steps to be taken by Parties . . . to achieve the full realization of this right" shall include the following. Article 1 of the UNIDO is entitled "Objectives." Article 2, "Functions," begins as follows. "In fulfillment of its foregoing objectives, the Organizations shall generally take all necessary and appropriate action, and in particular shall" employ eighteen means in Article 2 to fulfill its objectives. Article 4 of the constitution of the ITU sets forth in paragraph 1 "the purposes of the Union" and in paragraph two, "To this end, the Union shall in particular" with eight specific means to ends. Article 2 of the charter of the Organization of African Unity states that "The Organization shall have the following [five] purposes" to these ends in six fields of action. In brief, the constitutional construction of goals and means to goals is our basic guideline for appraising international organizations in the real world.

We now turn to the constitutional delineation of goals, especially those of shared security and shared and progressive well-being for states in the context of international organizations and then to means to goals through transactions and exchanges in the international marketplace. We conclude this chapter with a brief appraisal of goals and means to goals of states to demonstrate that states' quests for security and well-being as they define those goals present the historic challenge to international cooperation for goals of shared security and shared and progressive well-being. The United Nations and other international organizations in the system seek to bring state goals within the domain of organizations goals. However, the historic contention between state sovereign determination of goals and those of the organizations the states themselves established is a fact of international life up to the point when states in their sovereign capacity no longer can adequately achieve their goals of security and well-being.

GOALS OF UNIVERSAL AND
INTERNATIONAL ORGANIZATIONS

Shared security and shared and progressive well-being emerge as the goals of organizations in the U.N. system, both for their members and other states and for themselves as legal actors in the international marketplace. Shared security and shared and progressive well-being may be articulated in different combinations of words such as international peace and security woven throughout the U.N. Charter or the "objectives of international peace and common welfare of mankind" in the last sentence to the preamble of the constitution of UNESCO.

Shared Security

The United Nations is the flagship organization for shared security for its members and for shared security acting on its own authority. "International peace and security" as an overarching goal and condition for the international marketplace of states is set forth twenty-six times in the U.N. Charter. More limited security organizations such as the North Atlantic Treaty Organization (NATO) and the Warsaw Treaty Organization came under the aegis of "collective self-defense" as set forth in Article 51 of the U.N. Charter. We must distinguish, therefore, between shared or collective security for all states and collective defense for a specific group of states that organizes to defend itself against an identifiable common adversary.

Security

Security for the state and thus for states in the system is set forth in Article 2.4 of the Charter. "All members shall refrain in their international relations from the threat or use of force against the territorial integrity or political independence if any state, or in any other manner inconsistent with the Purposes of the United Nations." The condition of territorial integrity and political independence of states and means to establishing that condition provides for shared security for all against threats or uses of force. This even means that the United Nations itself may not "intervene in matters which are essentially within the domestic jurisdiction of any state" although the organization may if it elects to intervene with enforcement measures under the specific collective security pro-visions in Chapter 7 of the U.N. Charter. "Security" and "national security" are terms often found in international constitutional law. For instance, protection of "national security" may be more necessary than the enjoyment of specific human rights, as is the case in the United Nations Covenant on Civil and Political Rights, including such rights as liberty of movement in territory of state, treatment of aliens, public trial, freedom of expression, right of peaceful assembly, and freedom of association.[1] In Article 29 of the African Charter on Human and Peoples' Rights, "The individual shall also (along with individual rights) have the duty . . . not to compromise the security of the State whose national or resident he is." In brief, security as a condition of and goal for the state is acknowledged in international constitutional law.

Shared Security

Shared security is the bedrock of the United Nations and its vision "to save succeeding generations from the scourge of war" are the first words in the preamble to the U.N. Charter. Clearly unfettered quests by states for the goal of security as they may determine that goal is *a* if not *the* basic cause of uses of force when the state invades the territorial integrity or political independence of one or more states in the name of "security." The first purpose of the United Nations is "to maintain international peace and security" as set forth in Article 1, paragraph 1 and cited twenty-five more times in the Charter as we have noted. Article 1.1 continues with means to the end, the taking of "effective collective measures for the prevention and removal of threats to the peace, and for suppres-sion of acts of aggression and other breaches of the peace." It is thus the collective or shared responsibility of members to stand firm against aggression so as to advance shared security for all.[2]

Many other U.N. Charter provisions emphasize the shared or collective re-sponsibility of members for shared security. Article 2.5 calls on all members to "give the United Nations every assistance in any action it takes . . . and shall refrain from giving assistance to any state against which the United Nations is taking preventive or enforcement action." Article 2.6 requires all states "not Members of the United Nations to act in accordance with its principles." States share in decision making in the General Assembly and Security Council on measures to pursue shared security and under Article 25, members "agree to accept and carry out the decisions of the Security Council in accordance with the present Charter."

Shared and Progressive Well-being

This second goal of international organizations includes attaining conditions for nations and people that not only provide security from threats or uses of force but also the promotion of "social progress and better standards of life in larger freedom" as set forth in the preamble to the U.N. Charter. While the

United Nations is basic to the pursuit of shared security, shared and progressive well-being is the broad goal and task of all organizations in the U.N. system. We first examine the constitutional meaning of well-being, then turn to approaches to sharing well-being, and then to the promotion of progressive well-being, especially for nations and peoples whose "standards of life in larger freedom" are far below those of the relatively small number of states privileged with high levels of well-being.

Well-being

The preamble of the U.N. Charter calls for the promotion of economic and social advancement of all peoples. Article 1.3 on purposes calls for achievement "in solving international problems of an economic, social, cultural, or humanitarian character," as we observed in the previous chapter. Article 55 is of particular importance in the constitutional definition of well-being.

With a view to the creation of conditions of stability and well-being which are necessary for peaceful and friendly relations among nations based on respect for the principle of equal rights and self-determination of peoples, the United Nations shall promote: a) higher standards of living, full employment, and conditions of economic and social progress and development; b) solutions of international economic, social, health and related problems, and international cultural and educational cooperation; and c) universal respect for, and observance of, human rights and fundamental freedoms for all without distinction as to race, sex, language, or religion.

Article 55 is considerably amplified in the International Covenant of Economic, Social and Cultural Rights of 1966, which has been ratified by almost 100 nations. Some twenty-six articles spell out in concise detail such rights for well-being as those for labor, social security, family, health, education, and many other conditions of human well-being. Article 11 in particular deals with "the right of everyone to an adequate standard of living for himself and his family,"and especially the right to have food, which for Plato was the very basic human resource. Other international charters and treaties add to this compendium of well-being including the European Social Charter of 1961 and Rights of 1969 and the African Charter on Human and Peoples' Rights. The latter two treaties are of particular importance in that they demonstrate that conditions of human and national well-being are universal and not the monopoly of western nations. A goal of the IMF in Article 1 of its 1944 Articles of Agreement is to prevent measures "destructive of national or international prosperity."

The United Nations Declaration on the Granting of Independence to Colonial Countries and Peoples of 1960 cites "the need for the creation of conditions of stability and well-being and peaceful and friendly relations based on respect for the principles of equal rights and self-determination of peoples." Well-being is in many of the constitutions of organizations in the U.N. system. The ILO's— as reaffirmed in 1944—calls for the "promotion of health, education, and well-

being of all peoples.'' The 1972 Declaration of the United Nations Conference
on the Human Environment states that ''the protection and improvement (of that
environment) is a major issue which affects the well-being of peoples'' and the
first principle of this declaration, which led to the creation of UNEP, calls for
''an environment of quality that permits a life of dignity and well-being.''

The thirty-five nations subscribing to the principles of the East-West Helsinki
Declaration of 1975 ''recognize the universal significance of human rights and
fundamental freedoms, respect for which is an essential factor for the peace,
justice, and well-being necessary . . . to friendly relations and cooperation . . .
among all states.'' Other treaties cite well-being often, such as the treaty establishing NATO in April 1949, which calls for ''stability and well-being in the
North Atlantic Area.'' The goal of well-being is omnipresent in international
constitutional law.

Shared Well-being

Shared well-being as a goal is the sharing by states of conditions and international policy that is mutually beneficial to the quality of life of nations and
people. Such was the case with the eradication of the crippling disease of small
pox under the aegis of WHO in 1980, as well as the pursuit of shared well-being
from contamination on earth, which we surveyed in the previous chapter. Under
Article 56 of the U.N. Charter, ''all members pledge themselves to take joint
and separate action . . . for the achievement of the purposes [for well-being cited
above] set forth in Article 55.'' The extensive machinery provided for in the
Charter, especially under the Economic and Social Council as well as in other
specialized agencies, leave no doubt that ''international cooperation in solving
international problems'' affecting well-being in 1.3 of the U.N. Charter is the
essence of the quest for shared well-being, whether the state and its peoples are
very advantaged or disadvantaged. After all, as President Kennedy noted, the
most basic link of all peoples and nations is that ''we all inhabit this small planet.
We all breathe the same air.'' To cite only one more example, the constitution
of WHO states that ''the achievement of any State in the promotion and protection
of health is of value to all . . . and dependent upon the fullest cooperation of
individuals and states.''

Progressive Well-being

Progressive well-being is the gradual, step-by-step improvement of national
and human well-being as means to the end of a condition of well-being that at
least is an improvement over a previous condition of disadvantage and national
human suffering. Well-being is always a relative term, but international constitutional provisions emphasize the quest for constant improvement and progress,
whatever the definition. ''Progressive'' is a very basic theme in international
constitutional law as it underlines the often slow, step-by-step progress toward
higher levels of authority and capacity. As far back as the Hague Convention
of 1907, the parties signatory sought to serve ''the interest of humanity and the

ever progressive needs of civilization.'' Judge Green H. Hackworth's famous definition of international law in 1944 notes that ''it has developed with the progress of civilization . . . and must be governed by and depend on rules of law fairly certain and reasonable.''

The preamble to the U.N. Charter calls for ''social progress and better standards of life in larger freedom,'' as we have noted. The basic statement of well-being in the Charter is to be found in Article 55, which also includes the words ''progress'' and ''solutions.'' Progressive well-being is essential for developing nations—developing itself being a term of progress—but also for improving the conditions of all nations, such as environmental contamination of the industrialized democracies we reviewed in the previous chapter. Article 73 calls for the ''obligation to promote to the utmost . . . the well-being of the inhabitants'' of the trust territories. Progressive action toward the basic objectives or goals for the trusteeship system are specifically set forth in Article 76. Progressive well-being is enshrined in United Nations Development Decades of the 1960s, 1970s, and 1980s, for progressive development of nations in Africa, Asia, and Latin America.

In the Universal Declaration of Human Rights of December 10, 1948, ''every individual and every organization of society'' shall take progressive measures, national and international, to secure [the] universal and effective ''recognition and observance'' of the rights set forth in this famed document. The declaration progressed in turn to the U.N. Covenants on Economic, Social, and Cultural Rights as well as the Covenants on Civil and Political Rights of 1966, which are international laws for the pursuit of human and national well-being. Article 2 of the Economic, Social, and Cultural Covenant states that parties ''undertake to take steps . . . with a view to achieving progressively the full realization of [these] rights.'' In fact, many of the rights are stated first as goals and then followed by means to goals. Article 12 of the covenant recognizes in its first paragraph ''the right of everyone to the enjoyment of the highest attainable standard of physical and mental health,'' while paragraph 2 sets forth the ''steps to be taken . . . to achieve the full realization of this right.''

In the 1974 General Assembly resolution calling for the establishment of a ''new international economic order,'' members are called upon to ''promote the economic advancement and social progress of all peoples.'' In Article 35 of the charter of the Organization of American States (OAS), member states agree to dedicate every effort ''to accelerate their economic and social development'' to achieve a specific set of goals set forth in Article 31. Article 26 of the American Convention on Human Rights of 1969 calls for member states ''internally and through international cooperation'' to achieving progressively the full realization of the economic, social, and cultural rights or the goals of the convention. Article 2 of the 1957 Convention establishing the European Community (EC) calls for the establishment of a ''common market and progressively approximating the economic policies of Member states, to promote . . . harmonious development'' and a ''continuance and balanced expansion,'' and includes other wording clearly articulating the goal of progressive well-being. A timetable for the progressive policy is in Article 3. GATT in its protocol on developing nations in 1966 reaffirms the GATT objective of "raising the standards of living and progressive development of the economies of all contracting parties." The preamble to UNESCO calls for "advancing . . . the objectives of international peace and of the common welfare of mankind" through "educational, scientific, and cultural relations of peoples of the world."

In brief, with the passing of each year, more and more progress is and/or should take place to advance the condition of human and national well-being. In the area of human rights, which we explore in detail later in this book, the progressive movement for international protection of human rights is a cardinal feature of the U.N. system from the creation of the Commission on Human Rights in 1946 to the vast array of standards, conventions, and means of implementation by the early 1990s. Of particular importance is the concept of "developing," as in the abundant references to developing states, developing toward greater measures of shared and progressive well-being, reduction in dependence on others, and modernization as well. Clearly shared and progressive well-being needs no further documentation as the second goal for the universal structure of the U.N. system and related organizations.

Finally, the goals of shared security and shared and progressive well-being are not as discrete as is suggested by the Charter and the constitutions of other international organizations. Basically, security is a condition of physical protection against threats and uses of force while well-being is a condition of human and national economic and social welfare. But threats to physical well-being from depletion of the ozone layer or global warming as we examined in the previous chapter are key security issues, while nuclear waste and radioactive contamination usually associated with national security are global villains that must be countered to protect and advance human and national economic and social welfare.[3] Oil as the most valued resource in the international marketplace is essential to both goals of security and well-being. The separate yet interdependent goals were phrased well in the Yalta Conference of February 1945, the final meeting of Roosevelt, Churchill, and Stalin. The "Big Three" reaffirmed their "determination to build in cooperation with other peace-loving nations world order under law, dedicated to peace, security, freedom and general well-being of all mankind." Article 32, paragraph 2 of the American Convention on Human Rights unites the goals in declaring that "the rights of each person are limited by the rights of others, by the security of all, and by the just demands of the general welfare." The concept of "social security," widely embraced in the national policy of states and incorporated in international law in Article 9 of the International Covenant of Economic, Social, and Cultural Rights, is a nice combination of the concepts of security and well-being.

In the previous chapter, we noted that about all organizations considered their specific responsibilities—whether in education, health, or the broad goals of the United Nations itself—as producing conditions for peace, a union of security and well-being. We review the theory of functionalism in the next chapter as one that views states and officials working closely together toward a common international cause as reducing prospects of state confrontation. Cooperation and collaboration of states and people in the WHO for shared and progressive well-being contributes overall state practice of integration for a functional purpose and thus elevates shared security as well.

MEANS TO GOALS OF SHARED SECURITY AND SHARED AND PROGRESSIVE WELL-BEING

These noble goals can be more effectively pursued when states as the principal actors enjoy friendly relations and the reverse is true as well. The same is true with ourselves. Second, states find it absolutely essential for their own security and well-being to gain valued resources from others that they do not possess themselves in sufficient quality and quantity. Organizations provide an indispensable role in facilitating essential transactions between and among states. To perform that function, organizations seek conditions of security, well-being, and stability among others and then encourage and develop firm commitments between and among states to facilitate transactions and establish conditions essential to goals. Toward these ends, organizations seek to enhance cooperation between and among states, facilitate friendly competition, reduce unfriendly competition, manage and control confrontation, and seek to avoid conflict but manage and seek to resolve conflict as well. Again, we turn to the specific language of organizations' constitutions, treaties and practice to demonstrate this structure of means to goals.

Friendly Relations

The second purpose of the United Nations as set forth in 1.2 is "to develop friendly relations among nations based on respect for the principle of equal rights and self-determination of peoples, and to take other appropriate measures to strengthen universal peace." Friendly relations are the basis of the venerable term of "comity" in international law, which may be translated into courteous reciprocal relations between and among states. As noted above, amicable relations between and among states are essential to states gaining from others required resources and conditions and from foundations of state power offering to other states what may be wanted or needed through a friendly reciprocal relationship. The word "relations" in other words assumes a bilateral or multilateral transaction which is the very foundation of all international relations and the more friendly, the more effective the transaction.

The Charter states that friendly relations are rooted in a condition of *equality* between and among states, which is the first principle of the United Nations in Article 2.1, "The Organization is based on the principle of sovereign equality of all its members." This doctrine is basic to international law.[4] However, voting in the Security Council of the United Nations in Article 27 is weighted in favor of the five major powers or the council's permanent members. Voting in some other organizations, such as the World Bank, is not based on one vote for one nation—as is the case in the U.N.'s General Assembly and other organs.

Article 1.2 also locks "friendly relations" into self-determination of peoples, which is cited again in Article 55 and is the first "right" in Articles 1 of the U.N. Covenant on Civil and Political Rights and the Covenant on Economic, Social, and Cultural Rights. "Self-determination of peoples" lends itself to a rather imprecise interpretation. For the present, we take this concept to mean that unless a political community has sovereignty for its national self-determination, its condition of subservience to a nation controlling it is not conducive to friendly relations between the dominant nation and others.

Friendly relations are explicit in Chapter 6 of the Charter, which calls on nations to engage in pacific or peaceful settlement of disputes that are specifically enumerated in Article 33. Nations are to engage in friendly relations and transactions to avoid confrontation and/or conflict and to engage in peaceful negotiations and settlements before bringing any dispute to the United Nations. The preamble of WHO begins with the statement that its set of principles for health as "a state of complete physical, mental and social well-being" are "basic to the happiness, harmonious relations and security of all peoples." On October 24, 1970, the General Assembly passed an extensive Declaration of Principles of International Law Concerning Friendly Relations and Cooperation Among States in Accordance with the Charter of the United Nations. This declaration of considerable length goes into great detail with respect to the specifics of friendly relations. About every state has a bilateral treaty of "friendship and commerce" with about every other state, which provides abundant international law promoting friendly relations between and among states.

There is, of course, some ambiguity on degrees of friendliness. Justice Harlan noted that the Supreme Court would "hardly be competent to undertake assessment of varying degrees of friendliness or its absence" (between states, in this case the United States and Cuba in 1964) but suggested that a friendly relationship of some kind exists between states "short of war."[5] Friendly relations include "just and honorable relations" prescribed in the preamble to the covenant of the League of Nations and living together in peace as "good neighbors" in the preamble to the U.N. Charter. The "general principle of good neighborliness" is accentuated in Article 74. A major task of diplomacy as means to ends is to ensure the maximum of friendly relations between and among states in order that other objectives of diplomacy might better be pursued.

Exchange of Resources

No state, as we have noted, can successfully pursue its goals of security and well-being for its people, territory, governance, economic system, and sovereignty without gaining resources of various kinds from other states and offering, in turn, other states value in resources for their own security and well-being. The international transaction and exchange system, which we term the international marketplace, is fundamental to the very existence of states—which is enhanced by maximizing friendly relations. Valued resources include people such as military assistance, raw materials such as oil and food, manufactured products including cars and computers, capital such as loans and aid, and other physical requirements for state security and well-being. Invisible—as distinct from physical—resources include many kinds of services, such as banking, insurance, international shipping, and communications. Also invisible are other bodies of information, patents, copyrights, and trademarks. Because resources are so obvious an ingredient in the international marketplace, the term resources is used only once in the U.N. Charter. Under Article 26, we read that "in order to promote the establishment and maintenance of international peace and security with the least diversion for armaments of the world's human and economic resources, the Security Council shall be responsible for . . . establishing a system for the regulation of armaments." A reading of this provision, however, makes it quite clear the meaning and importance of human and economic resources in the international marketplace.

The U.N. Charter is the core. From the Charter and the United Nations have come treaties and practice that elaborate on the limiting language in the core constitution. Therefore, resources are often mentioned in U.N. resolutions and declarations as well as treaties. The United Nations Covenant on Economic, Social, and Cultural Rights of 1966 is such an extension and elaboration. Article 1.2 states that "all people may, for their own ends, freely dispose of their natural wealth and resources without prejudice to any obligations arising out of international economic cooperation, based on the principle of mutual benefit and international law." Under Article 2.1 of this covenant, each state is to take steps "to the maximum of its available resources" to achieve progressively the broad scope of economic, social, and cultural rights set forth in the covenant. Article 47 of the covenant states that nothing therein "shall be interpreted as impairing the inherent right of all peoples to enjoy and utilize fully and freely their natural wealth and resources.

UNCTAD has extensive policy, concerns, and programs for more equitable exchanges of resources, especially primary commodities. The vast majority of members of the United Nations, the developing nations, have advanced and voted for significant resolutions calling for "permanent sovereignty over natural resources," with resource protection and transactions being at the heart of the "new international economic order" cited above.[6] Article 3 of the General Assembly's Charter of Economic Rights and Duties of States of December 1974 states that "in the exploitation of natural resources shared by two or more countries, each state must cooperate on the basis of information and prior consultation in order to achieve optium use of such resources without causing damage to the legitimate interest of others."

GATT is the principal world trade legal authority, with rules for trade in resources amounting to over 2 trillion dollars a year. Its preamble calls for "developing the full use of resources of the world." WHO is charged with the development and distribution of health related resources for advancing the goal and condition of the "highest attainable standard of physical and mental health" as set forth in the preamble to its constitution. The 1944 Declaration of Aims for the ILO calls for a fuller and broader utilization of the world's productive resources necessary for the achievement of "the Organization's objectives." Principle 21 of the General Assembly's declaration establishing UNEP states that "states have, in accordance with the Charter of the United Nations and the principles of international law the sovereign right to exploit their own resources pursuant to their own environmental policies."

The FAO is charged with "the conservation of natural resources" in Article 1 of its constitution. Expanding international environmental law has as its central concern the quality of global resources. In the 1972 Declaration of the United Nations Conference on Human Environment, "natural resources of the earth . . . must be safeguarded" is in Principle 2. Principle 3 is concerned with "vital renewable resources" and with "non-renewable resources of the earth" in Principle 5. Principle 12 is concerned with resources to preserve and improve the environment, while Principle 13 deals with "a more rational management of resources."

The World Bank and the IMF have authority delegated to them by their members for transactions of monetary resources, especially for progressive well-being of developing states. Section 1 of Article 3 of the Articles of Agreement of the International Bank for Reconstruction and Development (World Bank) states that "the resources and facilities of the Bank shall be used exclusively for the benefit of members with equitable consideration to projects for development and projects in reconstruction alike." "The investment of capital for productive purposes" is the first and prime aim of the bank, and capital is the first and prime resource. In Article 1 of the Articles of Agreement of the IMF, its vital goal is "the development of productive resources of all members," made possible in part by the "general resources of the Fund." The 1982 Law of the Sea Treaty in Article 136 declares that "The Area and its resources are the common heritage of mankind," "the Area" being the location on and under the sea bed of valued minerals. Section 3 of the Treaty and Articles 150 to 156 elaborate on the "Development of Resources of the Area."

At the regional level, members of the OAS in Article 30 of the organization's 1948 charter "pledge themselves to mobilize their own national human and material resources . . . as fundamental conditions for their economic and social progress and for assuring effective inter-American cooperation." The OAS' "Charter of Punta del Este" of 1961—based on President Kennedy's Alliance for Progress—discusses the application of resources in Part 6, Title 2 of the convention.

In *The Republic* cited earlier, Plato held that food was the most valuable resource, "the first and greatest of necessities"—"and the necessity for food is the condition of life and existence.'' But as food is a finite resource within the state, imports and exchanges are necessary because (again) ''to find a place where nothing need be imported is well-nigh impossible.'' In brief, resource development and exchange go to the heart of relations between and among states. International organizations play an indispensable role for much of the orchestration of this vast exchange in the international marketplace.

Conditions

A condition is a state of affairs in international relations that nations pursue or seek to avoid for their security and well-being. States would like to have a condition of economic health and to avoid a condition of poverty. To return to the preamble of the constitution of the WHO, ''health is a state [condition] of complete physical, mental and social well-being and not merely the absence of disease or infirmity.'' The WHO thus seeks to fight, reduce, and as much as possible eliminate conditions adversely affect health. It is in full agreement with Article 12 of the International Covenant on Economic, Social, and Human Rights that there is a ''right of everyone to the enjoyment of the highest attainable standard of physical and mental health,'' including ''the creation of conditions which would assure to all medical service and medical attention in the event of sickness.''

The quest by international organizations for shared security and shared and progressive well-being requires conditions of friendly relations between and among states and then conditions for exchanges of all kinds of resources essential to state security and well-being. Conditions of international security, stability in international relationships, and states abiding by commitments to friendly relations and exchanges in the international marketplace are essential for fruitful pursuit of goals. In the wording of the preamble to the U.N. Charter, the founding authors are ''determined . . . to establish conditions under which justice and respect for the obligations arising from treaties and other sources of international law.''

In the domain of condition for security, we find in Article 2.4 of the U.N. Charter the condition of territorial integrity and political independence of states. Earlier statements of this prime condition include President Woodrow Wilson's thirteenth of his famous ''Fourteen Points'' of January 8, 1918, calling for a program for peace settlement, advocated for an independent Polish state whose ''political and economic independence and territorial integrity should be guaranteed by international covenant.'' Article 10 of the covenant of the League of Nations calls on members ''to respect and preserve as against external aggression the territorial integrity and existing political independence of all Members.'' ''Territorial integrity'' and ''political independence'' are cited as security conditions in Articles 27 and 28 of the charter of the OAS. The famous Resolution 242 of the Security Council of November 22, 1967, calling for ''peace for territory'' between Israel and its Arab neighbors, calls for the conditions of "sovereignty, territorial integrity and political independence of every state in the area" and their right to enjoy conditions of living "in peace within secure and recognized boundaries free of threats or acts of force."

Conditions for well-being are quite specific in Article 55 of the U.N. Charter. We cited earlier that the essentials of well-being in a, b, and c of Article 55 are essential "to conditions of stability and well-being which are necessary for peaceful and friendly relations among nations." The General Assembly Charter of Economic Rights and Duties of States of December 1974 calls for the "creation of conditions which permit the further expansion of trade and intensification of economic cooperation among all nations." The 1944 Declaration of Aims of the ILO states that

a. all human beings, irrespective of race, creed, or sex, have the right to pursue both their material and well-being and their spiritual development in conditions of freedom and dignity, of economic security, and equal opportunity.

b. the attainment of these conditions in which this shall be possible must constitute the central aim of national and international policy.

The above are rooted in the covenant of the League of Nations in Article 23, which calls for fair and humane conditions of labor for men, women and children. Article 22 speaks of "the strenuous conditions of the modern world" that are (were) not congenial to the "well-being and development" of peoples living in the colonies and territories of former enemy states. Article 1 of the constitution of the United Nations Industrial Development Organization (UNIDO) calls for the condition of promoting and accelerating "industrial development in the developing countries." The constitution of the ITV aspires to the condition of "rational use of telecommunications of all kinds" and GATT seeks a condition of liberal trade between and among nations.

The World Bank and the IMF lend capital on "suitable conditions" as set forth in Article 1 of the Constitution of the International Bank for Reconstruction and Development. The conditions they attach to loans especially and to developing nations in debt by over 1.3 trillion dollars is universally termed "conditionality," which reaffirms the significance of the term "conditions" in the language of international constitutional law. The 1972 global environmental declaration in Principle 8 speaks of "creating conditions on earth that are necessary for the improvement of the quality of life"—well-being. The negative "conditions of underdevelopment and natural disasters" cited in Principle 9 require attack while "better conditions for all" in developing countries should not be adversely affected by environmental policy and projects. The statute of the IAEA opens in Article 1 with "conditions" to follow for the objectives and functions of the agency. The third purpose for the FAO in the preamble to its constitution is to better the condition of rural populations.

On the regional level, the treaty of NATO of April 4, 1949, calls in the preamble and in Article 2 to promote "conditions of stability and well-being."

Under Article 29 of the charter of the OAS, "conditions essential to peace and security" include the ensuring of "social justice in the Hemisphere and dynamic and balanced economic development for their peoples."

For the thirty-five nations that signed the Helsinki Declaration at the Conference on Security and Cooperation in Europe, August 1, 1975, the condition of detente or relaxation of tensions between the superpowers and their allies was specifically articulated in the declaration. This document begins as follows:

Reaffirming their objective of promoting better relations among themselves and ensuring conditions in which their people can live in true and lasting peace free from any threat to or attempt against their security.

But this does not stand in isolation from the U.N. system to which the signatories vow "their full and active support" and seek "the enhancement of its role and effectiveness" in language that goes into some detail in seeking to relate the declaration to "the principles and purposes of the Charter of the United Nations."

Finally, we turn to human rights. The condition of international protection for human rights is set forth in great detail in the many statements of standards and in the treaties or covenants on human rights. Article 28 of the 1948 U.N. Declaration of Human Rights calls for an interesting condition: "Everyone is entitled to a social and international order (condition) in which the rights and freedoms set forth in this Declaration can be fully realized." What does the condition of "order" mean? One response is as follows. A condition of "order" is set forth in Article 3, paragraph b of the charter of the OAS.

International order consists essentially of respect for the personality, sovereignty, and independence of states, and the faithful fulfillment of obligations derived from treaties and other sources of international law.

As we shall discuss later, this definition of order, embodied in an international treaty or commitment, is basic to relations of states and international organizations. It also introduces us to commitments or treaties and other forms of obligations between and among states.

Commitments

A commitment is a binding agreement between two or among more than two states to establish conditions and mutual policy for the pursuit of their shared security and/or shared and progressive well-being. A commitment may be a charter, such as that of the United Nations, a treaty, and/or shared and progressive well-being. A commitment is most well-known as a treaty but it may have other names such as a charter (United Nations), covenant (the two principal United Nations Covenants on Human Rights), convention (the four Geneva Conventions of 1949 on humanitarian law), protocol (supplements to the Geneva Conventions), and even agreement itself (General Agreement on Tariffs and Trade). A treaty is the first and prime source of international law according to Article 38 of the statute of the International Court of Justice. The Vienna Convention on the Law of Treaties of 1969 is the overarching international law of commitments among states and other international actors.

The constitutions (charter, covenant, convention, etc.) of all international organizations are multilateral international treaties that contain specific obligations for signatories/members to comply with provisions of these extensive commitments. Clearly, then, commitments involve reciprocal obligations binding on all parties/members for relations, transactions, exchanges, and cooperative policy toward the specific goals of the particular organization and the broader goals of shared security and/or shared and progressive well-being. The commitment thus is some assurance of the condition of stability for orderly relations between and among states, reliability in the necessary exchanges of all kinds of resources, and some certainty that parties/members will indeed observe the provision of the commitments. The countervailing condition is instability, which almost always adversely affects organizations' and states' quests for security and well-being.

The constitutions and constitutional law of international organizations are commitments for states' and organizations' mutual pursuit of the goals of the organizations. Second, international organizations policy machinery is designed to produce continuous and progressive commitments to build on the foundation of the commitment of the organization. We thus read in the preamble to the U.N. Charter of the determination "to establish conditions under which justice and respect for the obligations arising from treaties and other sources of international law can be maintained." The covenant of the League of Nations in its preamble also emphasized binding commitments. The High Contracting Parties agreed to accept "obligations not to resort to war," firmly to establish "understandings of international law as the actual rule of conduct among Governments," and to maintain "a scrupulous respect for all treaty obligations in the dealing of organized peoples with one another."

The policy or output of international organizations thus is primarily designed to establish an ever-expanding set of commitments to increase the effectiveness of the organizations. The policy may be resolutions, such as those of the General Assembly that are not binding on members but do reflect broad desires by states to assume commitments to the resolutions that are passed by a substantial majority. Under Article 25, members of the United Nations "agree to accept and carry out the decisions of the Security Council." Article 13.1.a of the U.N. Charter calls on the General Assembly to promote "international cooperation in the political field and [encourage] the progressive development of international law and its codification." Thus the International Law Commission of the United Nations has been the genesis of a broad array of treaties or commitments that have substantially furthered the goals of the United Nations by establishing conditions to further exchanges of resources between and among states and to enhance international security and well-being.

As we observed in the previous chapter, almost all international organizations have specific provisions in their constitutions to generate new conventions or commitments to create and enhance fruitful relations and exchanges between and among states and with organizations as well. Thus constitutions parallel the provision in the constitution of the IMO for treaty generation. One example among many is the commitment-generation process of GATT as set forth in Article 37 of the Protocol Amending the GATT of 1966 entitled "Commitments." These include specific commitments by the developed states to create conditions enabling the developing nations to progressively sell more of their resources to the industrial democracies in the international marketplace. Under Article 38, the parties agree to "stabilize and improve conditions of world markets" for the enhanced sale and distribution of resources by the developing nations.

TRANSACTIONS AND EXCHANGES IN THE INTERNATIONAL MARKETPLACE

International organizations are required by their very nature to foster and to serve as arenas for the necessary transactions and exchanges between and among states toward the goals of security and well-being. Transactions are basically diplomatic relations and communications between and among officials of states and organizations, and exchanges are those of resources of many kinds between and among states. The Vienna Convention on Diplomatic Relations of 1961 is the international commitment to engage in orderly transactions. We find in the convention's preamble the parties' belief "that an international convention on diplomatic intercourse, privileges and immunities would contribute to the development of friendly relations among nations, irrespective of their differing constitutional and social systems." Exchanges of resources as we have seen through trade and aid, buying and selling, giving and receiving commitments, threat and counterthreat, force and counterforce are at the heart of the totality of international relations—a totality we call the international marketplace.

International organizations seek to enhance cooperation and friendly competition between and among states toward goals for the organization and for states, as well toward the end both sets of goals come closer together with the passage of time. The fourth purpose of the United Nations in Article 1 states it well. The United Nations is "to be a center for harmonizing the actions of nations in the attainment of" the purposes or goals of the organization. These include goals of cooperation and friendly competition and reduction or avoidance of confrontation and conflict. Other organizations similarly state this important concept, such as the purposes of the ITU, which include the harmonization of "the actions of nations in the attainment of those ends'' of the union. As in the second part of this chapter, these are means to ends.

Cooperation for Transactions and Exchanges

Cooperation between and among states and the organizations of which they are members is the essence of international relations. The friendlier the better, according to the second purpose of the United Nations in Article 1. Words such as "live together," "unite our strength," and "employ international machinery" for common goals as found in the U.N. preamble necessitate cooperation. "Collective measures" are required in Article 1, paragraph 1 and the purpose of achieving "international cooperation" in paragraph 3 for solving "international problems" accentuate the goal and process of cooperation. Promoting "international cooperation" is in Article 11 and 13 of the Charter. Article 33, with respect to peaceful settlement of disputes, requires cooperation especially through negotiation to prevent a dispute from sliding into confrontation or conflict. Cooperation is in the very first line in the preamble to the Covenant of the League of Nations.

We find in the General Assembly's Declaration of Principles of International Law Concerning Friendly Relations and Cooperation of October 1970 the provision that "states have the duty to cooperate with one another, irrespective of the differences in their political, economic, and social systems." The General Assembly's resolution on the "new international economic order" of May 1974 calls for "the broadest cooperation of all states . . . based on equity, whereby the prevailing disparities in the world may be banished and prosperity secured for all." The specific wording of the obligation to promote international cooperation is found in dozens of resolutions and commitments emanating from the United Nations and related organizations. Article 1 of the UNIDO cites as its prime purpose to promote industrial development and cooperation on global, regional, national, as well as sectoral levels. The preamble of the International Telecommunication Convention has the "object of facilitating peaceful relations, international cooperation and economic and social development among peoples by means of efficient telecommunications services." About all international organizations preach and practice international cooperation with each other in pursuits and policy in fields where they intersect. For instance, the conference of the ILO "pledges full cooperation of the Organization with such international bodies as may be entrusted with a share of responsibility . . . for the promotion of health, education, and well-being of all peoples." The first purpose of the IMF is to "promote international monetary cooperation through a permanent institution which provides the machinery for consultation and collaboration on international monetary problems." The preamble of the constitution of WHO states that "the achievement of any State in the promotion and protection of health is of value to all," which is also shared well-being.

The 1975 Helsinki Conference on Security and Cooperation in Europe and the declaration emanating from this conference is based entirely on new approaches to cooperation between the Western and Soviet bloc of states. Significant conferences have taken place since 1975, which have been attended by the thirty-five signatories that keep on reproducing new modes and commitments to cooperation in European relations. Section 9 of Cooperation Among States goes into considerable detail on the specifics of cooperation for this group of states. They do not constitute an international organization but call on the European Economic Commission under the U.N. Economic and Social Council to manage its activities and follow-up conferences. Cooperation also finds its way into the name of the principal organization for economic and development policy for the twenty-four industrialized democracies, the Paris-based Organization for Economic Cooperation and Development (OECD). In article 2 of the charter of the Organization of African Unity, the OAU shall "promote international cooperation" and members "shall coordinate and harmonize their policies, especially in the following fields: political and diplomatic cooperation, economic cooperation, educational and cultural cooperation, health, sanitation, and nutritional cooperation for defense and security." Cooperation is a firm tenet and obligation in international law.

Competition

International organizations as organizations of and for sovereign states recognize competition between and among states in their relations with each other and in pursuit of their own goals of security and well-being—which in many instances are competitive. Security for the United States and the Soviet Union have different bases of definition, interpretation, and practice and thus competition for conditions, resources, and commitments characterizes much of their relations. Well-being for the twenty-four industrial democracies who are members of OECD is something quite different than well-being for the vast majority of the developing nations. Both compete in the United Nations and other international organizations for conditions and commitments for advancing different definitions of well-being.

Competition in international organizations takes the form of diplomatic transactions leading to voting in organizations for resolutions and decisions advancing the goals of member states. The United States often claims that in the General Assembly and other organizations' assemblies, competition is unfair because the interests of the developing states are too often expressed in assembly resolutions based on one vote for one member according to Article 18 of the U.N. Charter. Other states claim on the other hand that the fact any permanent member of the Security Council can veto a council resolution by its negative vote tips the hand of competition to heavily toward the five major powers. Developing states also claim there is unfair competition in the World Bank and IMF, the voting is heavily weighted in favor of the wealthier industrial states, especially the United States with some 20 percent of the vote. It may be that there is some balance in the totality of these organizations and that the competition for resolutions and decisions often reflects the condition of sovereign states in contention in political organizations. In any event, the international civil service managing international organizations seeks to make the competition open, fair, and healthy because voting whether by count or consensus is the only way resolutions and decisions can be produced.

Other dimensions of competition in international organizations is competition in trade—the major exchange mechanism of the international marketplace—which is managed in large part by the Geneva-based GATT. GATT earnestly seeks to make this competition fair according to its rules and codes amidst many national claims of unfair competition by other states. States compete for receiving aid and services of organizations such as WHO, which like all other organizations has limited resources to respond to extensive demands for assistance. States compete for assistance from the U.N. Development Program, the World Bank and the IMF. The competition again takes place in the voting assemblies of organizations, which witness considerable and often intense diplomatic transactions for resolutions and policy favoring one nation or another or one bloc of nations or another bloc. We explore these processes in Chapter 4. Competition also is found in contention between and among states on interpretation of treaties and in judicial proceedings and other areas of relations that diplomacy seeks to resolve peacefully. Competition is a fact of international life and organizations and international civil servants as well as most diplomats seek to make competition as fair as possible and reduce damage of competition that is unfair and unfriendly.

Confrontation

A third principal relationship between and among states is confrontation. This condition dominated U.S.-U.S.S.R. relations after 1945. Confrontation takes place when conflictive demands for resources, conditions, and commitments required for security and well-being result in face-to-face dispute over such demands and claims. The United Nations is the prime international organization charged to deal with, prevent, manage, and control confrontational relationships.

Chapter 6 of the Charter provides for "Pacific Settlement of Disputes," and Article 33 concerns confrontation as well as "any dispute, the continuance of which is likely to endanger the maintenance of international peace and security." Confrontation in Article 33 is thus to be assuaged and mitigated by the parties "first of all, [seeking] a solution by negotiations, enquiry, mediation, conciliation, arbitration, judicial settlement, resort to regional agencies or arrangements, or other peaceful means of their own choice." Note the word "first." This means parties in confrontation should first try to settle their dispute by these time-honored peaceful means *before* bringing the dispute to the United Nations. Such a procedure thus keeps the dispute out of the limelight and provides the parties face-saving means to draw back from confrontation into a process and then condition of accommodation and, it is hoped, a return to a friendly relationship. Chapter 6 has five more articles dealing with United Nations options and programs for confrontation reduction, control, and management. In brief, if the oft-stated goal of the United Nations is the maintenance of international peace and security, its role in confrontation management and reduction is essential to the broader goals and the universal organization has performed most admirably in this important role.[7]

Conflict

Conflict is a relation between and among states involving the actual threats and/or uses of force. Again, the United Nations has the major global responsibility for the control and resolution of conflict and to prevent its continuation and expansion. This is in accordance again with the goal of international peace and security and many provisions in the Charter are consistent with Article 1: "to take effective collective measures for the prevention and removal of threats to the peace, and for the suppression of acts of aggression and other acts of peace." This again relates to the first words in the Charter, "to save succeeding generations from the scourge of war."

Chapter 7 of the Charter, "Action with Respect to the Peace, Breaches of the Peace, and Acts of Aggression," has specific and extensive provisions for the management of conflict and disputes involving threats and uses of force between and among states. These provisions have not been translated into actual mechanisms for conflict management due to the confrontation and competition between the two major power blocs. However, adaption of these provisions successfully brought forth collective measures under the aegis of the United Nations against aggression in Korea in 1950 and especially in the many peacekeeping missions of the United Nations, which effectively managed conflict in the Middle East, Congo (now Zaire), between India and Pakistan, Cyprus, and other areas and nations. At the end of the 1980s, the United Nations is involved more than any time in its history in conflict management and resolution especially in Afghanistan, Namibia, Kampuchea, and the Middle East.

The most powerful response by the United Nations under Chapter 7 on the initiative of the United States was the extensive collective measures against Iraq in response to its invasion of Kuwait on August 2, 1990. Beginning with Security Council Resolution 660 of August 2, 1990, and capped off by Resolution 678 of November 29, 1990, which called for "all necessary means" (read force) to evict Iraq from Kuwait, the United Nations military coalition was dedicated to the achievement of its goal through extensive military force.

Although Cicero noted that "inter arma silent leges" (in war the law is silent), there is much evidence that things have changed. Conflict is legally permissible in self-defense, in collective measures under the United Nations, and enforcement action under the authority of regional arrangements. It has traditionally been

widely used in the fight for national determination. The basic laws for humanitarian well-being are under the Geneva Conventions of 1949 dealing with war
on land, sea, prisoners of war, and conditions in occupied territory. These are
fortified by the Protocols of 1977, which are concerned with wars of national
liberation and civil wars not related to outside intervention. They are administered
by the same 171 states adhering to the treaties and by the International Committee
of the Red Cross as we observed in Chapter 2. Many international laws are on
the books dealing with terrorism, torture, and other international crimes. The
challenge to international law and organizations is to move more law into place
and to continue to develop legal and organizational capacity to implement the
law.[8]

Goals, Means, and Interdependence

In May 1974, in its resolution on a "new international economic order," the
General Assembly recognized "the reality of interdependence of all the members
of the world community." Interdependence obviously means increasingly dependence by all states on other states and the increasing need for international
organizations to play a powerful role in managing and facilitating quests by states
for resources, conditions, and commitments to ease their dependence and enhance
their security and well-being. The foundations are the organizations' constitutions, which are legal commitments subscribed to by their members. The organizations serve as arenas for multilateral transactions, diplomacy produced
through resolutions and decisions, and international legislation designed to enhance exchanges of resources between and among states and organizations. This
legislation also seeks to establish conditions, produce commitments, and in some
cases provide resources all toward advancing organization goals of shared security and/or shared and progressive well-being. In so doing, it is also an objective
to bring states' goals of security and well-being more into harmony with the
organizations' articulated goals of shared security and shared and progressive
well-being.

THE STATE AND THE INTERNATIONAL MARKETPLACE

Members of international organizations contribute many kinds of resources to
enable the organizations to pursue goals of shared security and shared and progressive well-being through the means or policies and the transactions and exchanges we have outlined in this chapter. We observed in Chapter 2 that states
have established international organizations and have contributed toward their
goals and policies because the organizations facilitate relations between and
among states and perform functions that states by themselves cannot accomplish.
From the evolution of organizations and their vast and manifold operations in
the international marketplace, we can better explain the role of the states them-

selves in this total system, especially when we derive from goals and means to goals of organizations to goals and means to goals of states.

The essential goals of states in relations with others is the security and well-being of their central interests, which are territory, the people, governance and its values, the economic system and resources, and the sovereignty of the state. A state cannot exist without these central interests, they are the raison d'etre of state policy of security and well-being and collectively provide the prime foundation of the power of the state to pursue goals in the international marketplace. Each state in its constitution has a basic statement about its goals, whether the constitution is in writing or not. The preamble to the U.S. Constitution thus states this nation's goals and means to goals: "We the people, in order to form a more perfect union, establish justice, insure domestic tranquility, provide for the common defense, promote the general welfare, and secure the blessings of liberty." These goals find their way into over 200 years of national legislation and Supreme Court decisions expressing basic United States interests.[9] Clearly they parallel organization goals of shared security and shared and progressive well-being.

We saw in the parable of Plato and in other commentary that no state has within its jurisdiction all that which it judges it requires for security and well-being. Thus the state through its national policy and national policy process must go to the external international marketplace for resources, conditions, commitments, and occasionally controls to enhance its goals of security and well-being. This parallels the role of organizations in pursuing friendly relations between and among states, facilitating resource exchange, and creating and expanding conditions and commitments to assist states in their necessary quests for their requirements. The power states possess to seek and gain these requirements is derived from their territory, people, governance (including the military), and economic system and resources—the currency they need to gain what they seek of others in the international marketplace.

The historic problem in the balance between the sovereign state and *its* quest for its security and well-being and the institutions of international organizations and law and *their* quest for shared security and shared and progressive well-being is the state's sovereign right to define the meaning of security and well-being for its central interests. The ideal is a coalescence between state definitions and organizations and laws defining shared security and shared and progressive well-being—which we examine more fully in the next chapter.

Four fairly stable factors, including the state's history, geography, economic system, and resources, comprise a mold that may dictate the more permanent character of state power. Four fairly fluid determinants include demands and supports of domestic sources of policy, conditions and events in the external international marketplace, governance and officials below top leadership, and top leadership itself. Each nation provides a case study on the relative importance of each of these eight determinants of national security and well-being.

Historic invasions from the west have substantially tempered the requirement by the Soviet Union today for controls over Eastern Europe. The geographic position of the United States for most of its history has immunized it from any great fear of direct attack. High levels of economic performance and access to resources provide the industrial states with high levels of well-being and the reverse for most of the world's states. Well-being for India cannot be understood without a basic knowledge of the nature of Hindu religion.

Domestic sources of policy in the democracies make many demands on how security and well-being are defined. External events in the international marketplace far more determine approaches to well-being for the developing states than their very limited capacity to influence those events, such as the global price of their primary resources. The bureaucracies and the Communist Party in the Peoples Republic of China have much to say about the nation's goals, as does the U.S. Congress. Security requirements for President Carter and President Reagan differed sharply, especially in strategic arms negotiations and commitments.

The national policy of states thus seeks in the international marketplace resources, conditions, commitments, and possibly controls to advance their interpretation and requirements for security and well-being. As the two superpowers so heavily influence security for our small planet, each seeks conditions to further its goals. President Truman declared when he announced the famous Truman Doctrine on March 12, 1947 that "one of the primary objectives of the foreign policy of the United States is the creation of conditions in which we and other nations will be able to work out a way of life free from coercion." Article 28 of the 1977 Constitution of the U.S.S.R. states that the nation's foreign policy is aimed at favorable conditions for building communism in the U.S.S.R., strengthening the position of world socialism.

Because of the differences in definitions of security, the kinds of conditions the policies these nations sought throughout the Cold War were clearly competitive and often confrontive. The demise of the Cold War has been marked by increased consensus by the two powers on the condition of security and thus shared security.

As we observed earlier with respect to organization goals of shared security and shared and progressive well-being, these two goals usually are not discrete and often depend on each other. Functionalism, an important theory in international integration, basically holds that economic and social cooperation between and among states will reduce tension and confrontation and will build the foundations of a secure world. In the famous Truman Doctrine of March 1947, U.S. aid to Greece and Turkey was framed on the premise that both economic and military assistance were required to bolster these nations and each depended on the effectiveness of the other. The Marshall Plan, announced three months later, was grounded in the same premise—that the security of the European nations—and thus United States—demanded an economically strong Europe.

Given vast differences between and among states in determinations of security and well-being in the framework of international organizations is an enormous task, especially for diplomats who have the responsibility in time and place to correlate state security of one or a few with shared security for the many. Twelve resolutions by the Security Council, between August 1990 and March 1991, did merge state definition of security with shared security under the aegis of the United Nations in the historic U.N. coalition of states which drove Iraq out of Kuwait in the Gulf War. Debate in the United States raged over this nation's votes in the Security Council for collective measures including force in Resolution 678 of November 29, 1990, as against many in Congress who felt that only that body has the authority to declare war. This issue revolved around political turf between the President and Congress and also whether "collective measures" should go beyond economic sanctions to include use of force for deterrent purposes under the authority of the Charter. As often happens, contending forces within the state may agree on the goal of security but not necessarily on the magnitude of the threat or the policy of response. The United States' final policy did merge its state security as a goal with shared security of the United Nations in this historic functioning of the United Nations, as its authors intended when they wrote the Charter in 1945.[10]

In any event, the overarching structure for goals and means to goals in the Charter and constitutions of most other international organizations of shared security and shared and progressive well-being is reflected in state goals of national security and well-being. The gaps between state and organizations' goals are many and varied, given the numbers of states and the variables that shape state requirements for the pursuit of those goals. We explore this central problem of relations between states on the one hand and international organizations and law on the other in the next chapter along with the spectrum of sovereign state authority to the authority of the sovereign organization.

NOTES

1. See Articles 12, 13, 14, 19, 21, and 22 of the covenant.

2. We prefer the adjective "share" to underline mutuality and reciprocity implicit in "share" rather than the aggregate joining of forces implied in the word "collective."

3. It is interesting to note that at the 44th General Assembly in 1989, the United States, the United Kingdom, and the Soviet Union, among other sponsors, sought for the Security Council to determine drug trafficking "a threat to international peace and security." Seven developing nations combined to defeat the draft resolution on the grounds that "the Security Council should deal only with direct threats and uses of force" (*New York Times*, October 11, 1989). Senator Sam Nunn, chairman of the Armed Services Committee of the U.S. Senate, declared that environmental destruction is a "growing national security threat." The late Vice President Hubert Humphrey always complained that "security" was taken to be military power. He held that it is "much broader than military power and much more complex. There can be no security without a commitment to social betterment." Ruth Leger Sivard (ed.), *World Military and Social Expenditures: 1987–1988* (Washington, D.C.: World Priorities, 1987). *Alternative Security: Living Without Nuclear Deterrence*, edited by Burns H. Weston (Boulder: Westview Press,

1990) presents seven approaches to security other than nuclear stand-off including Weston's chapter, "Law and Alternative Security: Toward a Just World Peace."

4. "No principle of general law is more universally acknowledged than the perfect equality of nations. Russia and Geneva have equal rights. It results from this equality, that no one can rightfully impose a rule on another." U.S. Chief Justice John Marshall in *The Antelope*, 1825. At that time, Geneva was a sovereign state and the smallest, while Russia was the largest.

5. *Banco Nacional de Cuba v. Peter L. F. Sabbatino*, United States Supreme Court, 376 U.S. 398, 1964.

6. Resolution on Permanent Sovereignty over Natural Resources, General Assembly, December 14, 1962: "full permanent sovereignty of every State over its natural resources and all economic activities." Assembly resolution of May 1, 1974, calling for a "New International Economic Order"; and "In the exploitation of natural resources shared by two or more countries, each must cooperate . . . in order to achieve optimum use of such resources." See General Assembly Resolution, "Charter of Economic Rights and Duties of States," December 14, 1974, among other declarations and resolutions.

7. See A. Le Roy Bennett, *International Organizations*, 4th ed. (Englewood Cliffs, N.J.: Prentice-Hall, 1988) for compilations of well over 100 disputes considered and in many cases resolved by the Security Council and General Assembly of the United Nations.

8. See Adam Roberts and Richard Guelff, *Documents on the Laws of War* (Oxford: Clarendon Press, 1989) for an impressive collection of primary resources on law of conflict.

9. The court speaks of the nation's "safety, independence, and welfare" in *Fong Yue Ting v. United States*, 149 U.S. 698, 1893; "peace and safety" in *Mahler v. Eby*, 264 U.S. 32, 1924; and "national well-being" in *Missouri v. Holland*, 252 U.S. 416, 1920.

10. See Thomas M. Franck and Faiza Patel, "UN Police Action in Lieu of War: The Old Order Changeth," *American Journal of International Law* (January 1991): 63 ff.

5

INTERNATIONAL ORGANIZATIONS: FROM HIGH STATE AUTHORITY TO SUPRA ORGANIZATION AUTHORITY

States devise international organizations because they cannot successfully achieve goals of security and well-being in a unilateral manner and because they accept the fact that sharing the pursuit of goals in an international organization can enhance their security and well-being. There is, however, a spectrum or continuum of international organizations concerning the extent to which states choose to share with other states the pursuit of common goals. Well over 90 percent of states are members of the principal organizations in the U.N. system and other international legal authorities such as the World Bank and WHO.[1] Each, however, may determine the extent it wants to retain and maximize its sovereign authority to determine its goals and policy, the extent to which it seeks a partnership role with international organizations of which it is a member, the delegation of substantial state authority to which it is a member, the delegation of substantial state authority to the organization within a framework of shared security and well-being, and finally whether it chooses to lock in and not withdraw delegated authority from the organization. The four basic positions on our spectrum are (1) high state authority, (2) partnership between state and organization, (3) high organization authority, and (4) supraorganization authority.

Caution is advised when using any classification system. There is no fully sovereign state at one end of the spectrum because all states have dependency on some others. There is no fully sovereign organization because the very concept of the sovereign state is not compatible with a "sovereign organization" with complete authority over its members. Gray areas abound along the spectrum. Any state may insist on sovereign authority to determine its security goals, assume a partnership goal with WHO for shared well-being, delegate considerable authority to the ITU to regulate radio frequencies, and accept considerable sovereign authority by the Commission and the Court of the European Community (EC) in many facets of its economic policy. France is such a state, and likewise many other states may have varying degrees or relations with or commitments to organizations.

Furthermore, states are free to alter those relations and commitments back and forth depending on the demands and policy objectives of domestic sources of policy and governance in the state (such as the U.S. Congress, events in the international marketplace, and especially the vision and commands of top leadership). Some of these variables motivated the United States temporarily to leave the ILO from 1977 to 1980 and in 1984 to withdraw from UNESCO. The United Kingdom followed suit in 1985. The United States generally dominated voting in the U.N. General Assembly from 1946 until the late 1950s, while the Soviet Union made abundant use of the veto in the Security Council during the same period to protect its interests. In the past several decades, votes in the General Assembly have not been congenial to U.S. determinations of its goals of security and especially well-being. It has bended to vote negatively in the council more than any other permanent member. U.S. support for the United Nations waned during the Reagan administration, but President Bush increasingly calls for a stronger United Nations.

As we observed in Chapter 2, the trend is definitely toward multilateralism and an increase in organizations' authority in moving toward greater sharing of security and well-being in proportion to states' increasing incapability to pursue their own goals in any independent or quasi-independent manner. Nevertheless, the state remains sovereign, has considerable reserved powers in the constitutions of international organizations as well as in its own constitution, and has forces within its governance and domestic sources of policy that jealously protect state sovereign authority. But turning from high state authority to state/organization partnership, we find abundant evidence of constitutional authority and cooperation between and among states and organizations to pursue more common goals. We then move along to examine such policy and practice in high organization authority and then a momentum toward supra-organization authority, especially in Western Europe.

This spectrum was explored in different ways as the English colonies in North America moved toward independence, confederation, and then federation with the constitution of 1789. *The Federalist Papers* continue to provide insights and wisdom with respect to the role of more centralized governance in ensuring enhanced security and well-being for people and units of government under its authority. The constitutional history of the United States is an example of co-operation and contention between the federal government and the powers "reserved to the States respectively, or to the people" in the Tenth Amendment. The more youthful constitutional history of international organization reveals similar patterns.

HIGH STATE AUTHORITY

There is no purely sovereign state although a few states exercise high and semi-exclusive authority over their goals of security and well-being as they define them. All states have some economic dependency on others and all states voluntarily enter into treaties or commitments that place limits on unilateral state policy and that constitute various patterns of cooperation and sharing with other states in areas of security and well-being. Any compendium of bilateral and multilateral treaties such as the United Nations Treaty Series provides a graphic illustration of ever expanding legal commitments and thus constraints on state sovereignty and on exercise of unilateral state policy.

We can cite very few states today that seek high state authority in most of their national policies. Myanmar (Burma) and Albania are hardly congenial members of the global community of states. The United Nations has repeatedly repudiated the goals and policies of the Republic of South Africa, which is a pariah for the most part. Israel's goals and policies likewise have been annually condemned by the vast majority of members of the United Nations. Based on his experience, former U.S. Ambassador to the United Nations, Daniel Patrick Moynihan, found the United Nations a very "dangerous place."[2] Germany and Japan marched out of the League of Nations in 1933 and the Soviet Union was cast out in 1939 over its war against Finland. There are not many other examples of high state authority in the comprehensive determination of state goals and national policy.

Although about all states are members of organizations in the U.N. system and other international legal authorities, there are at least four reasons why many states and especially the super and major powers retain high state authority in significant sectors of national policy. They have reserved powers in the constitutions of organizations and often in their own national constitutional law. Much state policy and legislation erect barriers to organization partnership, and in many nations there is a strong foundation of patriotism and national identity in public opinion, which is hardly supporting of any merger of national and international interests or policy.

Reserved Powers in International Constitutions

Somewhat like the Tenth Amendment of the U.S. Constitution, constitutions of international organizations and other international treaties and agreements afford their members or treaty adherents reserved rights to immunize themselves in part or whole from organization authority. The basic provision on state sovereignty in the U.N. Charter is "territorial integrity and political independence" in Article 2, paragraph 4. As we have earlier observed, conditions of statehood are guaranteed in this provision from threat or use of force by all nations. Sovereign equality of all members is ensured in Article 2, paragraph 1. In Article 2, paragraph 7, the United Nations may not "intervene in matters which are essentially within the domestic jurisdiction of any state" except in cases of enforcement measures in Chapter 7 of the U.N. Charter. The veto power of permanent members of the Security Council in Article 27 reserves to such states the right to block implementation of council decisions. Each state in Article 51 has the right of "individual or collective self-defense," a "right" usually invoked by any state using threats or actual force whether for actual defense of "preventive" (read, offensive) defense measures.

Security safeguards exist in many other international treaties. Article 21 of GATT states that nothing in this world charter for the rules of trade "shall be construed . . . to prevent any contracting party from taking any action which it considers necessary for the protection of its essential security interests."[3] A careful reading of the General Agreement reveals many escape clauses states may use to exempt themselves from the global rules for trade.

Five articles in the U.N. Covenant on Civil and Political Rights permit signatories to derogate their obligations on the grounds of security and public order. "Security clawbacks" from obligations are permissible with the liberty of movement by people within the state or leaving the state, freedom of expression, peaceful assembly, and freedom of association.[4] No derogation is permitted with respect to the rights of life; freedom from torture, slavery, or servitude; inability to fulfill a contract; being subjected to an *ex post facto* law; and being a person before the law.[5] It still is the prerogative of each state to define what security actually is although the momentum toward patterns of shared security and thus a common definition is a fact of international life in the late 1980s and early 1990s.

Therefore, the provisions we have cited are increasingly subjected to critical inquiry with respect to state guardianship of state sovereignty. States probably would not become members of the United Nations if their territorial integrity and political independence were not guaranteed in Article 2, paragraph 4. But states exercise sovereign authority to alter the condition of "territorial integrity" through treaties and practices such as permitting ships of other nations the right of innocent passage through their territorial waters as in the 1982 Law of the Sea Treaty or flights over their territory under the legal authority of the ICAO. "Political independence" is abridged by states abiding by the rules of trade under the aegis of GATT.

Sovereign equality of states in Article 2, paragraph 1, is a time-honored principle of international law. The right of permanent members of the Security Council to veto council resolutions is not exactly "sovereign equality." However, neither superpower would have signed the U.N. Charter without the veto that has been used most sparingly in recent years.

Article 2, paragraph 7, indeed has been invoked, especially by the Republic of South Africa, as the prime limitation on intrusion into "domestic jurisdiction." Increasingly, however, questions are being asked as to words in this paragraph. What are "matters?" What does "essentially" mean, and thus who is to say what is essentially within domestic jurisdiction and what is not? What is domestic jurisdiction in view of treaties such as the 1984 Convention Against Torture and Other Cruel, Unusual, or Degrading Treatment or Punishment, which makes the heinous crime of torture international in scope and jurisdiction and thus not protected by "domestic jurisdiction" if the culprit torturer is apprehended. There is no question that states demand safeguards against armed intervention as a violation of Article 2, paragraph 4. However, Article 2, paragraph 7, is increasingly less relevant against the claim and act of humanitarian intervention to uphold international human rights law in states where there are manifest violations of human rights. In brief, as states enter into more and more international organizations and treaty commitments to advance their goals, they give evidence of voluntarily yielding dimensions of state sovereignty.

Some organizations have copious provisions in their constitutions for member states to deviate from specific obligations. By whatever name—derogations, waivers, safeguard clauses for sovereign authority, or exclusions—they do protect high state sovereignty. As we have noted before, states usually will not accept absolutely binding commitments damaging to state definitions of security and well-being. Such is the case of GATT, which in addition to the "security clawback" in Article 21 contains many other articles enabling states to waive obligations seeking to maximize liberal trade relations. "Safeguard" clauses include "temporary" waivers for balance of payment problems, injury due to "market disruption" and exemptions "in exceptional circumstances not elsewhere provided for in this Agreement."[6] Similar provisions in constitutions of other organizations are safeguards for exercise of high state authority. However, states abide by their commitments under the GATT far more often than they deviate from them. The record of GATT is hardly perfect vis-a-vis the agreement's goals, but the record since 1948 reveals dramatic reductions in trade barriers including a thirty-fold expansion in world trade.

Reserved Powers in State Constitutions and Governance

It would require extended analysis to examine in the constitution of members of the United Nations and other organizations the legal limitations on states extending authority to the international organizations. The U.S. Constitution, which the president vows in his inauguration to "preserve, protect, and defend," has some specific provisions that preclude delegation of certain authority. In Article 2, "Executive power shall be vested in a President of the United States" and thus not in an international organization with respect to the vast executive authority of the president. The president is "commander in chief of the Army and Navy of the United States," a fact President Truman very much had in mind when he dismissed General MacArthur in 1951, who was then commander of U.N. forces in Korea. This authority, therefore, should be appraised within the context of possible military operations by the United Nations in the provisions of Chapter 7 of the U.N. Charter.

The U.S. Congress has the authority to declare war under Article 1. When Senator Henry Cabot Lodge and others read the covenant of the League of Nations in 1919, they found that the United States as a member of the league could be swept into war under certain conditions without authorization of declaration of war by Congress. This was one reason among many why Congress failed to give advice and consent to ratify the covenant. It also explains strong U.S. support for the right of veto in Article 27 of the U.N. Charter and the provision of Article 5 of the North Atlantic Treaty of April 1949 that participation in possible collective defense military measures under NATO is hedged by each state taking such action as "it deems necessary." In referring to this provision in Senate hearings on NATO, Senator Arthur Vandenburg proudly claimed that the American flag continues to fly over the Capitol.

Congressional authority to tax and appropriate monies hit the U.N. system like a brick in the mid-1980s when legislation specifically demanded sharp cuts in U.S. support of most intergovernmental organizations. Congress "regulates commerce with foreign nations" with authority as exercised in the Trade Act of 1988 for protectionist policy at some variance with U.S. commitments under GATT. The U.S. position, however, was that unilateral determination of what unfair trade is will force other nations with tariff obstacles to reduce their own barriers and to return, therefore, to the multilateral determination of trade practices under GATT.

The U.S. Senate has never given its advice and consent for ratification of the two principal U.N. covenants on human rights on the grounds that too many covenant provisions conflict with the U.S. Constitution or call for rights not so recognized by the United States, such as the right to work, health, and education.[7] Does the proposed U.S.–U.S.S.R. treaty banning chemical weapons violate the prohibition of "unreasonable searches and seizures" in the Fourth Amendment of the U.S. Constitution when it permits surprise inspections at chemical plants? How does an international treaty such as the 1984 agreement to limit liability for oil spillage affect the law in the state of Maine, which has no limit on liability of companies responsible for oil pollution? These and many other problems and issues could be reduced or eliminated by reservations, amendments, or "understandings" with respect to treaties and other international agreements. However, these obstacles are a reality and give support to those who vigorously guard high state authority.[8]

State Goals and Policy in Pursuit of Goals

In shaping policy through legislation or otherwise to advance goals of security and well-being, top state leaders have a difficult time gaining agreement or some consensus on goal definition, challenges to goals, and mobilization of resources of power to meet the challenges. Difficulties are even greater in seeking shared goals and policy as means to goals in conjunction with other nations, in or outside of international organizations.

Security

The rulers and the ruled within the state agree on the necessity of security for the central interests of the state. Differences and debate arise, however, on threats to security, requirements to meet those threats, which instruments of national policy to employ, mobilization of resources, and a host of other issues and logistics for state security. The great case study for the United States in the twentieth century was the evenly divided debate from 1937 to 1941 over whether Germany and Japan were threats to national security and how to respond, if at all. Churchill chronicles the same division in England between 1935 and the outbreak of war in September 1939.[9] Consider national debates in the United States over Vietnam, Nicaragua, and El Salvador, and Soviet construction of a natural gas pipeline to Western Europe. Discovery of offensive missiles planted by the Soviet Union in Cuba in 1962 led to the White House sessions in October on the nature of this threat and how to respond.[10]

Agreement and response on security goals and policy is nevertheless much easier and more manageable within the state than in conjunction with other states, especially under the aegis of firm top leadership. Shared security whether through a collective defense organization such as NATO or universal collective security under the United Nations basically implies state delegation of some decision-making authority to the collective organization. NATO is easier because fifteen states have agreed since 1949 that the Soviet Union poses a threat to their individual and collective security. But state leaders ask, can we really depend on others to make security decisions? Belgium relied on international law before Germany overran that unfortunate state in 1914. In 1938 and 1939, Czechoslovakia and Poland finally realized that the League of Nations and those with which they had mutual defense treaties would not prevent dismemberment by Nazi Germany (joined by the Soviet Union in the occupation of Poland). When the United States decided not to join the league, England and France immediately engineered understandings that shot holes through key collective security provisions of the covenant. The central problem of collective security under the League of Nations and United Nations is that of a collective definition of security, threats to security, and how to respond to those threats given different approaches to security by member states. Hitler knew too well in the 1930s how different states and their governance and domestic sources of policy disagreed on the nature of the German threat to them, rendering a collective definition and response highly unlikely.

Universal collective security under the provisions of Chapters 6 and 7 of the U.N. Charter and especially the voting formula in Article 27 imply and command an extraordinary convergence of Security Council members' definitions of security, the nature of threats to security, and policy and power to respond to those threats. If we take the four fairly stable and then the four more fluid determinants of security for the state outlined in the the previous chapter, it becomes quite clear what an enormous task it is for diplomacy to negotiate in terms of a convergence for collective security definition and response. On the other hand, consider this convergence in the collective measures taken by the United Nations Security Council in Korea in June and July 1950. Even more significant are the Council resolutions with respect to Iraq beginning with Number 660 on August

2, 1990, and especially Resolution 678 of November 29, 1990, which served as the legal basis for the commencement of U.N. use of force on January 16, 1991, to seek to drive Iraq out of Kuwait.

There have been many other Council resolutions based on unanimity of the permanent members on security and other issues. The many successful deployments of U.N. peacekeeping missions under the aegis of the Council and the extensive catalog of arms control agreements, especially involving the two superpowers. Peace can come in pieces as agreements on bringing state security into congruence with shared security reduce state options to violate the prohibitions on threats and uses of force in Article 2, paragraph 4.

Well-being

State pursuit of national and human well-being is moving from sovereign authority to increasingly high levels of cooperation and organizational authority for shared and progressive well-being. Organizing for economic stability, development and modernization, social and cultural well-being, international protection of human rights, and confronting global villains were appraised in Chapter 2. But the firm hands on high state authority have many problems with visions of shared and progressive well-being that are set forth in Article 55 of the U.N. Charter and in other organizations constitutions and policy.

There are many reasons why high state authority might place brakes on advancing shared well-being. The developing states, in their demands for a New International Economic Order in 1974, in years previous and in years hence, call for a major structural change in the international marketplace for transfers of resources of all kinds to advance their well-being and to give them more equity in the international system. The demands have not produced great results in the past fifteen years, largely because the industrial states and especially the more affluent ones do not view the 130 or so developing states as a collective grouping to receive and utilize their largess but rather as individual states meriting assistance in general accord with the goals of the potential donor states. About a third of all U.S. foreign aid goes to Israel and Egypt and well over two-thirds to bilateral aid rather than multilateral aid through international organizations. Bilateral aid serves the givers' interests, commands accountability for receivers' expenditures, and satisfies domestic sources of policy whose taxes flow into foreign assistance.

Furthermore, affluent nations, such as the United States, often view the deplorable conditions of well-being in many developing states as caused not by the indifference or tight purse strings of the "have" nations but more by conditions within the developing states themselves. Often cited are authoritarian governments, state controlled economies, bloated bureaucracies loaded with political favorites and appointments by nepotism, unacceptable financial management favoring the affluence of elites, few attempts at an equitable structure for taxation, and many other attributes of incompetent state policy. These conditions certainly apply in many but varied forms in probably most developing nations.

Certainly the thirty to thirty-five least developed states as identified by the United Nations have almost zero well-being for over 90 percent of their populations irrespective of mismanagement. However, many organizations in the U.N. system, such as WHO and ILO, make most significant contributions toward shared and progressive well-being irrespective of inadequate funding on a multilateral basis.

High state authority in well-being is not just a matter of developed–developing state relations. The reality of the interdependence of the economics of the international marketplace is hardly matched by international management of that interpendency. The lack of coordination between and among the Group 7 states— United States, Japan, West Germany, England, France, Italy, and Canada—in such areas as trade, interest rates, currency exchanges, their debt and deficits as well as Japan's huge surpluses, reduction of developing nations accumulated indebtedness of about 1.5 trillion dollars, and some controls over international banks and currency exchanges all reflect the inclination of these powerful nations to try to hold on to sovereign state management. This flies in the face of ever-expanding economic interdependence, which really necessitates enhanced international coordination and some management by organizations such as the IMF or even some supra-international economic organization yet to be created.[11] If the alternative is economic nationalism including trade protection of high levels, the fragile global economic system could well suffer a collapse that would make conditions of the late 1920s and early 1930s look like a nickel and dime crisis. Whither the well-being then?

A serious study should be undertaken of patterns of high state authority in a variety of states members of different kinds of international organizations. Three brief examples of United States high authority are illustrative. Some have expressed great concern about any major treaty and subsequent organization with respect to the abolishment of chemical weapons and essential monitoring and implication. Drafts of the central treaty being negotiated by the forty-nation U.N. Conference on Disarmament in Geneva include provisions for surprise inspections at sites where there is suspicion of cheating. This may contradict the Fourth Amendment to the U.S. Constitution, which forbids ''unreasonable searches and seizures.'' In addition to this possible constitutional roadblock to international authority is a concern by some states in the United States that a 1984 treaty imposing limits on liability by tanker owners for oil spills are unacceptable. U.S. Senate majority leader, George J. Mitchell of Maine, opposes limits that would supersede state laws, some of which have no liability limits. Senator Mitchell's powerful position in the Senate as well as his concern for oil spills damaging the long coast of Maine led to July 1990 legislation to allow states to impose unlimited liability on oil spill and pollution costs. This conflicts with the forty-three-nation treaty setting liability limits that the United States may now not be able to join. U.S. radio unions charge that the Pentagon's intention to use peacetime international satellite systems in war time violates the fifty-seven-nation treaty that established the International Maritime Satellite Organization

(INMARSAT), which has authority to "act exclusively for peaceful purposes." Other examples abound that reveal serious problems in the alignment of state and international authority.

In summary, state governance is often very reluctant to advance state goal formulations and policy toward furthering decision-making authority of international organizations and laws because such advancement is conveying authority to others. Governing officials in any polity—local, state, and national—seek to hold on to power and authority. In the United States, this is continually in evidence not only in the tugs of war between and among the three branches of the federal government but also bureaucratic turf fighting in the executive branch, confrontations by the two houses of Congress and between and among committees and subcommittees, and grumbling over Supreme Court decisions concerning powers of the other two branches.

A tight grip on power and authority is compounded when one considers that decisions by governments to yield through treaties and other means of authority to organizations means conveyance of power and authority to voting majorities in international organizations, exercise of executive authority by international civil servants, and often combinations of both. Should the IMF's international civil servants determine the meaning of well-being for debt-ridden Mexico? Should international secretariats, irrespective of how well qualified, make decisions when these officials are not in authoritative positions by the consent of the governed and not responsible or accountable to peoples over whom they exercise decision-making authority?

A brief case study illustrates these questions. In mid-May 1989, the health ministers of the EC voted eleven to one that all community members must carry health warnings on cigarette packages. The one vote against this regulatory and mandatory policy was cast by the United Kingdom. The British health minister upon instructions from Prime Minister Margaret Thatcher told her fellow ministers that "the compulsory language and type required on the packages is too much regulation and unnecessary detail." In opposing such policy and proposed EC law to impose taxes and establish a central bank, the prime minister declared that "My vision of Europe is one of sovereign states joined in association." She also denounced the EC's Executive Commission and its "bureaucrats" for proposing a charter for workers' rights as a "socialist charter full of unnecessary controls." Her adversary in her Conservative Party in Parliament, former prime minister Edward Heath, termed Thatcher's views as "absolute rubbish." Conservative member, Lord Plumb, president of the European Parliament, declared that Thatcher "misunderstands the nature of the community."[12] Here, we have these interesting themes. Members of the EC progressively have delegated increasing authority to the Executive Commission but Thatcher, on the grounds that the EC is only an association of sovereign states, stresses Great Britain's authority to oppose an EC decision. The avowed basis for opposition is too much regulation and detail, but here and elsewhere, Thatcher stresses the real reason, her apprehension of the EC intruding on Great Britain's sovereign decision-making authority. In addition, she does not favor community civil servants—"bureaucrats"—shaping policy and making decisions for sovereign Great Britain. But she is opposed by key people in her party and government who view British goals of well-being advanced in the arena of shared well-being in the EC.

Led by the United States in the mid-1980s, there was growing criticism of the U.N. secretariat and overall administrative decision-making structure and processes, which led in part to Secretary General Javier Perez de Cuellar to a major restructuring of the secretariat. The organization's fiscal crisis was part of this equation of reforms. Even prominent scholars such as Professors Donald J. Puchala and Roger A. Coate could make this observation:

[T]he word of the United Nations is at present being greatly hampered by the political crisis surrounding the institution and internally, the U.N. is wrenching, cranking, grasping and gasping through the throes of administrative "reform," and smarting, skimping, and worrying through its financial difficulties. What stands at Turtle Bay today is a rather far cry from the organization that was to beat the swords of 1939–1945 into the plowshares of a brighter future.[13]

If this is the reality of the United Nations and associated organizations in its system, it is no wonder that states and especially the industrialized democracies—and *especially* the United States—emphasize high state authority over organization authority.

Perhaps. But the Puchala and Coate assessment requires modest critique. Any *bureaucracy* has administrative problems and tangles. However, international bureaucracies have particular situations in administration and management. They include a hand-to-mouth financial existence in depending on annual contributions by members which too often are inadequate and in arrears. On the other side of the coin, states providing major financial support continually review budget levels, expenditure, and cost-effectiveness. The Geneva Group of thirteen major Western contributor nations that pay over two-thirds of the assessed budget of the three largest U.N. specialized agencies (World Health Organization, International Labor Organization, and the Food and Agricultural Organization) reviews budgets prior to making contributions in order to streamline the expenditure side in accordance with their expectations of administrative efficiency. Article 101, paragraph 3 of the Charter calls for a staff with the "highest standards of efficiency, competence, and integrity" and also requires "recruiting the staff on as wide a geographical basis as possible." Thus the Secretary General and high Secretariat officials must correlate high staff qualifications with staff representation from all members of the organization. Administrative efficiency and effectiveness are not always congenial with these mandatory correlations. Political pressures by important nations for high staff appointments for their nationals and other attributes of states' involvements with administrative operations render the entire management of international organizations a tremendous challenge to chief executive officers and high officials.

Further, the Puchala and Coate statement refers to the organization at "Turtle Bay," the name of the area on New York's East Side where the United Nations now stands. What about the European headquarters in Geneva and other organizations in Geneva and elsewhere in the U.N. system? The United Nations in New York is highly and visibly political as home of the General Assembly and Security Council. In Geneva and elsewhere, the United Nations and organizations in the system are far less political and far more productive, especially in advancing shared and progressive well-being. Former director general of the United Nations in Geneva, Eric Suy, told the author's class at the United Nations in Geneva that the United Nation is about 10 percent political and 90 percent involved in human and national services. This 90 percent, he added, consumes about 80 percent of the organization's annual budget and this output is often unseen, certainly not by the beneficiaries but by those who view the United Nations in unfriendly political and negative ways.[14]

Domestic Sources of Policy

Domestic sources of policy in the United States and most of the other industrialized democracies include public opinion and all kinds of political interest groups, the media, vast organizations and institutions in the private economic domain, private elites and other important personages, and governing officials at subnational levels. They have their own sentiments, visions, and expectations of national goals and policy, which in many cases are strongly supportive of high state authority over international law and organization authority. In part this is attributable to retaining in the homeland power and authority and to share that power and authority outside the state on as minimal level as possible. In past, nationalism, patriotism and its symbols of the flag and the anthem, national pride, crusts of history, and many other visceral and affective emotions and identities are part and parcel of national sentiment and sovereignty.

In part, many people simply are not familiar with the need and accomplishments of international organizations on the one hand and have a fear and mistrust of them on the other. Many are not in tune with the reality of global interdependence and the need to cooperate and associate for a shared security and well-being. The sovereign state increasingly cannot supply to its people and its other central interest. There are not many national interest groups supportive of international cooperation and collaboration but there certainly are many that would oppose such internationalism if and when their own goals and interests may be in jeopardy. Domestic sources of policy are politically powerful, especially in democracies. They have many tools and influences to steer their version of security and well-being for the nation into national policies that reflect their objectives in whole or part. Top leadership and governing officials responsible and accountable to domestic sources of policy are ever-sensitive to demands and supports of these sources. They are mindful of security for their own interest as well—especially the security of continuation in public office.

High state authority also means the capacity of a very few states to influence the international organization to pursue a policy congenial with the state's definition of its goals of security and well-being. The United States was able to exercise its national authority in shaping winning coalitions and votes in the General Assembly until well into the 1960s. Its role in the Security Council resolutions and decisions on the North Korean invasion of South Korea in June and July 1950 steered U.N. policy toward U.S. security goals, especially when the Soviet Union voluntarily abdicated its voting rights in the council at that time. It used the Security Council at the time of the Cuban missile crisis in October 1962 to legitimize its position in demonstrating to the world that indeed Soviet offensive missiles had been installed in Cuba. To give another example, the United States commandeered the vote of the OAS Council in May 1965 to multilateralize its unilateral intrusion into the Dominican Republic upon the occasion of a political crisis in that small nation. The voting formula for the World Bank and the IMF is based on numbers of shares held by members, thus giving the major shareholders, the United States, the EC, and Japan the overwhelming voting power in these institutions. These two financial institutions thus embrace liberal economic policies of the dominant states although officials in these organizations exercise a high degree of professional independence. High state authority is a fact of national and international political life in the mixture of state sovereignty and distribution of power in the international marketplace, but the trend in the early 1990s is in the other direction.

PARTNERSHIP: THE ORGANIZATION AND ITS MEMBERS

"The Organization and Its Members" shall pursue the purposes of the United Nations and "shall act in accordance with the following Principles" as set forth in Article 2. This partnership role of the organization and its members is fortified in the preamble where the "peoples of the United Nations" through their states *unite* their strength, and *combine* their efforts in the *pursuit* of the *aims* of the organization, shared security and shared and progressive well-being. The text of the U.N. Charter emphasizes the senior partnership role for the United Nations in the pursuit of shared security in Chapters 6 and 7. Article 49 is of particular importance: "The Members of the United Nations shall join in affording mutual assistance in carrying out the measures decided upon by the Security Council." In Article 55, the United Nations "shall promote" many dimensions of shared and progressive well-being. The partnership role of organization and members is reaffirmed in Article 56 where members pledge themselves to take the "joint and separate action in cooperation with the Organization for the achievement of conditions of well-being" stated in Article 55.

Article 1 makes it quite clear that it is the responsibility of the organization to pursue the purposes of the United Nations with words in each of the four goals emphasizing this obligation: *maintain*, *develop*, *achieve*, and *to be a center* for harmonizing *the actions of nations in the attainment of these common ends*.

In Article 2, the organization has specific obligations and responsibilities under paragraphs 1, 6, and 7 of the principles, while the members' obligations are set forth in paragraphs 2, 3, 4, and especially 5, where they pledge to "give the United Nations every assistance in any action it takes in accordance with the present Charter."

Partnership is confirmed by the fact that states need the United Nations and other international organizations to pursue state goals of security and well-being and organizations cannot progress toward goals such as shared security and shared and progressive well-being without state members. The state is sovereign and can come and go as far as organizations but none really "go" save the rare occasions when they leave an organization—such as when the United States left the ILO for a few years in the late 1970s and is currently on the sidelines of UNESCO. Also, the organization itself is an independent legal actor with full legal personality under international law. Thus the relationship between sovereign state and sovereign organization is one of necessary partnership and cooperation to advance mutually independent but interdependent goals of security and well-being.

Through diplomacy, voting, financial and other supports, members move the organization. The organization likewise moves its partner members through its outputs of law, resolutions, decisions, services, and other means to goals of shared security and well-being. As in any partnership relations, there is much give and take for both members and organizations with compromises, negotiated or in the process of organizational activity. The organization by majority vote may elect a specific course of action, hoping that most members will join in partnership and resources to attain goals. Such was the impressive majority vote calling for a New International Economic Order by the General Assembly on May 1, 1974. However, the United States and many other industrialized democracies did not view their goals of security and well-being to be furthered by a structural change in the existing international economic order. Partnership between majority resolution and members able to provide resources to affect the resolution did not ensue. But there were compromises including a common fund to support commodity prices, an integrated program for commodities, and other segments of the agenda for a new order that became modest partnership activities between organization and members.

The record of the United Nations and other organizations since 1945 demonstrates a progressive partnership between organization and members, which is an accretion of policy, practice, and achievements that proceeds into the 1990s. The lines of partnership between organization and members are not always clear and precise in this middle ground between high state authority and high organization authority. Each member has its own constitutional provisions on relating to international law and organization as we have observed, and these provisions may not be clear as well. Under Article 6, paragraph 2 of the U.S. Constitution, "The Constitution, and the laws of the United States which shall be made in pursuance thereof, and all treaties made, or which shall be made, under the authority of the United States, shall be the supreme law of the land.'' Thus we have three sources of the "supreme law of the land": the constitution (as interpreted by the Supreme Court), laws or legislation made in pursuance of the constitution, and treaties. In general, if there is conflict among the three, the most recent takes precedent over the other two. In the famous case of *Missouri v. Holland*, the Supreme Court held that a treaty may enable the federal government to do what legislation cannot do, thus emphasizing the primacy of the treaty under international law.[15] However, in the case of *Sei Fujii v. California*, the California Supreme Court overturned a lower court decision that held that the U.N. Charter was superior to state law in a case involving real estate discrimination. The higher court ruled that the U.N. Charter is not "self-executing" —automatically overriding state law—because it is a treaty and thus "supreme law of the land." The California Supreme Court thus said that the U.N. Charter as a treaty must be "executed" or fortified by state or federal legislation before it can be applied as law in California or other jurisdictions.[16] The partnership role between organization and law on the one hand and members on the other is constantly tested.[17]

Security

In the domain of security, states delegated considerable authority to the United Nations in the U.N. Charter for the taking of "effective collective measures for the prevention and removal of threats to the peace, and for the suppression of acts of aggression" in Article 1. The wide divergencies between and among the superpowers and other nations have generally prevented the full implementation of the collective security machinery set forth in Chapter 7 of the U.N. Charter. However, through usage, interpretation of the U.N. Charter, and other means to adapt the charter to existing and changing conditions involving "international peace and security," the members and the global organization have developed partnership roles that have contributed substantially to the prevention of major warfare.

When the Security Council voted on June 27, 1950, to recommend collective measures against aggression by the Democratic Republic of Korea (North) on the Republic of Korea (South), the United Nations was (1) taking action under Chapter 7 of the U.N. Charter, and (2) many members of the United Nations provided armed forces for the implementation of the Security Council's resolution and many other resources as well to confront the aggression. This partnership proved successful in deterring the aggression and restoring the fragile status quo between the two Koreas. In the many peacekeeping operations since the first major United Nations Emergency Force was dispatched to the Middle East in November, 1956, (1) the General Assembly and especially the Security Council took action upon votes by their members to establish and direct peacekeeping operations, and (2) some members supplied the armed forces to serve as peacekeepers. This partnership role has expanded greatly in the late 1980s and early

1990s with peacekeeping missions creatively and effectively reducing the tone and substance of hostility between disputing parties.[18]

Twelve resolutions by the Security Council of the United Nations in dealing with the Gulf War between August 1990 and mid-March 1991 have abundant references to partnership between the twenty-eight U.N. members that provided military forces to the Gulf coalition and over fifty other members dispatching other kinds of support and material. Resolution 661 of August 6, 1990, for instance, in calling for severe economic sanctions against Iraq, "decides that all states" and "calls on all states" with respect to sanctions policy. "Partnership" is also the central theme employed by President Bush in describing his vision of a new world order—appraised in the preface—including his call for a "new partnership of nations" in his address to the General Assembly of the United Nations on October 1, 1990.

Well-being

The partnership role for shared and progressive well-being, underlined by states' "joint and separate action in cooperation with the Organization" in Article 56 to take action well beyond cooperation in Article 1, paragraph 3, to achieve the specific conditions of stability and well-being in Article 55. The extensive outputs or policies and services of the United Nations and a vast array of their international organizations in the domain of shared and progressive well-being demonstrate the ever-increasing "international machinery for the promotion of the economic and social advancement of all peoples." The General Assembly's establishment of the UNEP in 1972 stated in its constituent resolution that "international cooperation programmes in the field of the environment must be undertaken with due respect for the sovereign rights of States and in conformity with the Charter of the United Nations and the principles of international law." There are many similar provisions in the constitutions of international organizations that emphasize the partnership equation.

Of course there are other approaches to expanding human and national well-being. Many regional organizations such as the OAS and the Association of Southeast Asian Nations (ASEAN), along with regional banks and the EC's relations with independent states—former colonies of EC members—are deeply involved in advancing progressive well-being in developing nations. Such also is certainly the case with the World Bank and the IMF. A number of industrial democracies, especially the United States, extend far and more bilateral aid to other nations as a "separate" action rather than multilateral aid through the United Nations and other international organizations. In its annual aid program toward progressive well-being, the United States sends out about four dollars to specific nations, usually associated with the United States in shared security, to one dollar through international organizations. U.S. annual aid to Israel and Egypt alone amounts to about one-third of its annual economic and military aid to other nations and organizations. There is more control and accountability with bilateral aid, it better pinpoints the donor's interests than the vague goals in the minds of some of shared and progressive well-being, and thus it better commands reciprocal congeniality from the recipient states. However, the United Nations and other international organizations are absolutely essential to shared and progressive well-being of all nations and their strength and capability in this area of partnership grows with each passing year.

Diplomacy

The task of enhancing the partnership between organizations and states is due less to constitutional texts, which are quite specific, but more to the men and women who have the diplomatic responsibility delegated to them by both states and organizations. The diplomat representing the state seeks to advance his/her state's definition of and requirements for security and well-being while the organization's diplomat is concerned both with the goals and purposes of his/her organization as well as the resolutions and decisions of the organization. Both seek to influence the other—as well as other states' diplomats—to develop a consensus that is a blend of states' goals and organization goals. All organizations' resolutions, decisions, covenants, and other outputs represent a masterful exercise of the craft of diplomacy in moving states' definitions of their goals of security and well-being toward organizations' goals of shared security and shared progressive well-being. A superb memoir of the goals, processes, frustrations, and achievement of international diplomacy is that by Sir Brian Urquhart, who served with great distinction as Under-Secretary General for Special Political Affairs at the United Nations until his retirement in 1985.[19]

In any forum where votes are taken or consensus is pursued, there will be minority voters who will not agree with the majority decisions. But only in the manner of diplomatic processes, negotiations, give and take, and final agreement can the partnership be advanced. As always, the superpowers and the major states play the primary roles in shaping outputs of decisions, resolutions, and the law. The early 1990s witnessed considerable agreement between the superpowers on the meaning of shared security through a host of Security Council resolutions on long-standing disputes and confrontations around the globe.[20]

Many other organizations and their policies reflect the partnership role between organizations and states. Here is a sampler. The preamble of the WHO states that "the health of all peoples is fundamental to the attainment of peace and security and is dependent upon the fullest cooperation of individuals and states." The 1944 Declaration of the ILO calls for the "effective international and national action" for the achievement of its objectives. The 1966 Protocol of GATT recognizes that "individual and joint action is essential to the further development of the economies of the less-developed contracting parties." The constitution of the Organization of Petroleum Exporting Countries (OPEC) states that the organizations's "principal aim . . . shall be the coordination and unification of the petroleum policies of Member countries." The 1961 Declaration of Punta del

Este of the OAS states that the parties "undertake to adopt measures, both internally and through international cooperation . . . to achieving progressively . . . the full realization of rights . . . in the Charter of the Organization of American States." The preamble to the constitution of the FAO reads: "The Nations accepting this Constitution [are] determined to promote the common welfare by furthering separate and collective action on their part for the purposes of," as set forth in the Preamble and Article 1 of the constitution. The December 1972 General Assembly resolution establishing the UNEP recognized that "international cooperative programs in the field of the environment must be undertaken with due respect for the sovereign rights of states and in conformity with the Charter of the United Nations and the principles of international law." Finally, the Convention of the Law of the Sea of 1982 recognizes the "desirability of establishing . . . a legal order for the seas and oceans" and "with due regard for the sovereignty of all States."

The state reserves the senior role in the pursuit of security irrespective of the senior role allocated by states to the United Nations in the U.N. Charter. The United Nations and other international organizations occupy the senior role in the march toward shared and progressive well-being. By the early 1990s, the line between security and well-being becomes more and more blurred as global events and conditions each day render enhanced higher levels of interdependence to meet state requirements for goals of security and well-being.

Partnership between organizations and states will continue to be crafted by processes of diplomacy to seek blends of state and organization goals. The trend is toward the senior role of organization. It is interesting to note in this vein provisions in the charter of the OAS that address this partnership. We find in Chapter 2 of the charter that "International order consists essentially of respect for the personality, sovereignty, and independence of States, and the faithful fulfillment of obligations derived from treaties and other sources of international law." This suggests an equal partnership but this provision is preceded by that which states that "international law is the standard of conduct of States in their reciprocal relations," a senior status for international law and organization.

Finally, the senior role of international obligations is found in the most widely embraced of all international conventions, the four Geneva Conventions of 1949 dealing with war and its victims, which we appraised briefly in Chapter 2. Each of these treaties incorporates the "Martens Clause," which came from the writings of the German jurist, Georg Freidrich von Martens (1756–1821) and which is also found in the Fourth Hague Convention of 1907. Should a state denounce its commitments under these treaties,

[I]t shall in no way impair the obligations which the Parties to the conflict shall remain bound to fulfill by virtue of the principles of the law of nations, as they result from the usages established among civilized peoples, from the laws of humanity and the dictates of public conscience.

Commitment to the principles of international law thus should prevail over the will of high state authority to walk away from the obligation.

HIGH ORGANIZATION AUTHORITY

High authority for organizations is agreement by and commitment of members to enable the organization to move the members toward enhanced levels of shared security and shared and progressive well-being, well beyond high state authority and further than organization-member partnership. High organization authority greatly influences and modifies state policy and in many ways places significant limitations on the exercise of high state authority.

Again we must be careful about generalizations. Some organizations by their constitution and membership voting have high authority, such as the IMF, while others are constructed much more to providing services of great significance than exercising decision-making authority over states such as WHO. Although a Swiss-chartered organization, the International Committee of the Red Cross, as an international legal actor under the aegis of the Geneva Conventions of 1949 and Protocols of 1974, has considerable authority in the domain of the laws of war and effects of war. Each organization is different with its own constitution, delegation and exercise of authority, and guidance by members. However, some major organizations and some sectors of other organizations continue the evolution of organizations we appraised in Chapter 2 in the continuation of necessity of organizations to advance security and well-being in areas that states neither can do by themselves nor not nearly as effective as can their organizations.

In his inaugural address of January 20, 1961, President John F. Kennedy expressed the progression toward organization authority very well. "To that world assembly of sovereign states, the United Nations, our last best hope in an age where the instruments of war have far outpaced the instruments of peace, we renew our pledge of support and to enlarge the area in which its writ may run." The esteemed scholar of international relations, Professor John Herz, put the issue another way. "Now that national interests are merging with a common interest by all nations in global peace and prosperity [security and well-being], we should observe and enforce the international system of rules without which those objectives cannot be obtained."[21]

The principal concept in the progression toward higher organization authority is the theory and practice of functionalism, which really is another approach to some of the central themes of our study. Nations form international organizations to perform functions to meet state requirements for their goals in ways states cannot adequately do for themselves. As units of governance, states are too small and inadequate to meet demands of their populace for progressive well-being. They thus constitute organizations to cooperate in advancing their economic and social welfare and, in so doing, create great benefits to states that should not be jeopardized by confrontation and conflict between and among states. Functionalism thus joins the goals of security and well-being by elevating cooperation for shared and progressive well-being and, in so doing, reduce tension and bellicosity toward shared security. Functionalism further holds that war itself is largely the product of economic and social disparities and disadvantageousness. Functional cooperation in international organizations also helps to reduce the appeal of sovereignty and furthers the concepts of international cooperation in the great laboratory of people working in organizations for common causes— for the "international interest" of shared security and well-being.

The major author of functionalism is David Mitrany, whose 1933 study, *The Progress of International Government*, captured the imagination of statesmen and scholars who could see how functional cooperation might and should erode state confrontation and conflict.[22] As we have observed, the League of Nations was primarily charged with collective security and the prevention of war. Only Articles 23, 24, and 25 dealt with the promotion of shared and progressive well-being, and the ILO was the only agency constructed basically on the premises of functionalism. In the 1930s Mitrany contributed to the vision of statesmen and scholars that the enhancement of economic and social cooperation might well spill over into increased political cooperation and thus shared security. A major committee under the leadership of Viscount Bruce of Australia submitted major recommendations to accelerate the work of the League of Nations and new agencies to foster economic and social progress. However, the Bruce proposals came in 1939, as did World War II, but they made a major contribution to the thinking and planning that led to the United Nations and other postwar organizations. An outstanding historian of the United Nations observed that the United States assumed prime responsibility as the major architect of the United Nations. As early as 1943, U.S. planners visualized an international organization that would combine "the negative function of preventing or punishing aggression with the positive function of promoting conditions conducive to peaceful relations among nations."[23] As with the functionalist theory itself, this vision demonstrates the interdependence of shared security and shared and progressive well-being.

Claude and others emphasize the virtue of functionalist theory but also provide critical analysis. The premise that wars begin because of economic and social inequities does not wash if we examine the origins of World Wars I and II. There is great intermixture between state goals of security and well-being but we observed earlier in this chapter that the roots of state definition of its security, security requirements, and security policy are difficult to transplant to international authority for determination of shared security and thus collective measures against threats and uses of force. States bring to organizations their own definitions and visions of goals of security and well-being. Where there is disparity between and among states on their goals, they seek to protect their interests in organizations and to gain support from other states through diplomacy and negotiation and voting as well. The higher the level of political confrontations, or what is referred to as "politicalization" in international organizations, the less able are states able to reach consensus on organization policy. Likewise, the lower level the political confrontation, the more likely consensus, agreement, and organization policy can be achieved.[24]

Functional theory, however applied, can hardly reduce political uses of international organizations by states that want to maximize high state authority over their goals. Politicization is often perceived through the eye of the beholder. The United States charges the Arab states of politicization at the annual June conference of the ILO when the latter accuse Israel of labor injustices in the Israeli-occupied territories. Other states have accused the United States of politicization of the U.N. Commission on Human Rights in making one of its prime goals in recent years the condemnation of Cuba for human rights violations. Politicization is receding in the early 1990s in the fora of international organizations but it must always be remembered that these institutions are arenas for goal striving by sovereign states.

The progressive integration of the EC since its inception in 1958 may be viewed as the triumph of functionalist theory and practice. Among the EC's accomplishments has been the blending of essential state goals of France and Germany, both of which were central to the origins of the wars of 1870, 1914, and 1939. But regional functionalism in geographic areas where states have so much in common is not necessarily transferable either to other regions or to states on a universal scale.

Functionalism has played a decisive role in the theory and practice of international organizations and we have drawn much from its lessons. However, it encompasses much idealism, or what ought to take place in international integration. Further, like many terms and concepts in the lexicon of academia, functionalism is a term rarely known or understood by nontechnical officials in international organizations, including political appointees often seen at the U.N. Mission in Geneva and advisers and others whose responsibility and accountability is more to their national government than to organization partnership or high organization authority.

Therefore in this study we have preferred to emphasize relations between state goals of security and well-being and the constitutionalism and practice of international organizations in advancing shared security and shared and progressive well-being. It is interesting to note however that functionalism and international constitutionalism are joined if we reverse the purposes of the U.N. Charter in Article 1 and work from the United Nation as a center for the harmonization of interests of states through economic and social cooperation and then to the provisions for maintenance of international peace and security in the first paragraph of Article 1.

High organization authority is based upon the constitutional provisions of international organizations, progression of that authority in the practice and productivity of organizations, and the domestication or incorporation into municipal law by organization members of the treaty law generated by organizations. The rapidly expanding body of international constitutional law progressively moves state goals of security and well-being toward organization goals of shared security and shared and progressive well-being.

Organizations' Constitutions and High Organization Authority

The U.N. Charter is—with some exceptions such as the IMF and the World Bank—the constitutional bedrock for international constitutional law—or, United Nations law—in the U.N. system of organization.[25]

Established by sovereign states in 1945, "We the peoples of the United Nations ... through representatives (of our respective Governments) ... do hereby establish an international organization to be known as the United Nations." This preamble is a close replica of the preamble to the U.S. Constitution, which we cited in Chapter 3 to demonstrate the blending of state goals of security and well-being. In both preambles, constitutional systems are established and both the United Nations and the United States have witnessed the expansion of these constitutional systems—and the process continues.

The distinct international legal authority of the United Nations was confirmed by the International Court of Justice in its famous advisory opinion of 1949, "Reparation for Injuries Suffered in the Service of the United Nations." This opinion, which has flowed into the mainstream of international constitutional law, confirms the United Nations and other international organizations as possessing constitutional authority independent of their members.[26] The court cited the "progressive increase in collective activities of states" as necessitating new international institutions, which we observed in Chapter 2. The court added that to achieve the purposes to which states agreed in Article 1 of the U.N. Charter "the attribution of international personality [authority] is indispensable." In brief, sovereign states created the United Nations and other international organizations to exercise authority that constantly grows in proportion to states' incapability to achieve goals of security and well-being under high state authority.

Shared Security

We traced the constitutional foundations in the U.N. Charter for shared security in Chapter 3, which is expressed in the preamble: "to unite our strength to maintain international peace and security and to ensure . . . that armed force shall not be used, save in the common interest." In Article 24, "members confer on the Security Council primary responsibility for the maintenance of international peace and security and agree that in carrying out its duties under this responsibility the Security Council acts on their behalf." Paragraph 2 of this article cites the chapters in the U.N. Charter that contain the "specific powers granted [by members] to the Council for the discharge of these duties." Article 25 states that the "members of the United Nations agree to accept and carry out the decisions of the Security Council in accordance with the present Charter." If we go by the text, these provisions demonstrate high organization authority for shared security, assuming, of course, unanimity among the Security Council's permanent members. We appraise in the next section U.N. practice under this delegated authority. Any reading of articles dealing with council authority in Chapters 5, 6, and 7 only reveals further confirmation of extensive council duties and responsibilities for shared security. Even a careful reading of the "escape clauses" in Article 51, with respect to self-defense, indicate that the Security Council if it chooses can immediately curtail individual or collective member action in self-defense. It has specific authority over regional arrangements taking enforcement action in Article 53. With national will, especially by the council's permanent members, the Security Council can exercise very high organization authority for shared security. High organization authority for shared or collective security, of course, requires Security Council members and especially the permanent members to delegate firm authority to the Council in this textual interpretation of high organization powers.

Well-being

High U.N. authority for advancing shared and progressive well-being stems from the preamble's statement on the employment of "international machinery for the promotion of the economic and social advancement of all peoples" toward the "end" or goal or promoting "social progress and better standards of life in larger freedom." Article 1, paragraph 3, calls for "cooperation" in solving international problems of an economic, social, cultural, or humanitarian character. However, Article 56 calls for all members to "pledge to take joint and separate action in cooperation with the Organization" for the achievement of the specific components for well-being which "the United Nations shall promote" in Article 55. These provisions are buttressed by Chapter 10 on the responsibilities of the Economic and Social Council and by Chapters 11 and 12 on Non-Self-Governing Territories and the International Trusteeship System. Of particular importance in the realm of high authority in shared and progressive well-being are the International Covenants on Civil and Political Rights and on Economic, Social, and Cultural Rights as well as a host of other international legal commitments and obligations states accept in a host of other human rights covenants we review in Chapter 6.

Beyond this are the numerous international legal authorities including specialized agencies such as WHO, financial institutions such as the World Bank, and the extensive activity of hundreds of nongovernmental international organizations that work collectively and separately with organizations in the U.N. system for the goal of "social progress and better standards of life in larger freedom." The joining of all these organizations and international legal systems demonstrates high organization authority in advancing shared and progressive well-being.[27]

The Progression of International Constitutional Law

We observed in Chapter 2 that when the U.N. Charter was signed on June 26, 1945, its authors did not and could not anticipate the cold war, the advent of the atomic era, the emergence of over 100 new states from the ashes of colonialism and the rapid strides in technology, all of which have made their deep imprint on the past forty-five years. To this list we may add much else, not the least global villains such as radioactivity contamination and AIDS. Nevertheless, the United Nations and international organizations old and new have adapted to an ever-evolving and changing condition of states and other international actors. Irrespective of deplorable conditions on many parts of our small planet—including wars, hunger, poverty, disease, illiteracy—the plight of some 15 million refugees, the progression of international constitutional law toward enhanced shared security and well-being cannot be denied.

Let us take the security of the person and also well-being with security against torture and thus well-being in a physical and psychological sense. Before World War II, many states had laws against torture but more did not. The definition of torture is that which is intentionally inflicted by a public official to produce a confession, to punish or to intimidate, and causing severe pain or suffering whether physical or mental.[28] In his famous "Four Freedoms" address of January 6, 1941, President Roosevelt cited freedom of speech and expression, freedom to worship, freedom from want, and freedom from fear as goals for the postwar era. These basic rights or freedoms flowed into specific wording in the 1948 Universal Declaration of Human Rights. The 1945 U.N. Charter speaks eloquently of "equal and inalienable rights of all members of the human family" and calls on all states in Article 55 "to promote universal respect for and observance of human rights and fundamental freedoms." Article 5 of the Universal Declaration of Human Rights and Article 7 of the International Covenant on Civil and Political Rights of 1966 provide that "no one shall be subjected to torture or to cruel, inhuman, or degrading treatment or punishment," a right from which no state can ignore or derogate.

In expanding on the 1941 "freedom from fear," the General Assembly continued this progression of international constitutional law in 1975 by passing the Declaration on the Protection of All Persons from Being Subjected to Torture. This declaration took the form of international law with the adoption by the General Assembly of the Convention Against Torture and Other Cruel, Inhuman, or Degrading Treatment or Punishment on December 10, 1984, the thirty-sixth anniversary of the Universal Declaration of Human Rights. The treaty became fully operative in 1987, has been ratified by the United States, and has an administrative structure including a Committee Against Torture responsible to states that are parties to the treaty and a Special Rapporteur on Torture accountable to the U.N. Commission on Human Rights. The administrative machinery is in full operation and torture as an international crime is being widely addressed around the world.[29] Examples abound on how international constitutional law has evolved and expanded so extensively from wording in leaders' speeches, the U.N. Charter, and other foundations.

Expanding Sources of International Constitutional Law

The legal foundation for sources of international law is found in Article 38 of the Statute of the International Court of Justice. In basic sequence of importance, they are treaties, customs, principles, judicial decisions, teaching of respected scholars, and equity if the court and parties agree to settle a dispute in this manner. The body of international treaty law generated by international organizations such as the Convention Against Torture was anticipated by the U.N. Charter in Article 13, which encourages the "progressive development of international law and its codification," and also in Article 62, paragraph 3, which authorizes the Economic and Social Council "to prepare draft conventions for submission to the General Assembly." The United Nations thus generated the Convention Against Torture, which established its treaty body, the Committee Against Torture—a new but limited international organization with responsibilities for state compliance to the treaty. As we observed in the anatomy of the IMO, most of the principal international treaties arising from international organizations have provision for the multiplier effect for new international law and limited organizations under that law. We examine this multiplier effect with respect to human rights law in Chapter 6.[30]

Customary international law has flourished since 1945 in the adoption by organizations and especially the General Assembly of a multitude of annual resolutions and decisions that are repeated so often they become legal norms, especially if positively supported by the overwhelming majority of states in member-nation assemblies.[31] Principles of international law such as human rights standards and declarations flow on into treaty law such as the Universal Declaration of Human Rights, which serves as the foundation for subsequent human rights covenants. Principles of international humanitarian law must be observed by states whether or not they are signatories to the Geneva Conventions and Protocols on international humanitarian law.[32] Judicial decisions with compliance authority flow from the European and Inter-American courts of human rights and both the United States and the Soviet Union have agreed that the International Court of Justice should have more compulsory jurisdiction. International case law is growing rapidly as a source of law to be used in subsequent arguments before international courts.

The writings of scholars, such as the "Father of International Law," Hugo Grotius (1583–1645) and Professor Leo Gross of the Tufts University Fletcher School of Law and Diplomacy, are evidence of international law. The International Law Commission of the United Nations is composed of thirty-four eminent scholars who have drafted many of the drafts of treaties subsequently adopted by the General Assembly and ratified by states. Of particular importance have been the Vienna Convention on Diplomatic Relations of 1961 and the Vienna Convention on the Law of Treaties of 1969.[33]

New Bodies of International Constitutional Law

These sources accompanied by others have produced evolving or new bodies of international constitutional law. International criminal law has deep roots because pirates have been historic international criminals and may be seized and disposed of by any state. Slavery likewise has been an international crime since the nineteenth century but is now covered by modern covenants. The Nuremberg

Charter and trials of the Nazi war criminals in 1945 and 1946 boosted international criminal law to new heights with the precedent of new law and a trial of men accused of the international crimes against the peace, crimes of war already on the books, and a new international crime, that against humanity. The war criminals were tried on the basis of their individual crimes irrespective of orders from superiors, and their claim of jurisdiction did not wash because the Nuremberg Court held their crimes transcended all jurisdictional issues. They were international.[34]

Under the U.N. system, new crimes were added to the books, including genocide under the U.N. Convention of 1948, apartheid in the International Convention of 1973, and torture in the convention of 1984. There are a number of international covenants on various dimensions of terrorism as well as much national legislation on the capture and trial of terrorists, including those under the ICAO and the conventions governing Europe and the Americas. These bodies of international criminal law parallel Nuremberg in that the crimes are international and not confined to the jurisdiction where they were committed and the state detaining the criminal may try the culprit or extradite him to his native state.[35] International criminal law is on the march.[36]

International economic law combines all the international economic and financial organizations and their constitutions and practice as well as the network of bilateral treaties almost all states have with others for reciprocities in commerce, finance, and economic cooperation. International economic law generated by GATT, the IMF, the World Bank and regional banks, the UNCTAD, the UNIDO, and the ITC among others make it difficult to keep up to the pace and increasing authority of international laws and organizations in the economic domain and thus shared and progressive well-being. Part of international economic law is international development law, which involves many of the above organizations as well as the United Nations Development Program.[37]

Other clusters of international law and thus high organization authority include international human rights law (to which we turn in Part 2 of our study), and international labor law, which is largely under the aegis of the ILO. We also add international social law including the extensive work of the subsidiary bodies of the U.N. Economic and Social Council and specialized agencies such as the WHO. International environmental law under the expanding authority of the UNEP and other new institutions and treaties cited in Chapter 3 to deal with transnational villains can best serve the erosion of so much of our small planet. International refugee law under the authority of the UNHCR, the seven major treaties establishing international law of space, and international communication law supervised by such organizations as the ITU and the array of nongovernmental organizations and transnational corporations associated with the union join these new categories of international constitutional law. Organizations generate law through treaties, which in turn generate new institutions and new law, all of which emphasize expanding high organization authority. This is an evolutionary process, not necessarily well-planned or coordinated, but nevertheless a response to states' needs and to advance shared security and well-being in preference to insecurity and reverse well-being, which is the condition rejecting high organization authority.

Domestication of International Constitutional Law

High organization authority is particularly manifested when organizations generate treaties and policy that commit states to incorporate them in their own municipal or national law. This is done through member states' processes of ratification of organizations' treaties and legislation for implementation into the law of the land. We noted earlier in this chapter the U.S. constitutional provision in Article 6, paragraph 2, with respect to treaties joining the U.S. Constitution and national legislation as comprising the "supreme law of the land." They become "supreme" with some exceptions when legislation incorporates them into national law. Article 25, or the Basic Law of the Federal German Republic, states that "the general rules of public international law are an integral part of federal law. They shall take precedent over the laws and shall directly create rights and duties for the inhabitants of the federal territory." Article 55 of the 1958 Constitution of the French Fifth Republic declares that "Treaties or agreements duly ratified or approved shall, upon their publication, have an authority superior to that of laws, subject, for each agreement or treaty, to its application to the other party."[38]

The Fourth Hague Convention of 1907 calls on signatories to "issue instructions to their armed land forces which shall be in conformity with the Regulations respecting the laws and customs of war on land annexed to the Present Convention." This early provision for domestication was carried on in the Geneva Conventions of 1949 and Protocols of 1974 to make the laws of war and international humanitarian law the most extensive area of international constitutional law to become domesticated by sovereign states.

The U.N. Charter has no provision for domestication but many articles call on members to "give the United Nations every assistance in action it takes in accordance with the present Charter" as in Article 2, paragraph 5. A more firm obligation is to be found in Article 25, which declares that members "agree to carry out the decisions of the Security Council in accordance with the present Charter."[39]

The 1969 Vienna Convention on the Law of Treaties has a number of provisions dealing with treaty compliance and domestication. Under Article 26, "Every treaty in force is binding upon parties to it and must be performed by them in good faith" (pact sunt servanda). Article 27 states that "A party may not invoke the provisions of its internal law as justification for its failure to perform a treaty." This rule is without prejudice to Article 46. That article in turn reads as follows:

1. A State may not invoke the fact that its consent to be bound by a treaty has been expressed in violation of a provision of its internal law regarding competence to

conclude treaties as invalidating its consent unless that violation was manifest and concerned a rule of its internal law of fundamental importance.

2. A violation is manifest if it would be objectively evident to any State conducting itself in the matter in accordance with normal practice and in good faith.

In the years since 1945, domestication provisions have become integral parts of many international treaties and policy produced by international organizations. We cite now only several of some major domestication provisions that incorporate international law into domestic or municipal law of the states that voluntarily ratify and accept those treaties as binding.

Genocide Treaty, 1948, Article V

The Contracting Parties undertake to enact, in accordance with their respective Constitutions, the necessary legislation to give effect to the provisions of the present Convention and, in particular, to provide effective penalties for persons guilty of genocide or any of the other acts enumerated in Article III [specific acts of genocide].

International Covenant on Civil and Political Rights, Article 2

Each State Party . . . undertakes to take the necessary steps, in accordance with its constitutional processes and the provisions of the present Covenant, to adopt such legislative or other measures as may be necessary to give effect to the rights recognized in the present Covenant.[40]

Convention Against Torture, Article 2, paragraph 1

Each State Party shall take effective legislative, administrative, judicial or other measures to prevent acts of torture in any territory under its jurisdiction.

Similar provisions are to be found in the 1956 Supplementary Convention on the Abolition of Slavery, the Slave Trade, and Institutions and Practices Similar to Slaves, Article 6; the International Convention on the Elimination of All Forms of Racial Discrimination, Article 2.1; the International Convention on the Suppression and Punishment of the Crime of Apartheid of 1973, Article 6, and Article 4 in the 1989 Convention on the Rights of the Child. The regional human rights conventions for Europe, the Americas and Africa all have articles requiring domestication. As with the African Charter, parties shall "undertake to adopt legislative or other measures to give effect" to the "rights, duties, and freedoms enshrined in this Charter."

The constitution of the ILO of 1919 and the supplemental Declaration of Aims and Purposes of 1944 have many provisions calling for domestication because the main thrust of ILO, as we have observed, is to produce conventions on labor and management issues that are to be adopted by member states as part of their municipal law. The United Nations definition of a refugee in the 1951 Convention and 1967 Protocol—a person outside his or her country who has a well-founded fear of persecution on account of race, religion, nationality, membership in a particular social group, or political opinion if he or she were to return to his/her country—is accepted by the United States. This definition is in the 1980 U.S.

Refugee Act—one example of U.S. domestication. Another example is the 1979 United States Trade Agreements Act, which authorized the United States to domesticate the trade codes of the 1973–1979 "Tokyo Round" of trade negotiations under the aegis of GATT. Domestication of treaties emanating from international organizations bind states together in the administration and enforcement of law common to all of them. In this manner, international law does become enforceable as long as states ratifying treaties truly accept their commitment to implement them as well.

Administration and Adjudication

High organization authority requires highly competent international civil servants with loyalty to the organization and organization goals of shared security and well-being rather than to the goals and policy of their national state. Further, high organization authority must have judicial organs to interpret treaties and international policy under those treaties and to make judicial decisions that are respected and accepted by states members of organizations.

International Administration

In all international organizations the international civil servant is bound by the wording of Article 100 of the U.N. Charter that means he or she may not take orders from the home state or "other authority external to the organization." This is accompanied by the demand that no government should seek to influence the international civil servant. The article stresses the "exclusively international character of the Secretary General and his staff." As we noted earlier, high state authority is manifested when states are apprehensive about the "exclusively international character of the international civil service."

International civil servants obviously carry the passport of the states of which they are citizens. Is it possible, then, to find people with an "exclusively international character"? The answer is and must be "yes." There are about 100,000 international civil servants in the international organizations we study and there is very little evidence that they deviate from the oath they must take to serve the organization and not any other state or authority, especially the one to which they retain citizenship allegiance. For a long time, Soviet international civil servants and those from some other socialist states were on a very short rope, but this too has changed under the leadership of President Mikhail Gorbachev.

The chief executive officer of the organization—secretary general, director general, or other title—sets the tone and pace for administrative integrity, impartiality, and dedication to duty. This is particularly true of the secretary general of the United Nations. Secretary General Javier Perez de Cuellar has provided inspired leadership for the United Nations in the 1980s, and with the warming of relations between the United States and the Soviet Union, has drawn to his high office, and to him personally, the confidence and desire by the superpowers for increased authority. His diplomatic leadership was vital to the Soviet pullout of Afghanistan in 1989, gradually resolving the protracted crisis in Namibia, bringing the Iran–Iraq war to a conclusion, and reducing conflict and tension on Cyprus, the Western Sahara, and other areas of the world. He is being called upon to play a major role in investigations of production of chemical warfare anywhere in the world and has inspired the staff of the United Nations to take increasing pride in their professional responsibilities.

Further, Secretary General Perez de Cuellar responded brilliantly in the late 1980s to the fiscal crisis faced by the United Nations in view of cuts of contributions by the United States. He further effected administrative streamlining to answer the charges of bureaucratic duplication and inefficiencies.[41] Officials in the World Bank and IMF exercise high organization authority in making decisions on loans to developing nations and in the restructuring of national economies of developing nations that are plagued with enormous indebtedness. The authority delegated to them by members is in recognition of their high level of professional expertise and credibility in organization administration. New leadership in institutions such as the WHO in the late 1980s has also elevated states' confidence in and respect for international civil service. All of this is not to say that leadership and administrative improvement translate readily into willingness of states further to delegate authority to international organizations. However, international civil service is gaining increasing credibility in response to the clear need for expanded international administration in all areas of shared security and well-being.

In addition to the mainline officials of international organizations are people chosen for their expertise in specific areas of organizations' operations but who do not represent their nations of citizenship or other authorities. Many examples abound. The assembly of the World Health Organization, which meets in Geneva each May, is composed of representatives of member states, but the executive board of WHO consists of experts in principal areas of health chosen on a global geographic basis. This board has extensive authority delegated to it by the assembly and its interests are striving toward the goals of the WHO, although clearly its policy directives come from the political processes and resolutions of the assembly. The executive board of UNICEF is composed of experts, as is the case of many executive boards of organizations. The forty-three member U.N. Commission on Human Rights is an intensely political organ in its annual six-week meeting in Geneva in February and March. However, the main day-to-day work of the commission is undertaken by its staff of international civil servants in New York, Geneva, and throughout the world, as well as its expert bodies (including the twenty-six-member Subcommission for the Prevention of Discrimination and Protection of Minorities and its two committees with responsibilities for the implementation of the two U.N. covenants on human rights, which we study in Chapter 6). The commission also engages outstanding international experts, "rapporteurs," and establishes working parties of experts to deal with allegations of violation of human rights by specific nations and to explore "themes" such as torture, disappearances, and summary or arbitrary executions. The reports of these experts have been annually considered by the commission and, on the whole, received considerable majority votes of approval of their findings and recommendations. In brief, organizations' policy are extensively influenced and guided by international civil servants and experts who serve the international interest, advance goals of shared security and well-being, and earnestly seek to promote organizations as centers to harmonize the interests of their members. Perhaps we can apply to the international officials the statement by President Washington, who warned his fellow Americans in several of the drafts of his Farewell Address not to be anxious to withdraw their confidence in public servants because that confidence is "the best incentive to a faithful discharge of their duty."

International Court of Justice

The International Court of Justice (referred to here as Court) with its Seat at the Peace Palace in the Hague, The Netherlands, is a continuation of the League of Nations' Permanent Court of International Justice. It has played an important role in juridical determination of a number of disputes between states and in delivering advisory opinions that clarify and contribute to the growth of international constitutional law. It has never realized its potential as "the principal judicial organ of the United Nations" in Article 92 of the U.N. Charter. However, there is agreement in the early 1990s that the Court should be delegated more authority. Moves by both the United States and the Soviet Union have elevated Court power to interpret treaties and make binding decisions in specific categories of disputes. Thus the Court may well play an increasing role in high organization authority.

The Court's constitutional foundations are to be found in Chapter 14 of the U.N. Charter and also in its own constitution, the Statute of the International Court of Justice. The U.N. Charter provisions are brief, but the statute and especially Articles 34, 35, 36, 37, and 38 (Chapter 2, Competence of the Court) provide the essential authority for the Court's performance of its delegated authority. All members of the United Nations are *ipso facto* members of the Court and only states may appear before the Court. Under Article 36 of the Statute, the Court's jurisdiction in legal disputes submitted to it by parties include interpretation of treaties, any question of international law, determination of facts that may relate to a breach of international obligation, and the nature of reparation in the event there is such a breach. The Court may also give advisory opinions as requested by the General Assembly and Security Council and by other U.N. organs and specialized agencies as well. We cited earlier in this chapter the Court's advisory opinion in the "Reparations Case," which confirmed the independent constitutional and legal status of the United Nations and thus subsequently similar status for other international legal authorities on the basis of provisions in their constitutions. The Court is also called upon in provisions in a number of constitutions of organizations and the treaties these organizations have generated to interpret the conventions and determine disputes submitted to the Court by any party to a dispute. In time, case law under such provisions will compile an extensive record of international judicial review.[42]

States appear before the fifteen members of the Court by agreement to accept the Court's jurisdiction in their particular case. Under Article 36 of the statute, states may declare that they accept the compulsory jurisdiction of the Court. Forty-four states have accepted this jurisdiction but often with hedging reservations. Article 94 of the U.N. Charter states that "each member of the United Nations undertakes to comply with the decision of the [Court] in any case to which it is a party." The Court has no enforcement mechanism but neither does the Supreme Court of the United States. The judges and staffs of the Court and other international juridical bodies are the same as international civil servants in being immune from orders from their states or others.

In 1989, both the United States and the Soviet Union moved toward strengthening the Court. The United States proposed that the other four permanent members of the Security Council join with it in enabling the Court to decide on disputes arising under treaties and other sources of international law and to accept as binding the judgment of the Court in such disputes. The kinds of disputes, however, would be carefully defined and would not include those relating to national security or threats or uses of force. Basically they would be disputes, especially interpretation of treaties, that would not be so important that any state could not afford to lose in the judgment. The United States has also recommended that the Court be more extensively used in arbitration. The Soviet Union, in turn, declared that it would accept as binding an arbitration decision by the Court in disputes involving some human rights treaties including the 1984 Convention Against Torture. This announcement was made at the 1989 session of the Commission on Human Rights and as an extension of Soviet policy under President Gorbachev to strengthen international organizations and juridical bodies.[43] Both superpowers in August 1989 signed an agreement to accept the binding arbitration of the Court in seven specific treaties, including those dealing with terrorism and drug traffic. These treaties require nations apprehending alleged violators either to extradite or to try them for their crimes. They will also seek to persuade the other three permanent members of the Security Council to take similar action to broaden the jurisdiction of the Court and especially its role in international judicial review in treaty interpretation.[44]

It will be some time before the Court will command the willingness of states to accept its compulsory jurisdiction as many states have with respect to the Court of the European Community and the European Court of Human Rights. Even those courts, however, have compulsory jurisdiction in very specific areas of disputes and treaty interpretation. In its judgments and advisory opinions thus far, the Court does speak for the international system of states as the principal judicial organ of international constitutional law. It has elevated judicial disputes between states to a judicial determination representing the international constitutional system. For instance, when Iranian citizens with the approbation of the Iran government seized the American hostages in November 1979, the United

States almost immediately took this profound violation of international diplomatic law and treaties to the International Court of Justice. The Court unanimously held in an interim decision on December 15, 1979, that the U.S. position must be upheld and the hostages released. This was reaffirmed in a strong ruling on May 24, 1980. Although the hostages were not released until January 20, 1981, the Court's decision converted a United States–Iran political/security confrontation into an international legal affirmation of a crystal clear violation of international law. In a sense, the Court legally multilateralized a bilateral conflict, which served notice on the world that the law shall be upheld.[45]

SUPRA-ORGANIZATION AUTHORITY

Supra-organization authority is exercised by an organization over its members in specific areas of policy and governance formerly held by the members and which they now specifically delegate to the organization. Once delegated, that authority cannot be retrieved by members unless they vote to do so or resign from the organization. The most conspicuous examples of supra-organizations' authority is that exercised by the EC over its twelve members and the European Commission and Court of Human Rights under the Council of Europe.

Many proposals for a "world federal government" and a "world constitution" were voiced at the end of World War II in the idealism to move the United Nations on to supra-organization authority. High state authority was terrified at such designs, which never materialized. The United States proposed the establishment of a United Nations Atomic Energy Authority in 1946—the famous Baruch Plan—which would have given the authority control over atomic weapons in time. However, the plan failed to impress the Soviet Union, which was furiously developing its own atomic weapons and which also did not trust the U.S. promise to destroy its atomic capability after the authority was established.

The call for a "New International Economic Order" in 1974 contained proposals for extensive regulation of the existing "liberal" international economic order managed basically by the industrial democracies.[46] We noted earlier in this chapter that proposals for a new order was and continues to be resisted by the industrial democracies as not congenial to the well-being they enjoy under the existing order.[47] The various agencies and means for transfer of resources to the developing nations from the affluent states imply on paper measures of supra-organization authority. However, by the early 1990s, the strident demands of the mid-1970s have receded into diplomacy and exchanges sponsored by many international organizations such as the World Bank, IMF, UNCTAD, and GATT in the vast and complex relationships between the developed and developing nations.[48]

The 1982 Law of the Sea Treaty was referred to in Chapter 1 when we briefly scanned 5,000 years of evolving laws of the sea. These five millenia flowed into the treaty, which was generated by the United Nations and encompasses all the previous treaty and customary law of the sea. It sets forth legal rights, obligations, and relations for states in the jurisdiction of the seas covering about 70 percent of the surface of the earth. The treaty is only another example of the progression of international constitutional law as we see from its preamble: "the codification and progressive development of the law of the sea achieved in this Convention will contribute to the strengthening of peace, security, cooperation and friendly relations among all nations."[49]

The treaty has not come into force, largely because twelve of the twenty-four industrialized states oppose elements of supra-organization authority explicit in it, and especially the United States, which contributes one-fourth of the U.N. budget. We observed in Chapter 1 that invention and discovery breed necessity and vice versa, and one necessity has always been law to deal with constant invention and discovery. Technology in the 1960s and 1970s led to the possibility of mining sea beds under the high seas, which are thick with vast mineral resources such as nickel, tin, lead, and manganese. How should evolving international law deal with the jurisdiction of the sea bed, which is now in the grasp of industry seeking valued primary resources?

On the one hand, a few industrial states and especially the United States were developing technologies for the exploitation and mining of the lucrative sea beds. On the other was the vast majority of states, especially the developing nations, which took lines from the 1979 Moon Convention we examined in this chapter under space law that stated that outer space "shall be the province of mankind." Should not supra-organization authority exercise regulatory power over that which belongs to all rather any "national appropriation" or "claims of sovereignty" that are prohibited in the outer space treaty? The technologically advantaged nations argued the parable of the "Father of International Law," Hugo Grotius, which we cited in Chapter 1. Both the fisherman and the slave agree that the sea is common to all purposes but disagree on who owns what is found in the common area. The fisherman or industrial states with sea bed technology declares "but what my net and hooks have taken is absolutely my own" in response to the technologically poor slave—and nations—who argue that "what is found in the common area is common property."

The common property of "province of mankind" claim was eloquently sharpened on November 1, 1967, when the ambassador from Malta to the United Nations declared in the General Assembly that the sea bed is the "common heritage of mankind." It belonged to all mankind and thus it was the obligation of international law through international organizations to guarantee access to the sea bed and its riches. On December 17, 1970, the General Assembly approved the concept of the common heritage of mankind, which then found its way into the final Law of the Sea Treaty that was signed in Jamaica on December 10, 1982, by 117 states. Twelve of the twenty-four industrial states that contribute to well over 50 percent of the budget of the United Nations have not signed the treaty.[50]

The industrial states support over 90 percent of the treaty's provisions, which are very much in their interests for security and well-being. They ardently oppose, however, the strong thrust of the treaty toward supra-organization authority in areas that they claim should be in the domain of free enterprise traditional international law. They oppose the concept of the "common heritage of mankind" that is "beyond the limits of national jurisdiction" in the preamble. The treaty refers to the sea bed as the "Area" which, again, is the "common heritage of mankind." Under Article 137, "all rights in the resources of the Area are vested in mankind as a whole, on whose behalf the Authority shall act." The "Authority" is the supra-organization International Sea Bed Authority, which under Article 176 "shall have international legal personality" to manage sea bed mining. The authority is to have its own organization of a council, assembly, and a secretariat and there is also to be an International Tribunal for the Law of the Sea, as indicated in Annex 6 to the treaty. The actual mining is to be carried out by the enterprise under control of the authority with compulsory transfer by the states having technology for sea bed mining to the enterprise and the sharing of sea bed resources extracted from the bottom of the seas. The thesis of the slave is thus ingrained in the treaty, so strongly opposed by the industrial states' fisherman.[51]

Supra-organization authority at the universal level is far into the future because of the diversity of requirements of goals of security and well-being among the world's nations and especially between the industrial and developing nations. The IMF and the World Bank have been delegated by their members considerable decision-making authority, which is the gray area between high organization and supra-organization authority. The United States in November 1989 endorsed considerable authority into the GATT having the final word on dispute settlement by its special juridical panels of experts and in other areas of supervision of the rules of international trade in merchandise. At the regional level, however, supra-organization authority flourishes.

European Supra-organization Authority

It is among the twelve members of the EC that supra-organization authority is moving forward with a startling momentum in the early 1990s. Further, the European Human Rights Commission and Court under the aegis of the twenty-four–member Council of Europe are exercising authority over civil and human rights law of its member states, which grows with each passing year. Although most of the organizations we study are universal in scope and membership, the European experience in supra-organization authority provides significant models for processes, diplomacy, treaties, and administration for champions of the expansion of supra-organization authority.

The European Community

The powerful EC was established as the European Economic Community in the Treaty of Rome of March 25, 1957 and entered into force on January 1, 1958. Its original goal of vast reduction of trade barriers between and among its six original members has been realized and extensively broadened into a vision of significant and, in some areas, supra-organization authority by 1992 in marked unity among its current twelve member states.[52]

The locale of the EC is truly European. Its headquarters are in Brussels, with its court located in Luxembourg and parliament in Strasbourg. The council of the EC represents the member states, while the seventeen-member commission is to serve the goals and processes of the EC and "be completely independent in the performance of their duties."[53] This structure provides balance between state and organization authority, although the latter tends to prevail. Policy and laws are shaped by the initiative of the commission, reviewed carefully by the parliament of the EC and accepted or rejected by the council. Under the Single European Act of 1985, council decisions are now made by the majority and not by unanimity, as was the case in the original treaty. Thus, there is no veto in the council and, in general, little opposition to policy and law that reaches the council for the enactment of legislation as law both for the EC as an international legal authority and the members as well.[54] The Commission is the legal engine and the Council the locus of supra-organization authority.

The 518-member parliament of the EC has been elected since 1979 on the basis of direct universal suffrage with each member representing a specific electoral district in his or her nation, as well as one of many political parties vying in the parliamentary elections. Great Britain, for instance, is allocated eighty-one seats in the parliament. In the elections of June 19, 1989, the Labor Party won forty-five seats, while the Conservatives garnered only thirty-two. This was attributed in part to Prime Minister Thatcher's displeasure with the growing authority of the EC on the one hand and Labor's enthusiasm for closer ties with Europe on the other. Parliament's governing powers have constantly been enlarged in the last two decades. It has authority to amend, delay, and, in some cases, veto measures submitted to it for review including the EC's budget. It reviews EC treaties and is often outspoken on issues of foreign affairs.

The court of the EC has specific supra-organization authority in areas of delegated jurisdiction. The thirteen-judge court is charged under Article 164 of the 1957 Treaty to "ensure that in the interpretation and application of this Treaty, the law is observed." Under Article 171, "if the Court of Justice finds that a Member State has failed to fulfill an obligation under this Treaty, the State shall be required to take the necessary measures to comply with the judgment of the Court of Justice." The court hands down over 200 decisions and issues hundreds of rules for compliance each year in the progressive expansion of its judicial authority over such areas as antitrust issues, trade, regulatory activity, operations of the EC's massive Common Agricultural Policy, which consumes about 66 percent of the EC's expenditures and other areas of EC law.[55] The EC is administered by some 12,000 civil servants, often labeled "Eurocrats" who, as with international civil servants, are pledged to serve the interests and law of the EC and not the policies of their native states. The EC often acts with one voice, especially in international organizations such as GATT. The president of the EC's commission represents the EC at the annual economic summit meeting of the Group of Seven industrial powers.[56]

The EC's governance enacted the Single Europe Act in 1985, which targeted 1992 as the year to complete the integration of the EC to effect free movement of goods, services, money, and people. The EC's office labeled this goal as its "manifest destiny" and compared 1992 with the first voyage of Columbus 500 years before as the second "milestone in European economic development." All twelve member states now adhere to the European Currency Unit (ECU), which is the fifth most widely used international unit of currency. Monetary collaboration will move on toward a single currency and thus the elimination of exchange of currency operations between and among the members, a European central bank, and elimination of exchange controls. In the summer of 1988, in an address to the European parliament, Jacques Delors, president of the commission, declared that within ten years, 80 percent of the economic, and perhaps social and tax legislation, will be decided at the EC level.[57]

Clearly, supra-organization authority is on the move for the EC and its members, before, during, and after 1992. It is the world's largest single market of some 330 million producing and consuming people and 20 percent of global trade, with 100 billion dollars of trade and goods and services between the EC and the United States. The European Commission observed in 1983 that "the supremacy of Community law is a fundamental requirement of the legal order of the Communities" and the autonomy of community law is therefore "the foundation of the Community's legal order."[58] Leaders of the EC in their meeting in Dublin in June 1990 agreed to enter negotiations by the end of the year on a vaguely defined "political union" in addition to their negotiations toward an economic and monetary union. A new supra-organization authority EC with a unified Germany and new liaisons with Central Europe and the Soviet Union may well revive Europe as the heartland of the international system as it was for so long before.

European Human Rights

The Statute of the Council of Europe was signed in London on May 5, 1949, and entered into force on August 3, 1949. The ten original members recognized in the preamble "the common heritage of their peoples," which certainly is central to the growth of supra-organization authority in Western Europe. The statute was and is the progression of hundreds of years of visions of philosophers and statespeople for a more united Europe and especially the drive and leadership of Winston Churchill to forge a European unity that would finally bring an end to war. Article 1 of the statute calls for a "further realization of human rights and fundamental freedoms."[59] The new Council of Europe completed its work on freedoms on November 4, 1950, and the convention and its machinery went into operation on September 3, 1953.[60] Twenty-two members of the council have ratified the convention and thus have voluntarily bound themselves to the supra-organization authority provisions of this treaty.

Under Article 1, the parties "shall secure to everyone within their jurisdiction the rights and freedoms defined in Section 1 of this Convention." The rights are essentially civil rights and freedoms, as well as legal rights and especially guarantees of the due process of the law. Section 2 provides for the European Commission and the European Court of Human Rights "to ensure the observance" by parties of the convention. The commission in Section 3 is composed of twenty-two members elected by the council's Committee of (foreign) Ministers, and they sit in their individual capacity and professionalism and not as nationals of the states from which they come. The commission is charged with the administration of due process of the law when they receive petitions of complaints from individuals, nongovernmental organizations, or groups charging that their rights have been violated by one of the member states. After considering the petition, the commission, by a two-thirds vote, may make a determination or decision which under Article 32, paragraph 4, "the High Contracting Parties undertake to regard as binding on them."

The issue may be appealed to the court by any of the parties to the dispute or by the commission itself under Articles 47 and 48 of the convention, with the court having the highest jurisdiction over the member states and the Commission.[61] Section 4 sets forth the jurisdiction of the court and its judgment as final in any determination or decision. The "High Contracting Parties" in Article 53 undertake to abide by the decision of the court in any case to which they are parties and the court's judgment "shall be transmitted to the Committee of Ministers [of the Council of Europe] which shall supervise its execution."[62] The domestication provision of the convention is in Article 57, which states that "any High Contracting Party shall furnish an explanation of the manner in which its internal law ensures the effective implementation of any of the provisions in this convention."[63]

Supra-organization authority under the convention has resulted in the commission and the court handing down to members and other parties thousands of decisions that member states have accepted as final authority even over the highest courts of their lands. About one-fourth of the decisions have been addressed to civil and due process law in Great Britain, which has no constitutional guarantee of rights other than what the parliament through legislation determines those rights to be. As a result, the European Court has altered and amended British civil and criminal law in many respects and some in Great Britain have expressed displeasure over a non-British court having such authority. But authority it does have, along with the court of the EC, which manifests in specific areas the marked erosion of high state authority and even state-organization partnership.

Inter-American Human Rights

The OAS emerged with the signing of its charter by its founding members on April 30, 1948, and entered into force December 13, 1951. It was preceded, however, by nineteenth-century movements toward some hemispheric unity and by the Pan American Union of 1890, as well as a number of multilateral treaties in the early twentieth century that were aimed at cooperation and "good neighbors" (as President Franklin Roosevelt put it) and away from the unilateralism of the 1823 Monroe Doctrine. A provision in the preamble to the charter states that the members are

confident that the true significance of American solidarity and good neighborliness can only mean the consolidation on this continent, within the framework of democratic institutions, of a system of individual liberty and social justice based on respect for the essential rights of man.[64]

The organization moved toward implementation of this goal with the U.S. Convention on Human Rights, which was signed on November 22, 1969, and became operational with its administrative and judicial machinery on July 18, 1978. Chapter 2 sets forth the civil and political rights guaranteed under the convention and domestication into municipal law is in Article 2 ("Domestic Legal Effects") and in Article 43 as well. Chapter 7 provides for a commission and Chapter 8 the court, in following the structure and due process procedures of the European Convention's commission and court for protection of human rights. Both the Inter-American Commission and Court have their own statutes, unlike the European Convention.[65] Under Article 67, the "judgement of the Court shall be final and not subject to appeal." In Article 68, supra-organization authority is expressed by the statement that "state Parties to the Convention undertake to comply with the judgement of the Court in any case to which they are parties."

The convention and its commission and court have been in operation for a relatively brief period of time but have and continue to make their mark on inter-American civil and legal rights jurisprudence. But supra-organization authority moved forward slowly in this continent for many reasons. There is enormous variety in the cultural heritage in the Americas and in the composition of peoples of many states, including the indigenous Indian populations. Military regimes have taken advantage of the provision in Article 27 of the convention that provides suspension of guarantees of rights for "time of war, public danger, or other emergency that threatens the independence of security of a State Party." Some specific rights in paragraph 2 of Article 27, however, may not be derogated including the right to life. In any event, the convention and its law, commission, and court are in place and functioning with ever-expanding authority.

As far as constitutions of states are concerned, Article 24 of the Basic Law of the Federal Republic of Germany provides for a full acceptance of supra-organization authority. "The Federation may by legislation transfer sovereign powers to international governmental institutions." It is assumed this provision will be included in a constitution for the new United Germany. This is being done by members of the EC which, by 1992 as we have noted, will exercise supra-organization "powers" in specific areas of policy formerly under state authority. In any event, the inevitable progression of authority and law in the direction of high and supra-organization organization authority will be the most significant attribute of international law in the 1990s and beyond. We referred earlier in this chapter to new clusters of international constitutional law including international refugee law based on the refugee Convention of 1951 and the Protocol of 1967. We end this chapter with a vignette on the significance of this branch of international constitutional law in the context of the awesome events in Eastern Europe in 1989 and 1990. On September 10, 1989, Hungary announced that all East Germans who had fled their state would be permitted to leave Hungary and proceed to West Germany through Austria. The legal basis for this policy was Article 33 of the 1951 Convention, which basically states that no refugee seeking asylum in another state may be forced against his/her will to return to the state from which the refugee fled—no "refoulement." East Germany demanded of Hungary that the East Germans be returned but Hungary relied on international constitutional law to protect the East German "refugees." The floodgates were opened and international law paved the way for the surge of Germans from east to west and all that followed in the dramatic and peaceful revolution for human rights and freedom in Central Europe.

NOTES

1. An exception is GATT, the principal international legal authority in world merchandise trade, which has 96 members, or about 60 percent of membership in the United Nations. However, thirty other states adhere to GATT trade law (about 80 percent of all nations).

2. See Daniel Patrick Moynihan, *A Dangerous Place* (New York: Berkley Books, 1980). A former U.S. ambassador to the United Nations, Senator Moynihan considered the United Nations "dangerous" with respect to the international interests of the United States.

3. Nicaragua sharply challenged the United States in the GATT for its trade embargo against Nicaragua and for the United States' invoking Article 21 as a security exception to free trade. Neither side won or lost in the GATT dispute settlement.

4. See Articles 4, 12, 18, 19, 21, and 22.

5. See Articles 6, 7, 8, 11, 15, 16, and 18.

6. Articles 12, 19, and 25. See Finlayson and Zacher's "The GATT and the Regulation of Trade Barriers Regime," in Paul F. Diehl (ed.), *The Politics of International Organizations: Patterns and Insights* (Chicago: Dorsey Press, 1989).

7. See Articles 6, 12, and 13 of the Covenant of Economic, Social, and Cultural Rights. Article 6, paragraph 5, of the Covenant on Civil and Political Rights forbids the sentence of death to be imposed on persons under the age of 18, a matter of state law in the United States and contrary to most state laws. Article 20 of the same covenant prohibits propaganda for war that would be considered an infringement on the right of speech in the United States. There are other contradictions. The 1979 Senate hearings on the two covenants revealed abundant testimony by U.S. political interest groups such as the American Newspapers Publishers Association on contradictions between the covenants and U.S. constitutional law, in this case between the Civil and Political Covenant

prohibition on the "propaganda for war" in Article 20 and freedom of speech and press in the First Amendment to the Constitution. *International Human Rights Treaties: Hearings Before the Senate Committee on Foreign Relations,* 96th Congress. 1st Sess., 35, November 14–16, 19. See also Philip Alston, "U.S. Ratification of the Covenant on Economic, Social, and Cultural Rights: The Need for an Entirely New Strategy," *American Journal of International Law* 84 (April, 1990), p. 365.

8. Such is the situation with other nations as well as is evidenced by the many reservations and amendments they submit even when ratifying these covenants.

9. See Winston Churchill, *The Gathering Storm* (Boston: Houghton Mifflin Company, 1948).

10. See Graham Allison, *Essence of Decision* (Boston: Little, Brown & Co., 1971).

11. An interesting exercise would be the construction of a new Bretton Woods set of institutions—or, one institution of super-authority.

12. *International Herald Tribune,* May 17, 1989; *New York Times,* May 23, 1989.

13. Donald J. Puchala and Roger A. Coate, *The State of the United Nations, 1988* (Hanover, N.H.: The Academic Council on the United Nations System, 1988).

14. This certainly is not true of Professors Panchala and Chote, whose 1988 assessment of the United Nations is extremely well-balanced and yet critical in a very constructive manner.

15. 252 U.S. 416, 1920.

16. 38 Cal., 2d 718, 1952.

17. For an excellent appraisal of the state-organization partnership role, see James McCormick, "Intergovernmental Organizations and Cooperation Among Nations," in P.F. Diehl (ed.), *The Politics of International Organizations,* p. 83.

18. See Ernst B. Haas, *The United Nations and Collective Management of International Conflict* (New York: U.N. Institute for Teaching and Research, 1986). See also, Indar Jit Rikhve and Kjell Skjelsbaek (eds.), *The United Nations and Peacekeeping: Results, Limitations and Prospects* (New York: St. Martin's Press, 1991).

19. Brian Urquhart, *A Life in Peace and War: Memoirs* (New York: Harper and Row, 1987). See also Johan Kaufmann, *Conference Diplomacy: An Introductory Analysis,* 2d ed. (Boston: Martinus Nijhoff Publishers, 1988).

20. Such were resolutions in the Security Council reducing or ending conflict in the Iran–Iraq war, seeking Palestine's acceptance of the 1967 Council Resolution 242 on conditions to bring Israel and the Arab states together in negotiation, and resolutions on Afghanistan and Namibia (Southwest Africa). Progress in arms controls negotiations also reflect growing conditions of shared security for the superpowers.

21. *New York Times,* April 23, 1988. The concept of the "international interest" is mentioned twice in Article 24 of the League of Nations Covenant.

22. Yale University Press, New Haven. See, especially, Mitrany's *A Working Peace System* (Chicago: Quadrangle Books, 1966). A superb analysis of functionalism is to be found in Chapter 17, "The Functional Approach to Peace", of Inis L. Claude's *Swords into Plowshares,* 4th ed. (New York: Random House, 1984). See also Ernst B. Haas, *Beyond the Nation State: Functionalism and International Order* (Stanford: Stanford University Press, 1964); Chapter 9, "Social and Economic Cooperation," in Robert E. Riggs and Jack C. Plano, *The United Nations: International Organization and World Politics* (Chicago: The Dorsey Press, 1988); "Functionalism," in David W. Ziegler's *War, Peace, and International Politics* 3d ed. (Boston: Little, Brown & Company, 1984). For a more current approach to functionalist theory, see R. J. Harrison, "Neo-

Functionalism," in A. J. Groom and P. Taylor (eds.), *Frameworks for International Cooperation* (New York: St. Martin's Press, 1990), p. 139 ff. This volume is a superb collection of studies of international organization theory.

23. Ruth B. Russell, *A History of the United Nations Charter* (Washington, D.C.: The Brookings Institution, 1958), p. 206.

24. For an analysis of high and low politics in international organizations, see the chapters by James McCormick, "International Governmental Organizations and Cooperation among Nations," and Werner Feld and Robert Jordan, "Patterns of Decision-making in International Organizations," in Paul F. Diehl (ed.), *The Politics of International Organizations,* pp. 83 and 117.

25. Louis B. Sohn's *Cases and Other Materials on World Law* of 1950 was the pioneering study in this field. It was revised in 1956 and the title changed to *Cases on United Nations Law,* with a second edition in 1967 (Brooklyn: The Foundation Press, Inc.).

26. International Court of Justice, Advisory Opinion, 1949, I.C.J. Rep. 174.

27. Sohn's *International Organization and Integration* (Boston: Martinus Nijhoff, 1986) provides the reader with the constitutions of the major international organizations for examination of provisions dealing with their delegated authority.

28. This is basically the international legal definition of torture, taken from Article 1 of the 1984 Convention Against Torture. See Sohn, *International Organization and Integration,* p. 418. See also *Methods of Combating Torture,* Fact Sheet No. 4, United Nations Center for Human Rights, March, 1989. A leading study is J. Herman Burgers and Hans Danelius, *The United Nations Convention against Torture and Other Cruel, Inhuman or Degrading Treatment or Punishment* (Boston: Martinis Nijhoff, 1988). The United Nations has established a Voluntary Fund for Victims of Torture.

29. See Part V, "Human Rights and Social Issues," in *Issues Before the Forty-Sixth General Assembly,* United Nations Association of the United States of America, New York, 1992.

30. Articles 102 and 103 of the U.N. Charter call for all treaties entered into by U.N. members to be registered at the United Nations and that members' obligations under the U.N. Charter "prevail" over other international agreements concluded by members.

31. See dissenting opinion of Judge Tanaka, South West Africa Cases (Second Phase), in Ian Brownlie, *Basic Documents on Human Rights,* 2d ed. (Oxford: Clarendon Press, 1981). A resolution of the General Assembly is not binding on members and thus is not international law *per se,* unlike decisions of the Security Council.

32. It might be added that the Martens Clause, which we cited at the end of Part 2 of this chapter, states that even if states do not sign or denounce treaties, they are bound by "the principles of the law of nations" as well as "usages," "laws of humanity," and "dictates of public conscience."

33. For the text of these two treaties, see Sohn, *International Organization and Integration,* pp. 55 and 64. See also the Statute of the International Law Commission, Sohn, ibid., p. 51. An excellent and comprehensive treatment of sources is by Professor David Kennedy, "The Sources of International Law," *The American University of International Law and Policy* (Spring 1987), pp. 1–96. A major contribution toward a broad interpretation of sources of international law to enable the United States better domestic human rights law is Richard B. Lillich, "The Constitution and International Human Rights," *American Journal of International Law* (October 1989), p. 851, which looks to customary international law when treaties present obstacles to domestication. On the

contemporary relevance of classical writers in such areas as the rights and law of humanitarian intervention to address violations of human rights, see Theodor Meron, "Common Rights of Mankind in Gentili, Grotius, and Suarez" in *American Journal of International Law* (January 1991), p. 110 ff.

34. There were twelve other trials in Nuremberg under Nuremberg criminal law and one trial in Tokyo for Japanese war criminals.

35. Most states have bilateral treaties of extradition with each other for a legal and orderly process to return people alleged to have committed crimes to their home state or where the crime was committed.

36. An exhaustive treatment of this field is by M. Cherif Bassiouni, *International Criminal Law* (Dobbs Ferry, N. Y.: Transnational Publishers, 1986). Volume 1 deals with international crimes, volume 2 with international criminal procedure, and volume 3 with enforcement. Chapter 12, "Measures to Deal with International Crimes," in *United Nations Action in the Field of Human Rights* (New York: United Nations, 1983), is a comprehensive survey of covenants, declarations, and definitions of international crime. This survey is updated in the 1988 edition of this indispensible and official collection of U.N. primary resources in the field of human rights. See pages 184–190 and 200–204. See also Chapter 14, "International Criminal Law," in Gehard von Glan's *Law Among Nations*, 5th ed. (New York: Macmillan Publishing Company, 1986). See also Brian Michael Jenkins, "International Terrorism: A New Challenge for the United Nations," in *The United Nations and the Maintenance of International Peace and Security* (Boston: Martinus Nijhoff, 1987), p. 407.

37. See in particular R. P. Anand, *International Law and the Developing Countries* (Boston: Martinus Nijhoff, 1987). Also, *Development, Human Rights and the Rule of Law* (Elmsford, N.Y.: Pergamon Press, 1981) (sponsored by the International Commission of Jurists, Geneva) deals with the "legal right to development."

38. See Paul Sieghart, "International Treaties as a Source of Domestic Law," in *The International Law of Human Rights* (Oxford: Clarendon Press, 1984), p. 40; Richard B. Lillich, "The Role of Domestic Courts in Enforcing International Human Rights Law (especially the United States)" in Hurst Hannum, *Guide to International Human Rights Practice* (Philadelphia: University of Pennsylvania Press, 1984); "Conference Report: Human Rights in American Courts," *The American University Journal of International Law and Policy* (Summer 1986): 137. The Permanent Court of International Justice in the Exchange of Greek and Turkish Populations case in 1925 held that "a state which has contracted valid international obligations is bound to make modifications as may be necessary to ensure the fulfillment of the obligations undertaken." It stated in the Greece and Bulgaria Case in 1930 that "the provisions of municipal law cannot prevail over those of the treaty" of two contracting states. Domestication is confirmed in Articles 27 and 46 of the 1969 Vienna Convention on the Law of Treaties. See Lillich citation in note 33, which deals with domestication in the United States of international human rights law as well as Elizabeth Zoller, *Enforcing International Law Through United States Legislation* (Dobbs Ferry, N.Y.: Transnational Publishers, 1985).

39. In December 1966 the Security Council in the first of a series of decisions imposed economic sanctions on white-dominated Rhodesia (now Zimbabwe) and President Johnson issued an executive order for a U.S. embargo as municipal law in conformity with Article 25.

40. This provision should be compared to the "domestication" article in the companion Covenant on Economic, Social, and Cultural Rights (Article 2), which provides for a

more complex process, given the nature of these kinds of rights that differ in terms of implementation from civil and political rights.

41. For a succinct review of U.N. administrative and financial reform, see the annual publication, *Issues Before the 41st General Assembly of the United Nations* (1986); for the 42nd to 46th General Assemblies, see years 1987–1991. See also John De Gara's *Administrative and Financial Reform of the United Nations: A Documentary Essay*, The Academic Council on the United Nations System, Reports and Papers, Dartmouth College, Hanover, N. H., 1989. Antonio Donini, Research Office, U.N. Joint Inspection Unit, has written a splendid essay, "Resilience and Reform: Some Thoughts on the Processes of Change in the United Nations," in Philip Alston and Raul Pangalangan's *Revitalizing the Study of International Organizations* (Medford, Mass.: Fletcher School of Law and Diplomacy, Tufts University, 1988). See also, *Leadership at the United Nations: The Roles of the Secretary General and Member States* (New York: United Nations Association of the United States, 1986).

42. See, for instance, Article 37 of the constitution of the ILO, Article 9 of the Genocide Convention, and Article 30 of the Convention Against Torture, all in Sohn, *International Organization and Integration*, and Article 12 in the International Convention on the Suppression and Punishment of the Crime of Apartheid, in Brownlie, *Basic Documents on Human Rights*.

43. *New York Times*, February 12, 1989, and March 9, 1989.

44. See the article by Thomas M. Franck, "Soviet Initiatives: U.S. Responses: New Opportunities for Reviving the United Nations System," *American Journal of International Law* (August 1989), for a masterful analysis on how the expanding and closer relationship between the superpowers may greatly enhance the authority of the U.N. system.

45. The Court's decision did not lead to the immediate release of the hostages. However, Iran greatly suffered from this legal condemnation and legal processes and agreements of great complexity lead to the hostages' release in return for the United States lifting its freeze of Iranian assets. For a major and recent study of the Court, see Lori F. Damrosch (ed.), *The International Court of Justice at the Crossroads* (Dobbs Ferry, N.Y.: Transnational Publishers, 1987). See also Rosenne Shabtai, *The World Court: What It Is and How It Works*, 4th ed. (Boston: Martinus Nijhoff, 1989).

46. We cited the classic study by Arthur Lewis, *The Evolution of the International Economic Order* (Princeton, N.J.: Princeton University Press, 1978) in Chapters 1 and 2, which appraised the current international economic order of some 100 years with demands for a "new" order.

47. See the "Declaration on the Establishment of a New International Economic Order" of May 1, 1974, in Sohn, *International Organization and Integration*, p. 430; also the December 12, 1974, "Charter of Economic Rights and Duties," ibid., p. 433.

48. It is interesting to note that Article 1 of the constitution of the UNIDO of 1979 states that "the primary objective of the Organization shall be the promotion and acceleration of industrial development in the developing countries with a view to assisting in the establishment of a new international economic order." Current membership of 151 states thus adhere to this international constitutional provision.

49. For the text of the treaty, see Sohn, *International Organization and Integration*, p. 89–200. The continental shelf is the underwater territory of a nation that protrudes from its coast to the point where the ocean floor drops off precipitously. A contiguous zone is twelve miles further out to sea from the twelve mile territorial seas of a state.

50. Article 22 of the 1981 African Charter on Human and Peoples' Rights states that members share in "equal enjoyment of the cultural heritage of mankind." See Frederic L. Kirgis, Jr., "Standing to Challenge Human Endeavors That Could Change The Climate," *American Journal of International Law* (April 1990): 525, on the U.N. debate on climate as part of the common heritage of mankind.

51. Negotiations, however, proceed in Jamaica in the Preparation Commission for reaching some accommodation between the treaty signatories and the opponents. The commission is under the aegis of the United Nations Office of Ocean Affairs and the Law of the Sea, which issues annual reports. See also *Issues Before the General Assembly* for annual reviews.

52. For the text of the 1957 Treaty, see Sohn, *International Organization and Integration*, pp. 742–882. Sohn also annotates treaty articles with commission decisions and court cases that represent the growth of EC constitutional law. On pages 740–741, Sohn describes the EC's predecessors, the European Coal and Steel Community of 1951 and the European Atomic Energy Community. The treaty merging the three organizations of 1965 is also included, pp. 893–910. See also Jerry M. Rosenberg, *The New Europe: An A to Z Compendium on the European Community* (Washington, D.C.: Bureau of National Affairs, 1991).

53. Article 10, paragraph 2, see Sohn, *International Organization and Integration*, p. 897

54. This authority is located in Article 100 of the Treaty of Rome of 1957.

55. A leading study published by the Commission of the European communities is *Thirty Years of Community Law*, Luxembourg, 1983. See in particular, "The Elements of Community Constitutional Law," p. 71. Chapters 4 and 5 treat "The Sources of Community Law" both in a constitutional analysis and also through the acts of EC institutions. See also Francis Jacobs (ed.), *Yearbook of European Law*, vol. 1 (Oxford: Oxford University Press, 1981). Two recent studies are J.G. Merrills, *The Development of International Law by the European Court of Human Rights* (Manchester, N.H.: Manchester University Press, 1988); and T.C. Hartley, *The Foundations of European Community Law*, 22 ed. (Oxford: Clarendon Press, 1990).

56. Canada, Federal Republic of Germany, France, Italy, Japan, United Kingdom, United States.

57. *New York Times*, November 4, 1988.

58. *Thirty Years of Community Law*, Chapter 6. Of course much more law has accumulated since that study was published in 1983.

59. Statute, in Sohn, *International Organization and Integration*, p. 920.

60. Convention, in Sohn, *International Organization and Integration*, p. 929; Protocols, p. 943. Sohn adds commission and court decisions to give an idea of the extensive jurisprudence over members exercised under the convention.

61. Article 49.

62. Article 54.

63. See Andrew Z. Drizemczewski, *European Human Rights Convention in Domestic Law* (Oxford: Clarendon Press, 1983); Francis C. Jacobs, *The European Convention on Human Rights* (Oxford: Clarendon Press, 1975).

64. Charter, in Sohn, *International Organization and Integration*, p. 977.

65. Statutes, in Sohn, *International Organization and Integration*, pp. 1030 and 1038. The commission and court are organs of the OAS.

Part 2
Human Rights: Organization and Pursuit of Mission

The role of international organizations and especially the United Nations in pursuit of the mission of international protection of human rights provides a valuable case study of the harmonizing purpose of the international organizations explored in Part 1. Theology and philosophy articulate the earliest concern for the rights of humans which flow into the domain of the authority of political communities and, much later, on to international law and organization. The following charts for Chapters 7 and 8 illustrate state—organization dynamics in the quest for protection and enhancement of human rights.

CHAPTER SEVEN - THE MEMBER STATE

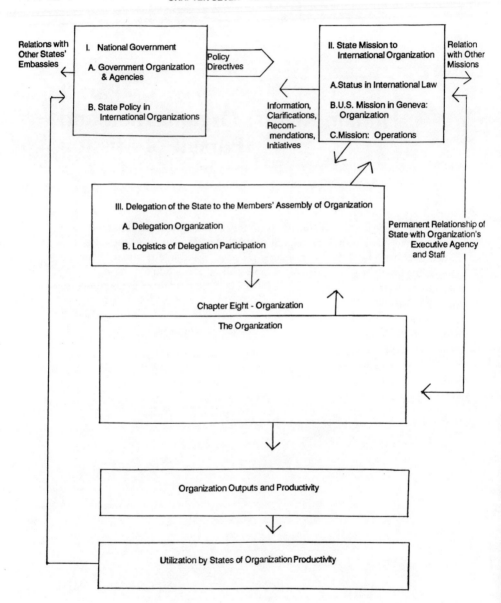

Relations with Other States' Embassies

I. National Government

A. Government Organization & Agencies

B. State Policy in International Organizations

Policy Directives

Information, Clarifications, Recom- mendations, Initiatives

II. State Mission to International Organization

A. Status in International Law

B. U.S. Mission in Geneva: Organization

C. Mission: Operations

Relation with Other Missions

III. Delegation of the State to the Members' Assembly of Organization

A. Delegation Organization

B. Logistics of Delegation Participation

Permanent Relationship of State with Organization's Executive Agency and Staff

Chapter Eight - Organization

The Organization

Organization Outputs and Productivity

Utilization by States of Organization Productivity

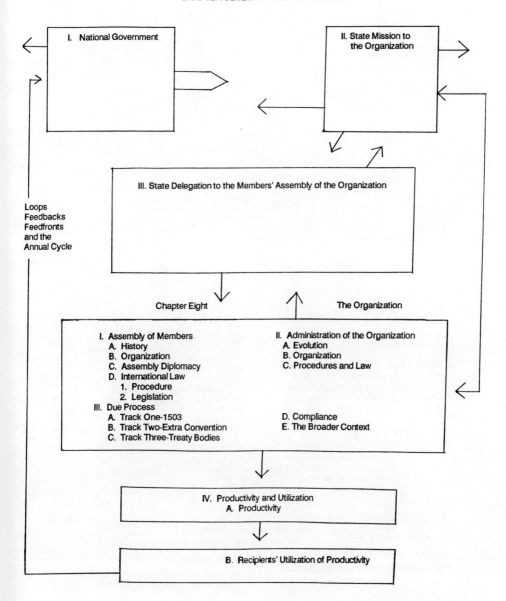

I. National Government

II. State Mission to
the Organization

Loops
Feedbacks
Feedfronts
and the
Annual Cycle

III. State Delegation to the Members' Assembly of the Organization

Chapter Eight

The Organization

I. Assembly of Members
   A. History
   B. Organization
   C. Assembly Diplomacy
   D. International Law
      1. Procedure
      2. Legislation
III. Due Process
   A. Track One-1503
   B. Track Two-Extra Convention
   C. Track Three-Treaty Bodies

II. Administration of the Organization
   A. Evolution
   B. Organization
   C. Procedures and Law

   D. Compliance
   E. The Broader Context

IV. Productivity and Utilization
   A. Productivity

B. Recipients' Utilization of Productivity

INTERNATIONAL ORGANIZATIONS AND THEIR MEMBERS:

ORGANIZATION, POLICY AND THE ANNUAL CYCLE *

Other
state
embassy
relations

THE MEMBER STATE ORGANIZATION
Top leadership, high officials,
foreign ministry, other
ministries, legislatures, NGOs, other.

POLICY

MISSION TO IO
Ambassador, professional staff,
IO specialists, public affairs,
other.

Other state
m i s s i o n
relations

POLICY DETERMINATION
National goals & IO goals, policy
process, costs & benefits?

Communications

POLICY DETERMINATION
Orders & directives from government,
policy for IO assembly & for other
organs of IO during the year

Policy

Communications

Feedback of how IO outputs
are being utilized with
evaluation of uses and
relevance to goals of the
state of security & well-being.

MEMBER STATE DELEGATION TO IO ASSEMBLY
Head of delegation, delegates from government
and from mission, consultants and experts,
support staff - daily meetings at mission to
shape daily policy

Relations between
mission & executive
& staff of the IO
throughout the year

Policy

Communications

THE INTERNATIONAL ORGANIZATION

ASSEMBLY OF IO MEMBERSHIP
Organization, officers & by-laws,
agenda of annual meeting & revisions,
addresses & floor debate on agenda issues,
framing issues for vote, lobbying & political
diplomacy, voting with pre-post explanations
of votes, role of NGIOs & other IOs, protocol

OTHER ORGANS OF THE IO
Governing or executive board Secretariat:
Secretary or Director General, official staff
hierarchy management of the business of
the IO, execution of IO policy (assembly
outputs, wide range of international
administration, work with recipients of
outputs (below)

PRODUCTIVITY or OUTPUTS Services (aid, financial, training, preventive
(hunger, poverty, disease, illiteracy) advisory, many other;
RULES (standards, laws, compliance supervision; research, publications,
field operations, etc.)

RECIPIENT OF OUTPUTS
Role and policy of top leadership & officials in relating outputs to national
policy & needs, are outputs used for intended purposes & audiences?

* Symbols: IO is international organization; NGO is non-governmental organization at the state level;
NGIO is non-governmental international organization at the organization level.

6

THE EVOLUTION OF RIGHTS FOR HUMANS

Current international law of human rights is basically the product of the post-World War II era. However, when we explore the religious and philosophical roots of protection and enhancement of human rights going back thousands of years and then the gradual emergence of political thought that flowed into proclamations of human rights and constitutional and legal foundations, we begin to realize that the human rights provisions in the U.N. Charter and the historic Universal Declaration of Human Rights of 1948 have firm roots. Belief and value systems, emergence of national protection of human rights, and then the flowering of international protection of yesterday, today, and tomorrow are the landmarks of the evolution of international human rights law.

THE BASIC ORIGINS

When did the concept of a just and equal treatment of humans begin? One place to start is in the Book of Isaiah and the word of the Lord: "learn to do well, seek judgment, relieve the oppressed, judge the fatherless, plead for the widow," and in Micah: "what doth the Lord require of thee but to do justly, to love mercy, and to walk humbly with thy God."[1] Doing "justly" is to give justice or fair and (it is hoped) equal treatment. As such, establishing "justice" is the mission of "We the people" in the preamble to the U.S. Constitution. The commandments of Moses are norms of moral law to be embraced by believers in the faith. Historically, they were preceded by the moral precepts of Hinduism as the oldest religion, the eightfold of "right" behavior such as views and resolves in Buddhism (which also proscribed the taking of human life), and the teachings of Confucius that stressed virtousity, especially by rulers, and high levels of ethical obligations by all.

These great religions and their teachings flowed into governance in various ways, in large part because it was not until Christianity that church and state were to have different masters. "Render unto Caesar that which is Caesar's and unto God that which is God's," exhorts Jesus in Matthew 22:21. Theology and statecraft were joined in political communities all over the world and continue to be so today for some 800 million Moslems ("true believers") on the one hand and over 3 million Jews in the state of Israel.

In ancient Greece, philosophy made significant contributions to the evolution of human rights theory and practice. The early Sophists taught that it is man who is master of his fate and not the rule of the gods, an affirmation basically that a right is not the monopoly of unquestionable determinism. Plato brought forth universal norms or "ideas" that apply to all and are universals in opposition to particularism. This may be interpreted today as the universality of human rights in opposition to those who claim that different societies and religions may determine what is "right" for them. We return to this theme later because some in developing nations question whether the present structure of human rights law overly emphasizes the human rights of the western world and especially the theory and practice of democracy. The Stoics joined the universalist position by holding that there is a natural law binding all people who must construct secular law to follow natural law. The great Roman statesman, Cicero, embraced natural law and worked with others to channel its teachings into the law of the Roman Republic and after his time, the Roman Empire. For Cicero, natural law is "right reason," an elastic term to be sure but it emphasizes thinking and rationality as against precipitous behavior or state policy. This also has its roots in Isaiah's request, "Come now, let us reason together." We make no claim, of course, that Cicero read the words of Isaiah.

There is much in the *Koran* of Islam that expresses concern for humane treatment by humans of other humans and an emphasis on brotherhood and egalitarianism not found in other religions. Allah is the author and giver of all rights, leaving no question for the Moslem of today to question the foundation of a "right." We read in the *Koran*, "Be just. That is next to piety." There is, of course, considerable difference and contention between and among different sects of Islam over the interpretation of the *Koran* but nevertheless Islamic nations have voluntarily accepted the law of human rights in the U.N. covenants.[2] In the thirteenth century perhaps the greatest Christian theologian, Saint Thomas Aquinas, outlined the central role of human beings in a just and social order. Although for Saint Thomas and the Roman Catholic Church (some eight hundred million people), the source of human law is derived from natural and revealed law, which in turn stems from the eternal law of God. In brief, human law must conform to the higher levels of law. This raises one burning question of our day: when does the right to life begin, at conception, at birth, or somewhere in between?

Saint Thomas had a great design for a holy Christian empire and his near contemporary, Dante, favored a secular empire. Both visions expired in the

Thirty Years' War, which reduced the Holy Roman Empire to a glorified paper organization and brought forth the Peace of Westphalia in 1648 and the state. The Peace of Westphalia was the "magic portal which leads from the old into the new world. In the political field, it marked man's abandonment of the idea of a hierarchial structure of society and his option for a new system characterized by the coexistence of a multiplicity of states, each sovereign within its territory, equal to one another and free from any external earthly authority. . . . This new system rests on international law and the balance of power, a law operating between rather than above states."[3] The inconsistency between the state "free from an external earthly authority" and the system resting on "international law" continues.

Even the Peace of Westphalia presents this contradiction. It confirms the sovereign state on the one hand but recognizes that the sovereign state has the affirmative responsibility to protect some basic rights of people under its jurisdiction on the other. The two treaties marking the end of the first major war among European states provided for rulers to tolerate the religion of their subjects who could worship as they had prior to 1624. Thus law as some earthly authority—law of treaties voluntarily accepted by sovereign states—carved out the beginnings of modern international human rights law.

THE CONTRACT FORMULA

1648 marked the beginnings of high state authority but also the emergence of the authority of international law with sovereign states' commitments to honor some basic human rights within the state. That authority was quite limited in 1648 and is today, unless sovereign states voluntarily accept high organization and legal authority for human rights, respect, and protection. That authority did not exist in 1215 when the Magna Carta introduced a fundamental contract between the sovereign states and its subjects for guarantees of some basic rights, especially in the domain of due process of the law. Philosophers, such as Grotius, wrote about the contract formula, but the authors of the Mayflower Compact of 1620 converted philosophy into legal commitment in establishing for the Pilgrims a "civil body politik" for "just and equal laws".

John Locke combined the contract formula within the state to a fundamental principle of international law. That principle, the inherent rights of humans as a central theme of natural law, is the basis of the contract within the state between rulers and the ruled. His *Second Treatise on Civil Government* of 1689 declared that if the ruler cannot protect the essential and unalienable rights of people—especially life and liberty—the ruler has broken his social contract to protect and enhance these rights of the people. He thus is to be cast out and replaced by another ruler who can and will honor the contract. Although this was seen as a rationalization for the expulsion of James II from England in 1688 for violations of civil and religious rights, Locke really was expanding on the existing contract formula of theory and practice.

What followed is history, including the rephrasing of Locke's contract formula in the U.S. Declaration of Independence of 1776 and the three famous "bills of rights": in England in 1688; France in 1789; and the U.S. Constitution's Bill of Rights, in 1791. Sieghart writes that "for the first time [these texts] set forth principles which are instantly recognizable as propositions of modern human rights law, properly so called." Those principles may be summarized as follows:

1. The principle of universal inheritance: Every human being has certain rights, capable of being enumerated and defined, which are not conferred on him by any ruler, nor earned or acquired by purchase, but which inhere in him by virtue of his humanity alone.

2. The principle of inalienability: No human being can be deprived of any of those rights, by the act of any ruler or even by his own act.

3. The Rule of Law: Where rights conflict with each other, the conflicts must be resolved by consistent, independent, and impartial application of just laws in accordance with just procedures.[4]

The two U.N. Covenants state that basic human rights "derive from the inherent dignity of the human person." The American Convention on Human Rights declares that the "essential rights of man are not derived from one's being a national of a certain state, but are based upon attributes of the human personality." Thus the constitutional law of human rights is grounded in "the principle of universal inheritance."

THE NINETEENTH CENTURY AND BEYOND

The era between the confirmation of the rights of people at the end of the eighteenth century and the advent of the League of Nations in 1919 witnessed the progression of international law and organizations, as we surveyed in Chapter 2. It would require many volumes to record adequately the slow processes of national laws advancing human rights, as well as international efforts including the abolishment of slavery and slave trade. Four areas of human rights merit our attention, however, because they illuminate some of the recurring issues and problems in the contemporary international law of human rights.

Perhaps the most important contribution of the American and French Revolutions was to the principle of national self-determination—freedom from England's external determination for the Americans and freedom from the internal determination by an unaccountable "divine right" monarchy for the French. National self-determination progressed throughout the nineteenth century and was a basic principle of President Wilson's "Fourteen Points" calling for the end of World War I. The concept of self-determination is woven throughout the U.N. Charter and is the very first article in the two U.N. Covenants on Human Rights. The article in both covenants states that "all peoples shall have the right to self-determination." In other words, there should not be an external determination or an internal determination of governance because people may not enjoy the other rights guaranteed to them in the covenants if someone else determines what those rights are and to whom they are guaranteed—and to whom they are not guaranteed. But, who are "peoples," and is "self-determination" possible without democratic institutions and processes? The covenants do not answer these questions with any degree of certainty and do not include the word "national." The 1950 European Convention in its preamble declares that the fundamental freedoms "are best maintained on the one hand by an effective political democracy and on the other by a common understanding and observance of the Human Rights on which they depend."

The U.N. Charter affirms the nation-state as the principal actor in international law and calls on all states to uphold the territorial integrity and political independence of the state and freedom from external political determination. The covenant on Civil and Political Rights, in turn in Article 25, guarantees to every citizen of a state essential guarantees and processes of democratic governance, including voting and being elected at "genuine periodic elections which shall be by universal and equal suffrage and shall be held by secret ballot, guranteeing the free expression of the will of the electors." From these constitutional provisions, self-determination thus means what both of the American and French Revolutions produced: a sovereign and basically democratic state. About everyone on earth, with the exception of over 10 million refugees, lives under the authority of a state but the vast majority of people do not enjoy democracy or internal self-determination. We still debate and contend with this historic issue.[5]

Second, the nineteenth and early twentieth century debates included the question: What are *rights*? The U.S., English, and French declarations were civil and legal rights for the most part, guaranteed by governments of very limited democracy. They placed limits on governmental control and authority and guaranteed government administration of due process of the law. However, social reformers in the French Revolution and the decades that followed were more interested in economic and social rights. The British social reformer, Robert Owen (1771–1858) was among the first to declare that individual rights had to be accompanied by social justice because the individual is so molded by his or her environment and that environment for many was hardly compatible with any definition of "rights." He and others thus pressed for government policy to begin to rectify deplorable economic and social conditions and successfully pressed for the early nineteenth century "factory acts," which led after about 100 years to the ILO and decades of ensuing international labor law. There were few economic and social rights in the Universal Declaration of 1948 but the two covenants extend the declaration into international human rights law and confirm Owen's theme of individual freedom with social justice, especially in the Covenant on Economic, Social, and Cultural Rights. Nevertheless, these two covenants are quite different in terms of provisions for implementation and are viewed differently by blocs of states. The democracies strongly favor the Civil and Political Covenant, while the developing and socialist nations champion the

Economic, Social, and Cultural Covenant but not to the detriment of the Civil and Political. This is due, in part, to the fact that this covenant in Article 4, paragraph 2, lists provisions from which states cannot derogate or reject. The fundamental rights that must be recognized and protection irrespective of demands of security or "public order" include the "inherent right to life," freedom from "torture, cruel, inhuman or degrading treatment or punishment," freedom from "slavery and abolishment of the slave trade," no ex post facto law or punishment for violating a law that was crafted after arrest, no imprisonment for not fulfilling a contractual obligation, right to recognition everywhere as a person before the law, and right to freedom of thought, conscience, and religion.[6]

Third, although Sieghart affirms the "universal inheritance" of the three great bills of rights, most people were left out of the will. The "men" the authors of the U.S. Declaration of Independence identified as being born with unalienable rights were white, educated, over twenty-one years of age, and usually owned considerable property. Women, non-whites, and especially blacks and Indians, people under twenty-one, and these holding little or no property by inference did not have the complete set of rights. Democratic societies have witnessed a progression of victories for the other "men" down through the decades, but at a slow and often hard-fought pace. It was only twenty-five years ago that black people and other minorities in the United States gained some very fundamental civil, political, and economic rights. Sessions of the U.N. Commission on Human Rights in the 1980s testify to the continuation of this fight to guarantee to all the "universal inheritance" promised to all in the U.N. Covenants.

Fourth, may a state unilaterally intervene in or on the jurisdiction of another state with the claim that it is upholding international law as against violations of that law by the other state? Should a state sit by and permit violations of international law to take place? Should a state not unilaterally intervene in another when gross violations of human rights take place? Hugo Grotius, the "Father of International Law," gained great legal fame when he justified for the Dutch East India Company the 1604 seizure by a Dutch ship of a Portugal vessel on the grounds that the Portugese were violating international law in claiming jurisdiction over the high seas. His treatise in justification led to his masterful work on law in general and specifically *Mare Liberum*, or freedom of the seas, in 1609.

Unilateral "humanitarian" interventions spread in the nineteenth century when England penetrated the Ottoman Empire in 1827 to prevent Turkish atrocities on the Greeks and later in 1876 in response to Ottoman massacres of Christians in what is now Bulgaria. The French intervened in Syria in 1860 and 1861 for the same humanitarian purposes. The United States unilaterally searched and seized foreign ships in the nineteenth century alleged to be engaged in slave trade because such trade was offending against slave trade acts and "against the general law of nations."[7] In 1941, the U.S. Congress passed the Lend Lease Act, which authorized the President to sell, transfer, lend, or lease war materials to a nation that was important to U.S. defense (read, "beleaguered England"). In return the United States could receive any kind of property or benefits important to this nation. Challenged by opponents at home and abroad as a unilateral violation of international law by a self-declared neutral state, the government replied that as Germany had grossly violated international law, "lend-lease" was a permissive sanction unilaterally imposed by the United States to uphold international law.

Today, we witness claims for just unilateral humanitarian interventions into Lebanon, several states in Central America, and even in the United States bombing of Tripoli on April 14, 1986, to punish the governance of that nation for state terrorism. Did Vietnam have the right to invade Cambodia in 1979 to quell the genocide by Pol Pot of 1 to 3 million of his fellow nationals? What of unilateral support by the United States and the Soviet Union in support of national liberation fronts in pursuit of the "right of self-determination"?

The concept is intervention to uphold international law and protection of human rights. The law against the concept is in Article 2, paragraph 4, of the U.N. Charter guaranteeing states territorial integrity and political independence. However, in this article, violations of this dual expression of sovereignty may not be "inconsistent with the Purposes of the United Nations." In other words, may humanitarian interventions be consistent with the purposes, especially when the purposes have been amplified by considerable international human rights law since 1945, especially where evidence appears to reveal "a consistent pattern of gross and reliably attested violations of human rights and fundamental freedoms"?[8] Added to this is the U.N. confirmation of the Nuremberg Charter and Tribunal judgment concerning the authority of the international community, organization, and law to assume international jurisdiction over crimes against humanity. Debate on these issues continues.[9]

THE LEAGUE OF NATIONS YEARS

World War I did not begin over issues of superiority or inferiority of human beings, as did World War II, and thus the peace settlements of 1919 and the years thereafter did not have the protection of human rights high on the agenda. Nevertheless, the League Covenant, the constitution of the ILO, and peace treaties between the victors and the vanquished significantly contributed to the progression of international human rights law. We have referred to this period and treaty provisions earlier in our study and our main objective now is to place them in the context of the evolution of that law.

Article 23 of the League of Nations Covenant deals with a number of areas that have come under international law such as fair and humane conditions of labor, just treatment of native inhabitants in colonies, concerns for traffic in women and children and in opium and drugs, and the prevention and control of disease. Article 25 encourages and promotes the humanitarian work of voluntary national Red Cross organizations, while Article 24 seeks to draw the work of "international bureaus" closer to the league in the "international interest." Article 22, as we have observed, has extensive provisions for the league's mandate system for supervision by mandate powers in the colonies that were possessions of enemy states in World War I. This was a pioneering provision in law of a modicum of international protection and surveillance over the basic human rights of millions of peoples in colonial areas by the new universal organization. It was therefore a legal prohibition on any sovereign treatment of these peoples who were under the jurisdiction of the protecting mandatory powers. The Permanent Mandates Commission approved by the League Council in November 1920 established protection and surveillance procedures that became foundations for subsequent U.N. and other organizations' capability to bring about compliance to international human rights law. They included an annual report by the mandatory power to the commission, which was provided in Article 22, the right of peoples in the mandates to petition the commission for complaints or seeking redress of grievances, and periodic visits to the mandate territories by commission members and experts to inspect at first hand the conditions there as well as verify and address themselves to information contained in the reports and petitions. This was an unprecedented outreach for international organizations to move goals toward practice and compliance and served as models and foundations for subsequent human rights practice.

We explored the origins of the ILO in Chapter 2, which was the first international organization charged with the development of new and advancing international law through treaties and covenants. The charge for international human rights in the work place is in Article 23, paragraph A, of the covenant as well as in the constitution of the ILO of 1919. The organization continues to expand on international labor law and has set many precedents for international due process and international compliance with the international human rights law of labor.[10]

Third, a number of treaties at the end of World War I provided for protection of minorities both in the new states carved out of the peace settlement and in some other states as well, such as Greece. President Wilson's call for self-determination brought forth Poland, Yugoslavia, Czechoslovakia, Austria, and Hungary out of the Austro-Hungarian Empire. The senior statesmen at the Paris Peace Conference decided in May 1919 that there should be new treaties for the guarantee of minority rights of national blocs now finding themselves under the jurisdiction of new states. The treaty between the war's victors and Poland of June 28, 1919, was basically the model treaty with Poland committing itself to treat new minorities in the revived Polish state, especially Germans, the same as Polish nationals. They were to have all the rights Polish citizens had and should not be discriminated against in any manner. Poland further agreed that the League of Nations would be authorized to guarantee minority rights although the minority issue was not incorporated in the provisions of the League of Nations Covenant. The impressive German-Polish Convention on Upper Silesia of 1992 guaranteed to minorities the rights of life, liberty, and freedom of religion among others in its Article 4. Sieghart observes that the effect of these treaties was to establish personal rights by private citizens against a state for violation of human rights guaranteed in a legal covenant.[11] Many other similar treaties followed including those with Austria, Bulgaria, Czechoslovakia, Greece, Hungary, Rumania, and Turkey, to name the principal nations.

The council of The League of Nations established a Minorities Committee to which the states protecting minorities reported and communicated and to which minorities reported and communicated and to which minorities could send petitions of complaints and other information. This process gradually became stronger in the 1920s and the league's secretary general was fully involved in this initial international human rights law "due process." With the rise to full power of Italy's Mussolini and then Japan and Nazi Germany by the mid-1930s, the reversion to high state sovereignty set in. Poland paved the way for the deterioration of the minority rights process by withdrawing from its commitments in 1934. This fundamental and pioneering international law of protection finally died with so much else as war replaced human rights and their laws in 1939 for six years of human malignancy.

Nevertheless, the covenant's recognition of the league's obligations to the advancement of some rights, especially in the social domain, provisions for protection of peoples living under the mandate system, organization and treaties for protection of rights in the workplace, and laws and procedures for international protection of minorities laid significant foundations for international human rights laws created later in the twentieth century. It is also important to note that the League of Nations generated the Slavery Convention, signed in Geneva on September 25, 1926, which was the first modern treaty protecting human rights in committing signatories to abolish slavery and slave trade.[12]

1945 AND BEYOND

Adolf Hitler and the Nazi creed were the antithesis of the core of human rights—the right to life, justice, and equal treatment. In large part, World War II had its genesis in the conflict between the thousands of years of gradual progression of human rights and the doctrine of racial superiority. The eloquence first of Winston Churchill and then others in the 1930s to unite in opposing the gradualism of Hitler's designs were unheeded by governance in England and France until it was too late.[13] Americans were divided over President Roosevelt's suggestion in October 1937 that the aggressors be quarantined much like the doctrine of containment only ten years later. Roosevelt pronounced his famous "Four Freedoms" of speech and religion and from want and fear as the foundations for a "secure" world in the "future days" in the address to Congress on January 6, 1941, thus engraving in the purposes of the then-raging war in Europe the cause of basic human rights. In their historic meeting at sea in August 1941, Churchill and Roosevelt pledged a peace "which will afford assurance that all men in all lands may live out their lives in freedom from fear and want."

As the war in Europe rolled toward a conclusion in the spring of 1945, the revelations of the Nazi atrocities unveiled by Allied armies marching into the death-filled concentration camps made their painful imprint on the men and women convening in San Francisco to write the charter of peace and world organization and into the reality of international protection. The Charter of June 26, 1945, came to life when it entered into force on October 24, 1945, and the Nuremberg Charter and indictment moved on to the famous trials that ended in judgment and sentence executive in October and November 1946. The charter and Nuremberg dramatically moved human rights forward from protection generally under high state authority to the level of state-organization partnership and, as far as "Crimes Against Humanity" to high organization authority. Security and well-being as goals could no longer be solely determined by the sovereign state as far as treatment of humans and protection of their rights were concerned. With goals of shared security and shared and progressive well-being, international law and organizations in the U.N. system now had authority in their constitutions to move ahead with international protection and enhancement.

The progression from words to law in the last forty-five years has been historic, but there is still so far to go. We fully recognize that international protection of human rights is much too frail as we survey the human and inhumane landscape of the globe in such areas as the Republic of South Africa, parts of the Middle East and Central America, and the plight of over 10 million refugees around the world. We are aware of the tragic figures of starvation and malnutrition as compared to the right to adequate food in the Covenant on Economic, Social, and Cultural Rights—or those figures of disease in contrast to the "right of everyone to the enjoyment of the highest attainable standard of physical and mental health" as written in the same covenant. However, the progression of international human rights law in the past forty-five years is a striking demonstration of how international organization and law modify state authority, advance human and national shared and progressive well-being, and give hope of continued progress in the 1990s and into the twenty-first century.

The Commission and the Universal Declaration

One of the first tasks of the new Economic and Social Council was to establish the Commission on Human Rights to translate the provision in Article 68 of the U.N. Charter to the reality of an assembly of eighteen states to move forward the challenging agenda for international protection of human rights.[14] The resolution constituting the commission included marching orders for the "Functions, Composition, and Working Method" of the Commission, which included the mandate to compose an "international bill of human rights." The resolution also called on the commission to establish a Subcommission on Protection of Minorities and one on the Prevention of Discrimination, which were united in 1947 to constitute the important Subcommission on the Protection of Minorities and Prevention of Discrimination.

The roots of international human rights law we have surveyed now flow into the trunk formed by the roots, the Universal Declaration of Human Rights resolved by the U.N. General Assembly on December 10, 1948. The many branches of this noble tree are the two basic covenants of 1966 as well as the many other international treaties at the universal and regional levels that provide articulation of internationally recognized human rights as well as the organizational machinery for international due process, implementation, and procedures for compliance.[15]

The eloquent words of the declaration are widely available for all to read, appreciate, and practice. However, some analysis of the declaration is of value within the context of our study. The opening lines of the declaration expresses the dual and interrelated goals of shared security and well-being.

Whereas the recognition of the inherent dignity and of the equal and inalienable rights of all members of the human family is the foundation of freedom, justice and peace in the world.

The preamble recognizes that implementation of the rights will require "progressive measures, national and international, to secure their universal and effective recognition and observance." The progression of universal and effective recognition since 1948 is recorded in part in this chapter as a study of the preamble's command that "human rights should be protected by the rule of law."

The legislative history of the declaration is extraordinarily interesting. Most of the drafting and negotiation took place in the newly-formed U.N. Commission on Human Rights, appropriately chaired by Eleanor Roosevelt, the widow of President Roosevelt. One of the principal participants was Charles Malik of Lebanon, who identifies some of the basic themes and confrontations in the shaping of a document that cuts across and through deeply held value systems of diplomats and their nations representing most of the world's religions, ideologies, and cultures.[16] As Malik notes, "everything in our debates revolved around the nature and destiny of man" including "his rights and freedoms." Three themes he identifies are especially important.

The two and a half years of negotiations brought forth "the basic ideological confrontations of this age," including representatives of democracy and communism, of socialist states and the Republic of South Africa (then, Union of South Africa), and of strong religious convictions and clashes. Malik asks, "Are they [human rights] original and inherent or are they granted and derived? Do they belong to the nature of things, or are they gifts of governments and systems? Are they absolute or are they relative to conditions and circumstances and stages of historical development? Are they man-made or do they derive from a source other than and higher than man?"

Second, what hierarchy of importance should be established in any listing of human rights? Which take precedence, civil and political—as favored by the democratic nations—or economic, social, and cultural—as championed by the socialist and developing nations. Civil and political won out (Articles 1 through

22) over economic, social, and cultural (Articles 22 through 27). This debate continues today and between the same blocs of nations. However, as Malik points out, they are mutually dependent, citing the imperative of freedom of thought and inquiry for developing states' "modernization" as one example among many.[17]

Shashi Tharoor, a high official with the UNHCR, provides a vivid example of the interdependence between the two categories of rights. He observes that the right to life is in the civil and political set of rights but views right to life as something more than the opposite of death just as peace is more than the absence of war. The right to life is the "right to live," which implies conditions of human and national well-being "for the full development of the human person."

These include food, shelter, adequate medical attention, education, productive employment, freedom to move about and express oneself freely, and the chance to grow in a healthy, tolerant, and peaceful environment free from ill treatment and persecution—in other words, a combination of both sets of human rights.[18]

As we have observed, however, the two sets of rights in the Covenants of 1966 have different modes for implementation and domestication, especially in Article 2 of both covenants. The provisions of the Economic, Social, and Cultural Covenant state goals and means to goals, recognizing that a disadvantaged state does not have the resources and conditions to guarantee to all the right to health in Article 12. Civil, legal, and political rights do not require resources but do necessitate political will and wisdom.

Third, debates over the wording of the declaration raised at many junctures the scope of universality of human rights, an issue we have already briefly appraised. Some claimed that there was too much of a Western imprint on civil and legal rights for societieis that do not have a historical tradition or structure rooted in the political contract between people and their inherent rights and rulers to protect those rights. More collectivist societies stressed group rights and duties, which the West would hardly consider universal.

The universal concept of rights won out, as we have observed. The declaration's preamble "Proclaims this Universal Declaration of Human Rights as the common standard of achievement for all peoples and all nations." As Malik states, the declaration

measures the stature of man and the degree of freedom realized by any people or nation. The world as a whole has spoken in this Declaration . . . after the most careful, responsible, authoritative, and joint consideration of every word, iota, and meaning in this document. This is the only world declaration of its kind in history.

It is interesting to note that a step to the 1948 Declaration and human rights law of today was President Roosevelt's "Four Freedoms" address of January

1941—freedoms he said were to apply "everywhere in the world." Tharoor, a citizen of India, makes a most impressive argument for universalism as against arguments by some in developing nations that many human rights do not apply to them. He concludes his brilliant paper by declaring that

Those of us Third Worlders who have experienced the enjoyment of human rights in our own countries—and in some cases, faced the loss of them—know what it means and why we do not wish to be denied our share of their universality. Human rights are not just "relevant" for us; they are essential.[19]

Nevertheless, debate over the universality of human rights in the declaration continues. Iran, in particular, has claimed in recent years that the declaration was written during the previous regime of the Shah and was illegitimate in the eyes of the new regime established by the Ayatollah Khoumeini. It was a secular document, whereas contemporary Iranian law places the rule of Allah above human law, and in any event, Iran "should disassociate itself from it, preparing instead an 'Islamic Declaration' of Human Rights."[20] The Human Rights Commission Special Rapporteur for appraising human rights compliance and transgressions in Iran, Galindo Pohl, completely rejected this argument, charged Iran with selective adherence to human rights law, and stressed again the global agreement by nations with different histories, ideologies, cultures, and religions subscribing to the universality of the human rights in the declaration.

The question of whether the declaration would be binding international law was another penetrating issue in the debates over the drafting of the declaration. Another essential source for the legislative history of the declaration is Professor John P. Humphrey, who was the first director of the United Nations Division of Human Rights. Professor Humphrey, a Canadian but also an international civil servant, records that Canada almost abstained in the final vote on the declaration on December 10, 1948, because of its apprehensions of the binding nature of the declaration.[21] Clearly, this "Magna Carta of Mankind," as Eleanor Roosevelt put it, is basically a General Assembly resolution that does not have the force of law. However, Professor Humphrey points out that the declaration expresses international customary law, has been woven into the constitutions of many new states, has been sued as a source of law in many national and international court decisions and concludes that "I am satisfied in my own mind that the Declaration is now [1984] binding on all nations."

The generation of international constitutional law through international organizations, a major theme of our study, is so obvious in appraising the declaration as the trunk from its historic roots and its importance as the source of expanding international human rights law. Alexandre Kiss phrases this phenomenon most eloquently.

When one walks in the mountains, the views change very often; lower peaks and ridges can conceal the highest mountains and make them seem less impressive. The true dimensions appear at a certain distance. The same applies to historical events, the real significance of which can only become clear some time later. It may be affirmed that the Universal Declaration of Human Rights, which was hailed after its proclamation as a major instrument, but considered to have no binding legal force and hence to impose no real obligations on States, is an example of this phenomenon. Today, the principles of the Declaration are considered to have become rules of positive international law and even to constitute law which takes precedence over other rules. International law is also indebted to the Declaration for a new process for elaborating rules in a new field with which it is confronted. Thus the true dimensions of the Declaration, which constitutes a summit in international life, become clear.[22]

It is remarkable that the European Convention on Human Rights was concluded less than two years after the declaration as the first binding human rights treaty with extensive provisions for international due process and compliance by governments. The two major U.N. Conventions were embraced by the General Assembly in 1966 and entered into force in 1976. The progression of many other universal and regional conventions is a matter of history and the process continues with new subjects in human rights law and expanded due process, means of compliance, and administration of human rights law. Many developing states envisage their proclaimed "right to development" as a collective right beyond human rights. The 1981 African Charter on Human and Peoples' Rights stresses the doctrine of "peoples" rights in Articles 19 through 24, which reflects as the U.N. Charter's preamble states "the virtues of their historical tradition and the values of African civilization" and the sociology and/or religions of many African groupings of peoples.[23]

The legislative history of the drafting of the declaration brought forth basic issues and themes that continue to permeate the political and legislative debates in the Commission on Human Rights and other U.N. organs, in the assemblies of the specialized agencies, and the commissions and courts of human rights organizations, whether universal or regional. Confrontations continue over basic philosophical issues about humans, contentions on the hierarchy of rights, issues of universality versus particularism, the questions of the binding and thus enforceable dimensions of human rights, and the conceptualization in debates and law of expanding rights beyond those in the declaration. This reflects the progression and clarification of international human rights in an international constitutional framework analogous to the progression and clarification of national constitutional law. We now turn to the shaping and administration of international human rights law based on organizations and conventions that constantly seek to advance protection of human rights.[24]

Finally, the declaration calls on "every individual and organ of society [to] strive by teaching and education to promote respect for these rights and freedoms . . . to secure their universal and effective recognition and observance." This exhortation is essential for the advancement of international human rights because unawareness or ignorance of one's rights is also ignorance of the right to be protected. This is a distinct challenge as there are well over a billion people who are illiterate and many more who in all probability know nothing of international protection of human rights let alone their own inherent rights. In brief, education and teaching for promoting respect for human rights is a task and responsibility for all of us.

Commission on Human Rights: 1948–1990

The 1946 Economic and Social Council resolution constituting the formal structure and policy orientation of the Commission on Human Rights requested the commission "to submit at any early date suggestions regarding the ways and means for the effective implementation of human rights and fundamental freedoms."[25] Already, the secretary general and U.N. Headquarters were receiving communications and pleas for help from people alleging violation of human rights. What should be the responsibility of the central commission at the global organization with respect to such communications? As early as August 1947, the council told the commission it had no power to respond to such messages. As late as July 1959, the council approved "the statement that the Commission on Human Rights recognizes that it has no power to take action in regard to any complaints concerning human rights."[26] However, in the 1959 resolution, the council did authorize the commission to compile before each annual session a nonconfidential listing of the substance of communications dealing with the promotion of human rights and a confidential list of "other communications." Thus, a process was actually begun for the commission to receive and compile an appraisal of messages about human rights, pro and con.

As the situation on protection of human rights deteriorated in the Republic of South Africa and in what we now call Namibia and Zimbabwe, the council, in June 1967, "welcomes" the decision of the commission to give annual consideration to the "Question of the violation of human rights." It authorized the commission and subcommission to examine information "relevant to gross violations of human rights and fundamental freedoms," as exemplified in the three areas of South Africa and to report back to the council with recommendations.[27] In a commission resolution of March 6, 1967, it had already established an Ad Hoc Working Group of Experts on Human Rights in Southern Africa, which was the first such agency established by the commission to gather experts to examine a specific country, area, or situation and report back to the commission.[28] Resolution 1235 also gave the commission and subcommission authority to review the thousands of complaints of human rights violations streaming into U.N. headquarters. In the following twelve months, the subcommission developed machinery to handle complaints. It established a working group to process and screen the communications to test for evidence of a consistent pattern of gross violations and admissibility for further consideration by the subcommission and then the commission. In brief, a process is now evolving that moves toward machinery for international due process of the law.

The dramatic change in the gradual enhancement of the commission's authority is to be understood largely in the events in the world and nations between 1947 and the early 1960s. The political dimensions of international relations and the progression of international law always act upon one another and this is particularly the case in the 1950s and especially the 1960s. The rise to independence and sovereignty of the many new nations in Africa and Asia led to the famous General Assembly Declaration on the Granting of Independence to Colonial Countries and Peoples in 1960 and the establishment of the Special Committee on Decolonization the next year. Civil rights action and new laws in the United States in the mid-1960s stimulated forward direction by the most powerful nation in the United Nations toward international action on civil rights as well. The mandate of the new Working Group on Southern Africa was quickly broadened, thus paving the way for improved machinery in what is now to become international human rights due process. This structure was buttressed by the completion in 1966 of the two principal United Nations Covenants on Human Rights that also established due process procedures (to which we turn later in this chapter).

Another part of the equation emerged in 1968 when the commission was called upon in a number of resolutions to establish machinery to examine the conditions in the territories Israel occupied as the result of the June 1967 Israel-Arab War. This led to the creation by the General Assembly on December 19, 1968, of the Special Committee to Investigate Israeli Practices Affecting the Human Rights of the Population of the Occupied Territories.[29] The committee, after considerable information gathering in this area, consideration of oral and written reports, and review of other substantial bodies of evidence, has written a report each year to meet its mandate. The report is received and debated by the commission each February and conveyed respectively to the Economic and Social Council and then the annual session of the General Assembly. Each year Israel is condemned by an overwhelming vote because of the Special Committee's findings of consistent patterns of gross violations of human rights and especially of the international law of occupied territory of the Fourth Geneva Convention of 1949.[30] Commission actions in South Africa and the Middle East not only set the precedent of targeting specific states for violations of human rights, but also for sending experts into the field for investigation and reporting purposes.[31] The Israel and South Africa issues remain the first two substantive issues on the commission's annual agenda, in part because they deal with issues of self-determination, which is the concern of the first article of the two United Nations Covenants on Human Rights.

A major step was taken by the Economic and Social Council on May 27, 1970, with the passage of the famous Resolution 1503. It is an elaboration on the 1967 Resolution 1235 and strengthens the commission's responsibilities and viability to respond to complaints of consistent patterns of gross violations of human rights.[32] The resolution established stages for receiving, screening, and taking action on communications from any source complaining of human rights violations. Communications must be addressed to the secretary general and are then forwarded to a working group of experts of the subcommission for processing. If they are found admissible and are likely to conform to the standards required for consideration in Resolution 1503, they are passed on to the subcommission for review and recommendation if all evidence points to consistent patterns of gross violations and then to the commission for appropriate action. That consists of a continuation of confidential negotiations between commission representatives and officials of the targeting nation. If the latter is not responsive, the commission may consider a resolution dealing with the situation on the open floor and/or name a working group or special rapporteur to continue to negotiate, secure evidence of violations, and report back to the commission.

The resolution established stages for receiving, screening, and taking action on communications from any source complaining of human rights violations. Communications must be addressed to the secretary general and are then forwarded to a working group of experts of the subcommission for processing. If they are found admissible and are likely to conform to the standards required for consideration in Resolution 1503, they are passed on to the subcommission for review and recommendation. If all evidence points to consistent patterns of gross violations and they are sent to the commission for appropriate action. That consists of a continuation of confidential negotiations between commission representatives and officials of the targeted nation. If the latter is not responsive, the commission may consider a resolution dealing with the situation on the open floor and/or name a working group or special rapporteur to continue to negotiate, secure evidence of violations, and report back to the commission.

With the entering into force in 1976 of the two major conventions on human rights, Civil and Political and also its Optional Protocol and the Economic, Social and Cultural, the United Nations law for international protection of human rights was established. Standards of the 1948 Declaration now had evolved into law for states choosing to ratify these conventions. The Covenant on International Civil and Political Rights created a Human Rights Committee to which ratifying states are to submit reports on the condition of human rights in their jurisdiction. The Committee monitors how these states domesticate the Convention into their municipal law under Article 2 and it submits reports to the General Assembly on its deliberations, evaluations of reports, recommendations and interpretations of the law of the covenant. States ratifying the convention's Optional Protocol permit individuals to petition to the committee. With more and more states signing on to the Convention and Protocol in the 1980s, its work load has greatly increased. It was and is compiling an expanding body of interpretative and case law and sharpening international due process of the law in terms of procedures and evidence. The Committee on Economic, Social, and Cultural Rights under the Economic and Social Covenant was established in 1986. We review treaty bodies under due process in Chapter 8.

The specific country targeting continued to evolve in the 1980s as the result of the Resolution 1503 process and findings and the commission's judgment that public exposures and condemnations were important tools for improving human rights protection. In 1978, the commission declared it was privately reviewing complaints against a number of states including Bolivia, Uganda, and Uruguay, which was the first public action on the floor of specific country targeting. Chile became an annual target and in 1980 the commission condemned the Soviet Union for its invasion of Afghanistan and condemned Cambodia (Kampuchea) for the horror and terror of mass extermination of hundreds of thousands of Cambodians, in addition to other human rights degradations. The United States claimed the commission was engaging in double standards by accusing some Latin American nations; and the Soviet Union, in turn, declared the commission was invading its domestic jurisdiction with the Soviet condemnation. Nevertheless, the commission rolled on with "country specific" charges and created more and more working groups and rapporteurs who were considered objective experts for investigations, reports, and recommendations on alleged violations of human rights.

In addition to country targeting was the evolution of a thematic approach to investigation and reporting. This was considered important because too many members of the commission of sovereign states said country targeting was "sanctimonious posturing" and "gratuitous political point-scoring," while the thematic approach would quietly include a number of countries but deal with an across-the-board problem.[33] In February 1980 the commission appointed five members to examine for one year the theme of enforced or involuntary disappearances. This group was to receive complaints, especially numerous from families of the missing and nongovernmental organizations, process the information, and make recommendations. The one-year mandate was renewed and became firmly established as the Working Group on Enforced or Involuntary Disappearances. Other working groups and rapporteurs were added to the list for specific country targeting and themes that we appraise shortly. The Convention Against Torture provided for its own Committee Against Torture in Article 17 with provisions for receiving and processing complaints and taking appropriate action. The commission also has its special rapporteur for the crime of torture to set up a dual system of a treaty body reporting to treaty signatories and an expert reporting to the commission.

The evolution of the commission was not smooth and its annual sessions today continue to be marked by accusations, acrimony, and intense debate. But, as we have observed, there was remarkable institutional and legal progression toward commission capabilities from its origins in 1946. Standard setting led to international human rights laws, international due process, and, in many cases, substantial changes in nations' behavior and leadership—toward the better. Equatorial Guinea overthrew its dictator Bokassa, largely because of human rights violations. New leadership in Argentina, Uruguay, Uganda, and some other states have removed these nations from annual country targeting. But the basic argument in the early 1980s turned on demands by some for a stronger and more activist commission and U.N. approach to international protection of human rights.

The director of the U.N. Division of Human Rights, Theo van Boven, was, perhaps, the strongest voice in this respect. His initiatives led in part to the development of working groups to investigate allegations of human rights violations and to seek to take remedial, if not punitive, action. He supported the creation of a High Commissioner for Human Rights, somewhat like the High Commissioner for Refugees, with authority and commission support to deal more effectively with complaints about human rights violations. Costa Rica proposed an office of the High Commissioner as early as 1965, but the Soviet Union consistently opposed such an office on the grounds it would infringe on state sovereignty. He repeatedly spoke up against too much confidentiality on the Resolution 1503 process and charged that some members of the commission and others feared bringing into the open verifiable "consistent patterns of gross violations of human rights." He undoubtedly had Argentina in mind, which did not sit well with the United States.

Following what became a public condemnation of human rights transgressions in several Latin American nations, van Boven announced his resignation on the floor of the commission on February 10, 1982. He cited major policy differences with U.N. leadership in New York. He had considerable support from some members of the commission and from experts on the subcommission. However, it is assumed that a sufficient number of states persuaded the secretary general to accept the resignation. It was a case study in international organization politics of differences between policies and goals of some nations and policy and goals of international civil servants and experts in a specific area, in this case the policy and law of protection of human rights.

Secretary General Perez de Cuellar appointed the Austrian diplomat, Kurt Herndle, to head the Division of Human Rights but did praise von Boven's record and continued to support the proposal to bring human rights administration under the authority of a high commissioner. Herndle's title was elevated to that of Assistant Secretary General to elevate the status of the human rights organization. Jan Martenson followed Herndle as Assistant Secretary General upon the latter's resignation in 1988, and this office was combined with the Directorship of the United Nations Office in Geneva resulting in a gravitation of administrative authority to Geneva. As we shall see, there is also a constant movement of authority to the international civil servants and experts and thus somewhat a devolution of power from the member-state commission itself.

The ever-expanding responsibilities, delegated authority, and productivity of the commission is evidenced by its growth from 18 members in 1946 to 21 states in 1961, 32 in 1966, 43 members in 1979, and up to 53 in 1992. The latter increase provides ten seats for developing nations and was opposed by the United States and most other Western nations on the grounds that such strong developing state representation could dilute accusations of alleged violations in those nations. They, in turn, justified the vote to increase their presence by claiming the Western states with ten seats are overrepresented as among the 159 members of the United Nations.

Each annual session of the commission of six weeks in February and March sees an overloaded agenda, meetings often going on into the night, and vibrant diplomacy on the floor of the assembly of members. The forty-fifth session of the commission in 1989 included the 43 delegations of members, 77 delegations from U.N. members not presently on the commission, and almost 1,400 representatives of states engaged in the commission's activities. Representatives from other international organizations, from about 133 nongovernmental organizations, and official observers from Palestine, the Southwest African Peoples' Organization (SWAPO/Namibia), the African National Congress, and a range of experts were also present. An unprecedented number of senior statesmen and women addressed the commission, including the Prime Minister of France, Michael Rocard; Dante Caputo, the Minister of Foreign Affairs from Argentina and president of the General Assembly; and Francisco Fernandez Ordonez, the Foreign Minister of Spain who spoke on behalf of the EC. This testifies to how highly states regard the importance of the commission in enhancing international protection of human rights and that importance increases with each passing year.

Today, unlike the beginnings, no nation in the world can go unscathed in the commission's sessions. The accused do not hide behind the legal protection for domestic jurisdiction but seek to respond to accusations irrespective of the often high level of acrimony on the floor. John Pace, secretary of the commission since 1979, observes that even though the commission's reach must take "mini-micro" steps, its reach over sovereign borders and into the sources of human rights violations demonstrates a remarkable progression of nation-sponsored international law to advance human well-being.[34]

The 47th session of the Commission on Human Rights drew to a close on March 8, 1991, with a host of decisions and resolutions on a wide range of issues and human rights abuses which make their annual trip to meetings of the Economic and Social Council and then to the General Assembly later in the year. They dealt with alleged atrocities by Iraq in Kuwait as well as within its own boundaries, a forthcoming investigation of rights violations in Cuba, and concerns over transgressions in the Soviet Republics of Latvia and Lithuania. The Commission spent considerable time in discussing measures to improve its procedures and due processes of the law as well as providing its executive arm, the Centre for Human Rights, with more administrative capability and authority. It furthered plans for the 1993 World Conference on Human Rights which, among other objectives, will seek to improve the implementation of existing human rights standards and law. A preparatory committee for the Conference was established and scheduled to convene in September 1991, for deliberations and planning which will be reported to the General Assembly. The machinery for moving rights from theology and philosophy to standards and law and implementation continues.

NOTES

1. Isaiah 1:17; Micah 6:8.
2. See *Human Rights in Islam*, International Commission of Jurists, Geneva, 1982.

3. Leo Gross, "The Peace of Westphalia," *American Journal of International Law* (January 1948).

4. Paul Sieghart, *The International Law of Human Rights* (Oxford: Clarendon Press, 1983), p. 8 of his Section 1, "Historical and Juridical Background." See also Asbjourn Eide (Director, Norwegian Institute of Human Rights), *Guide to the Development of Human Rights, Institutions, and Mechanisms*, Council of Europe, Strasbourg, May 1989. It is interesting to note that the four Geneva Conventions of 1949 on the rights and humanitarian protection of people who are victims of warfare specifically say that such people "may in no circumstances renounce in part or in entirety the rights secured to them." Thus the manifold rights of victims of warfare in these conventions, the most widely ratified treaties in existence, are so firm that even those who have them may not sever themselves from these rights.

5. See "Measures to Ensure the Right of Self-Determination," *United Nations Action in the Field of Human Rights* (New York: United Nations, 1988), pp. 16–38. See the bibliography for the importance of this comprehensive volume on the U.N. record in human rights. Two essential studies in this area are Hurst Hannun's *Autonomy, Sovereignty, and Self-Determination* (Philadelphia: University of Pennsylvania Press, 1990) and Heather Wilson's *International Law and the Use of Force by National Liberation Movements* (Oxford: Clarendon Press, 1988). Both have incisive legal analysis of self-determination and excellent bibliographies for this pervasive issue of the early 1990s.

6. Articles 6, 7, 8, 11, 15, 16, and 18.

7. *United States v. The Schooner Eugenie*, 2 Mason (U.S.) 409 1st Cir., 1822.

8. Economic and Social Council Resolution 1503 (XLVIII), May 27, 1970, implemented by the Human Rights Commission.

9. Michael Howard, *War and the Liberal Conscience* (New Brunswick, N.J.: Rutgers University Press, 1986), places unilateral humanitarian intervention within the context of liberal idealism in opposition to war and the causes of war. See also Fernando R. Teson, *Humanitarian Intervention: An Inquiry into Law and Morality* (Dobbs Ferry, N.Y.: Transnational Publishers, Inc., 1988).

10. See especially Francis Wolf, "Human Rights and the International Labor Organization," in Theodor Meron (ed.), *International Law of Human Rights* (Oxford: Clarendon Press, 1984).

11. Sieghart, *The International Law of Human Rights*, p. 13.

12. The 1926 Convention was buttressed by the 1953 United Nations Protocol amending the convention and provisions against slavery in the Covenant on Civil and Political Rights cited under international criminal law in the previous chapter.

13. While in Munich in 1932, Churchill was invited by an associate of Hitler to meet "der Führer." Churchill asked, "Why is your chief so violent about the Jews? . . . What is the sense of being against a man simply because of his birth?" The meeting never took place. Winston Churchill, *The Gathering Storm* (Boston: Houghton Mifflin Company, 1948), p. 84.

14. The Economic and Social Council in a resolution of February 16, 1946, set forth terms of reference for the new commission. In a resolution of June 21, 1946, the council fully described the functions, composition, and working method of the commission. Sohn, *International Organization and Integration*, p. 351. The first "nuclear" session of the commission met in April 1946 and the first plenary session in January 1947.

15. The declaration is General Assembly Resolution 217 (III), see Sohn, *International Organization and Integration*, p. 362. See also *United Nations Action in the Field of Human Rights*, 1988 for the official U.N. review of the International Bill of Human

Rights, including the origins and preparation of the declaration and the two ensuring covenants of 1966, p. 31.

16. Charles Malik, "The Drafting of Universal Declaration of Human Rights," *Bulletin of Human Rights* 1(1986): 18. Malik is particularly authoritative. At that time, he was rapporteur of the Commission on Human Rights, president of the Economic and Social Council to which the commission reports, and chairman of the General Assembly's Third Committee—which is responsible for issues of human rights. See also "A Magna Carta for Mankind," in Joseph P. Lash, *Eleanor: The Years Alone* (New York: W.W. Norton & Company/Signet, 1972).

17. Islam, the religion of over 900 million people, recognizes no distinction between the two categories of rights that comprise the two U.N. covenants of international human rights. See *Human Rights in Islam*.

18. Shashi Tharoor, "The Universality of Human Rights and Their Relevance to Developing Countries," keynote address at the Friedrich Naumann Stifung Conference on Human Rights, Sintra, Portugal, November 14, 1988. See also Boutros Ghali, "The Third World and Human Rights," *Bulletin of Human Rights* (1988).

19. Tharoor, "The Universality of Human Rights." This unpublished paper posits eights arguments against universalism that are followed by persuasive counterarguments. See, however, the report by the Council of Europe publication in its colloquy on "The Universality of Human Rights in a Pluralistic World," which hails the doctrine of cultural relativism and the pre-eminence of the European regional human rights authority over the universal, at least in the short run (Strasbourg: Council of Europe, July 1989).

20. *Issues Before the 43rd General Assembly* (New York: United Nations, 1988) p. 144.

21. John P. Humphrey, *Human Rights and the United Nations: A Great Adventure* (Dobbs Ferry, N.Y.: Transnational Publishers, 1983), pp. 63–77. Another important source is an interview with Mrs. Roosevelt recorded by Folkways Records (Album No. FH 5523, 1958) on some of these issues as she viewed them as chair of the Human Rights Commission.

22. Alexandre Kiss, "The Role of the Universal Declaration of Human Rights in the Development of International Law," *Bulletin of Human Rights* (New York: United Nations, 1988), p. 47. Dr. Kiss is Secretary General of the International Institute of Human Rights, Strasbourg. See also Fausto Pocar's "Considerations on the Legislative Function of the Universal Declaration of Human Rights in International Law," ibid., p. 64. Professor Pocar is vice chairman of the Human Rights Committee, United Nations.

23. The charter is in Sohn, *International Organization and Integration*, p. 1061. See also Richard N. Kiwanuka, "The Meaning of 'People' in the African Charter of Human and Peoples' Rights," *American Journal of International Law* (January 1988): 80; and Professor Emmanuel Bello, *African Customary Humanitarian Law*, (Geneva: Oyez Publishing Limited, 1980).

24. An outstanding publication in commemoration of the fortieth anniversary of the declaration is the *Bulletin of Human Rights* (New York: United Nations, 1988), special issue. with an introduction by Under-Secretary-General for Human Rights, Jan Martenson, and papers by some of the leading statesmen and academics in international human rights law.

25. Economic and Social Council Resolution 9 (II), June 21, 1946, in Sohn, *International Organization and Integration*, p. 315.

26. Council Resolution 75, August 1947, and Resolution 728, July 1959.

27. Council Resolution 1235, June 1967, in Sohn, *International Organization and Integration*, p. 357; *United Nations Action in the Field of Human Rights*, p. 283.

28. A commission delegation and staff did go into the field in Vietnam in 1963 to review some sixty-three allegations of government violation of religious rights of Buddhists, and they held some 106 interviews. This mission came to an end with the overthrow of the government of the Republic of Vietnam in November 1963. Humphrey, *Human Rights and the United Nations*, p. 302.

29. General Assembly Resolution 2443.

30. Israel claims it is not bound by the Fourth Geneva Convention because it is administering these territories and not occupying them. It refuses to accept the validity of the annual report and to permit the Special Committee to enter the State of Israel for discharging its mandate.

31. A historical footnote is that Namibia (or Southwest Africa) and the occupied territories in the West Bank are former mandate territories under the League of Nations.

32. For the full text of Resolution 1503, see Sohn, *International Organization and Integration*, p. 359.

33. *Issues Before the 35th General Assembly of the United Nations*, p. 107.

34. Perhaps the best comprehensive study of the commission is Howard Tolley, Jr., *The U.N. Commission on Human Rights* (Boulder, Colo.: Westview Press, 1987). This fine historical and legal/political appraisal of the commission emerged from the noted Urban Morgan Institute for Human Rights at the College of Law, University of Cincinnati. He also illuminates for us the work of the Subcommission on the Prevention of Discrimination and Protection of Minorities.

7

THE STATE

The international organization is constituted by states but once the constitution of the organization is legally in force over time the state-organization relationship takes on varying patterns as we have observed. The state may retain high authority in preference to significant organization participation or may seek a dominant role to bend the organization toward its goals. The partnership role may be the state's preference or high organization authority may take place, especially in proportion to the state's inability to meet its needs by its own sovereign authority. Finally, the state may choose to accept supra-organization authority in certain areas of national policy—now, international policy. Or, there may be combinations of all these points on the spectrum and gray areas in between, depending on the state's appraisal of the value of the organization to its goals or its needs for the organization to pursue goals. The sovereign state may always choose to depart from the organization or international treaty obligation but this may be an act of national suicide. In any event, the state is the locus of decision-making authority on the determination of its role in international organizations.

THE NATIONAL GOVERNMENT

We thus turn first to the state and its organization and policy with respect to the international organization. Our prime case study is the United States' organization and policy toward international organizations and specifically organization and policy toward the United Nations Commission on Human Rights. In addition to the national government of the state, we also review the mission of the state to the organization as well as its delegation to the assembly of member states, again in a general sense, the U.S. experience, and its participation in the Commission on Human Rights. Each state, of course, has its own government organization and policy, its mission and the delegation to the organization. The U.S. experience and its participation in the Commission on Human Rights is the general framework of the other states' roles in international organization and that framework lends itself to inquiry and research on other states' roles in international organization.

Government Organization and Agencies

Top leadership by whatever title—president, prime minister, general secretary, or king—has the obvious authority, responsibility, and accountability to determine policy toward and within organizations. As we have observed many times, the top leader is the bottom line in shaping state goals of security and well-being and determining requirements to pursue those goals. The top leader is assisted by leadership office organization—such as the executive office of the White House in the United States—and advisers from within and outside of government.

The president of the United States thus sets the tone that reflects his version and vision of national security and well-being. President Carter was oriented toward state-organization partnership and multilateralism, especially in human rights policy. President Reagan took a more ideological approach to organization policy and more unilateralism in foreign policy in general.[1] In any event, policy directives and orders go forth from the White House and all officials in the domain of bureaucracies having responsibilities for and with international organizations had better keep this fact well in mind.

The foreign ministry of the state is where organization policy is crafted under top leadership direction and the foreign secretary by whatever title heads this bureaucratic pyramid. The U.S. secretary of state presides over a vast array of offices and bureaus. Some have responsibilities for geographic areas and then states within those areas, such as the Office of Near East and South East Asian Affairs. Others deal with specific fields of foreign policy, such as the Office for International Organization Affairs and the Office of Human Rights and Humanitarian Affairs. The department's Policy Planning Staff certainly has analogs in other states' foreign ministries as do other offices and bureaus.

The organizational structure in the state that relates to international organizations is necessarily complex, given the thousands of intergovernmental organizations and subagencies, the treaties produced by organizations such as the United Nations Covenants on Human Rights, and the constant growth of new organizations and treaties to deal with new needs for state cooperation, as we observed at the end of Chapter 2. For the United States, some basic national agency-organization relations are as follows:

Department of State	U.N. Commission on Human Rights, among others
Department of Treasury	World Bank; International Monetary Fund
Department of Commerce	General Agreement on Tariffs and Trade

Department of Labor	International Labor Organization
Department of Health and Services	World Health Organization
Department of Agriculture	Food and Agricultural Organization
Department of Defense	U.N. Military Staff Committee and collective measures, e.g., Korea
Department of Education	U.N. Educational, Scientific, & Cultural Organization
Federal Communications Commission	International Telecommunications Union Commission
International Trade Commission	General Agreement on Tariffs and Trade

Each department or government agency will have more than one bureau concerned with a specific issue under the aegis of an international organization. For instance, top representatives of the Office of Human Rights and Humanitarian Affairs and of the Office of Near East and South Asian Affairs appeared before the Subcommittee on Human Rights and International Organizations of the House of Representatives Committee on Foreign Affairs on June 1, 1989, to testify and make policy recommendations in hearings on "Human Rights in Lebanon." This reflects interests and policy concerns on human rights in a specific area in addition to the universal responsibilities of the Human Rights Bureau.

Beyond intra-agency bureaus are agency cooperation. We draw from two organization concerns, finance and food, to provide examples of interagency coordination in the United States government. For *finance*, the Department of Treasury coordinates the National Advisory Council on International Monetary and Financial Policies (NAC). Participants include appropriate officials at the Treasury, as well as those from the Federal Reserve Bank, the Department of State, Agriculture, and Commerce Agency for International Development, and others from time to time. They shape policy toward and in the World Bank with its affiliates, the International Development Authority, International Finance Corporation; regional banks in Latin America, Africa, and Asia; the Bank for International Settlements; the OECD; the Group of Seven major industrial democracies; and others.

For *food*, the U.S. Department of Agriculture coordinates policy, especially through the office of the Under Secretary for International Affairs and Commodity Programs. Interagency participants include the relevant bureaus at Agriculture, State, Agency for International Development, and others. The host of organizations the department-coordinated Interagency Working Group works with is awesome. They include the FAO, the U.N. Development Program, the World Food Council, the World Food Program, the IFAD, the WHO (food health standards), the ILO (agricultural labor), the UNCTAD (agriculture in developing countries), the OAS, and all the financial international organizations associated with the NAC and Treasury that have responsibilities for supporting food policies and programs. President Carter's administration did have an interagency procedure for human rights policy but this was basically disbanded under the Reagan administration, which did not give the priority to human rights policy embraced by his predecessor. There was a considerable coordination between the Department of State and the United States Information Agency in shaping policy on the accusations of Cuban violations of human rights in the Commission on Human Rights in 1986 through 1989, but not with respect to across-the-board policy. Of course during these years, the U.S. targeting of alleged Cuban violations was its top priority in the commission.

It would be most valuable to have solid scholarship on how states that are members of the principal international organizations structure and orchestrate their policies with respect to the variety of organizations to which they belong. This would be particularly enlightening for Denmark, which is a member of 164 intergovernmental organizations at last count. There is no overall coordination of U.S. executive departments, agencies, bureaus and subbureaus. As we shall see when we relate organization of government to policy in international organizations, the fragmented structures can, and often do, produce fragmented organization policy. This situation within the state is reflected in the structure of international organizations. In Geneva, we asked the official at GATT why don't GATT, the IMF, the World Bank, and UNCTAD form a super coordinating agency to provide coordination to international trade and finance, which are so interdependent? His response was two intriguing questions. (1) How many agencies in Washington have constitutional and/or legislative authority for United States trade policy? (Answer: about 24). (2) Do the Department of Treasury, the Federal Reserve Board, and the president's Special Trade Representative sit in the Cabinet Room of the White House and coordinate the interdependencies between and among monetary, fiscal, and trade policy? (Answer: no, Congress aside).

In a speech on June 29, 1989, John Bolton, the Assistant Secretary of State for International Organization Affairs, called for a "Unitary U.N. policy that would treat the global organization in a comprehensive, orchestrated manner rather than a series of unrelated policies toward each U.N. component . . . this would permit us to redefine the proper limits of each U.N. component's responsibilities and help avoid both empire building and turf fighting."[2] An excellent speech and we look forward to unitary organization policy.

Most states' management of international organization policy is in the executive or administrative branch of government. The U.S. Constitution and its division and separation of powers conveys much authority to Congress including that over international organizations and multilateral diplomacy. The Senate Committee on Foreign Relations, the House Committee on Foreign Affairs, and their respective subcommittees on international organizations have considerable authority with respect to the U.S. role and policies in international organizations. They also generate legislation dealing with U.S. human rights positions and policies, both in organizations and on a bilateral basis with other nations, especially those receiving economic and military aid. The House Appropriations

Committee and subcommittees, as well as the Senate Ways and Means Committee and subcommittees, play pivotal roles in appropriation levels of financial support to international organizations, which we appraise shortly under state policy.

Members of the judiciary and other legal professionals serve terms on courts of organizations such as the United Nations' International Court of Justice and those of the European and inter-American human rights courts. They also participate in judicial agencies and determinations of some international organizations. Former U.S. Supreme Court Justice, Earl Warren, spoke highly of his experiences with the ILO.

Standing before us is the basic fact that a body of international law now exists. . . . For the past three years, I have had the good fortune to be associated with a judicial review panel of the ILO. I have been impressed at the extent to which the basic features of effective implementation are built into the constitutional structure of the ILO—fact-finding, exposure, conciliation and ajudication. The handling of complaints, which is the heart of meaningful enforcement of human rights, has been carefully structured in a precise, procedural manner [which have] produced concrete results. . . . The ILO experience can be applied to the entire range of human rights concerns.[3]

Furthermore, courts of states that are members of international organizations are called upon to make determinations in municipal law of legal issues relating to state-organization relations. Such was the case when the U.S. Federal District Court of the Southern District of New York held in 1989 that the United States could not close the mission of the Palestine Liberation Organization (PLO) at U.N. headquarters. The court said that such action would be in violation of the 1947 agreement between the United States and the United Nations, and under the U.S. Constitution, this treaty takes precedence over congressional legislation seeking to close the PLO office.

State Policy in International Organizations

State policy is dictated in part by the obligations and commitments it voluntarily accepts when it ratifies the constitutions of international organizations and if and when it is bound to conform to the organizations' decisions and resolutions. The state also seeks to shape the policies that are the products of the organizations' decision-making organs in the complex politics of international organizations. As a member of the United Nations and many other international organizations, the United States is obliged under international law to pattern much of its policy to conform to the organizations' constitutional law and policy. This is a member-organization partnership role and, in some areas, adherence to high organization authority, especially when significant treaties, such as those against genocide and torture, are domesticated into U.S. municipal law. Such is the merger of state goals of security and well-being with the organization's goals of shared security and shared and progressive well-being. Naturally, the more powerful the state, the more able it is to influence organization policy and goals to harmonize with the state's goals of security and well-being. Any study of the U.S. role in the Congo crisis in the early 1960s reveals that there was a distinct blend of U.S. goals with U.N. goals, including the peacekeeping forces that served the U.S. goal of security and the U.N. goal of shared security.[4]

State policy that stems from the structure and machinery of government is a combination of unilateral policy initiatives and multilateral diplomacy in conjunction with one or more other states, especially those that share basic goal definitions. The prime focus is on international legislation in the assemblies of the organizations or in other membership forms such as the forty-three–member U.N. Commission on Human Rights. Initiatives on developing resolutions, diplomacy in framing resolutions in such a manner that the resolution might gain necessary voting support, lobbying for favorable votes and defusing criticisms, the actual vote, and various kinds of follow-ups comprise much of the politics of the organization and the shaping of organization policy. State policy is also aimed at influencing the management of organizations by international civil servants to advance state policy. The organs of the organization are most serviceable for representatives of states to articulate the policy of the state, to appeal to broader audiences, and to address specific issues of importance to the state. U.S. Ambassador Adlai E. Stevenson brilliantly used the forum of the Security Council in October 1962 to demonstrate to council members and the world that the Soviet Union had indeed placed offensive nuclear missiles in Cuba.

Policy includes money and contributions to international organizations. For the vast majority of states, the assessed contribution based on assessments of the financial capability of the member is fairly pro forma. For the states making the large contributions, policy and money go hand in hand, especially in the 1990s. The United States contributes 25 percent of the central budget of the United Nations and to many other organization as well. Thirteen democracies in Geneva, which are assessed about 70 percent of the United Nations's biennial budget of around $1.8 billion and which contribute about 70 percent of the total contributions to agencies such as UNICEF and UNHCR, comprise the "Geneva Group" that meets regularly with organizations in Geneva to review budgets and to make strong recommendations for budgetary controls and efficiencies. The U.S. Congress passed the Kassebaum Amendment on October 1, 1986, which stated that the United States would not pay more than 20 percent toward the assessed budgets of the United Nations and the specialized agencies unless their member states (especially the Geneva group and *especially* the United States) had more influence over U.N. budget priorities and construction of budgets. It was felt such a policy would lead to the enhancement of that authority and especially a better correlation between budget and spending controls on the one hand and cost-effective administration on the other. Most agree the policy did work. The fact, however, that the United States continues to be hundreds of millions of dollars in arrears hits and hurts most line items on the U.N. budget, not the least the Centre for Human Rights and its global operations and responsibilities.

The multiple government bureaus and agencies within government organizations are managed by officials who often do not agree on state policy in international organizations. Disagreement over the correlation of state goals with organization goals and policies may be among officials within one bureau such as the Office of Human Rights and Humanitarian Affairs at the U.S. Department of State and between bureaus such as the Human Rights Office and the Office of Near East and South Asian Affairs. The former may strike out for better humanitarian treatment of Palestinians in Israeli-occupied territories, while the latter may argue that Israel's security demands a lower priority for human rights in the midst of the "Intifadah," or the Palestinian uprising. Which view wins in U.S. policy in the U.N. Commission on Human Rights? The Department of State and the Department of Health and Human Services may come up with opposing views on votes in the annual May assembly of WHO. Do you have the right to smoke where you please and/or do you have the right to be free of inhalation of cigarette smoke? This question and dilemma travels from the state to debates on the floor of the assembly, a debate over a human right and the condition of human well-being.

Officials who have policy responsibility and authority have their own views and convictions about the goals of national security and well-being and how the pursuit of these goals relate to international organizations. In authoritarian governments, officials generally make proposals and decisions based on the position of top leader. In a democracy, there usually is a healthy discussion and debate about state policy in organizations. In the United States, they are abundantly aware of the fact that the parameters and texture of policy are fairly well defined by the president's overall determination and vision for the U.S. role in the world. They can, of course, seek to convince higher officials and the White House of the wisdom of their policy proposals. But it is only natural and healthy that there be "in-house" policy differences and turf battles. Reconciliation of differences move on to officials higher up the bureaucratic ladder and then to the secretary of state and the president if necessary.

The shaping of policy toward any organization is also influenced by reports and recommendations from officials at the embassies and missions of the state throughout the world. The reports on nations' human rights policies that come regularly to the Department of State pour into the bilateral and multilateral policy determinations by the United States. Further, policy makers regularly consult with their counterparts at the embassies and missions located in the capital of the state. Well before the opening of the Commission on Human Rights sessions each February in Geneva, officials from the Human Rights Bureau at the U.S. Department of State will review policy proposals with their colleagues at embassies of states closely associated with the United States to review proposed resolutions, policy proposals, and voting strategy.

We now turn to a more detailed examination of U.S. human rights policy. Over the forty-five years of U.N. activity in the area of human rights, the United States has waxed and waned with respect to its human rights policies in the organs of the global organization. President Truman and Mrs. Roosevelt provided great and historic leadership in creating the Commission on Human Rights and gaining such significant U.N. support for the 1948 Declaration on Human Rights. President Eisenhower's secretary of state, John Foster Dulles, succumbed to demands from Congress and important domestic sources of policy to veto U.S. participation in crafting covenants on human rights out of the Declaration on Human Rights. He added that the United States would not ratify such covenants if they were to be negotiated and entered into force. They did enter into force in 1966, but the United States still has not ratified them and most other international human rights covenants except for those against torture and genocide.

In presidential administrations down to Jimmy Carter, it cannot be said that the United States made significant contributions to international human rights law. The Helsinki Declaration signed by thirty-five nations, including the United States, did have pioneering provisions for human rights enhancement and protection that led to human rights dissident activity in the Soviet Union and follow-up conferences that have added substantially to the global human rights system.[5] However, the U.S. civil rights movement of the 1960s and the aftermath of Vietnam in the 1970s led to major congressional initiatives for strengthening U.S. human rights policy—on a bilateral basis for the most part. Representatives Don Fraser, Chairman of the House Subcommittee on Human Rights and International Organizations, provided leadership for amendments to the Foreign Aid Act of 1961 and subsequent foreign aid acts that conditioned the dispensation of economic and especially military and security assistance to other nations on the recipient nations' human rights records.[6]

Congressional initiatives and leadership late in the Ford administration brought about changes in human rights policy and organization at the Department of State. Legislation of 1975 and 1976 led to the establishment at the Department of State of the Bureau of Human Rights and Humanitarian Affairs and the requirement that the secretary of state transmit each year to the U.S. Congress a "full and complete report regarding . . . the status of internationally recognized human rights . . . in countries that received [U.S.] assistance [and] in all other foreign countries which are members of the United Nations."[7] Human rights officers were appointed to the five geographic offices of the Department of State to infuse in area and foreign national policy human rights considerations and concerns. Human rights officers in U.S. embassies and missions abroad write reports that comprise the total of 169 reports in the 1988 volume. The impact of this extensive legislation has, in the words of the 1988 report, "made human rights concerns an integral part of the State Department's daily report and daily decision making."[8]

President Carter made human rights policy central to his total foreign policies and his Assistant Secretary for Human Rights and Humanitarian Affairs, Patricia

Derian, was a forceful leader in extending human rights policies. President Reagan from 1981 to 1989 declared he preferred quiet diplomacy and persuasion. U.N. Ambassador Jeanne Kirkpatrick and Human Rights Assistant Secretary Eliot Abrams upheld the idea of not condemning "traditional authoritarian nations," especially in Latin America, but rather to aim condemnations at totalitarian nations. In 1988 and 1989, the U.S. delegation to the U.N. Commission on Human Rights was led by Armando Valladares, a Cuban poet incarcerated by Castro who finally arrived in the United States to become an ambassador assigned to the commission. In these years, the main priority of the United States at the commission meetings was to condemn Cuba for human rights transgressions. The results were a mixed success, but attention to other critical human rights issues was quite limited.

Two human rights policy issues in particular have raised much debate at home and abroad. The U.S. main focus on human rights are those in the civil, legal, and political domain. Human rights for the United States are defined in Section 116 (a) of the 1961 Foreign Assistance Act as amended and basically are concerned with "flagrant denial of the rights of life, liberty and the security of the person." Added to this are internationally recognized worker rights as defined in Section 502 (a) of the Trade Act. With the exception of workers' rights, others in the economic and social areas are generally not considered by the U.S. to be rights, but rather entitlements that nations may offer citizens through domestic legislation.[9] Second, do concerns for human rights violations in some other nations diminish where and when security issues become paramount? For all but a few rights we have identified in the previous chapter, states may derogate or depart from protection of some rights on the groups of security threats or disturbance in public order. The United States under legislation may also overlook violations such as those in El Salvador and continue security aid if the situation warrants. Some say there is no way around this dilemma and others charge that this selectivity undermines a consistent human rights policy. What does or should happen if and when security policy intrudes on human rights policy and violations? The debate continues.

State policy in organizations and foreign policies in general are subject to change with shifts of view and policy of top officials, new people assuming top leadership, and a host of changing conditions both within the state and in the world outside. Policy has its seasons. It may be registered in the very short run with a vote in an emergency meeting of the Security Council, in annual membership meetings such as that of the conference of the ILO or the Commission on Human Rights, or in more durable forms such as the negotiation and conclusion of the Convention Against Torture. The central and constant factor is the continuous assessment by the state of the correlation of its definitions of and requirements for national security and well-being with the goals and policies of the many organizations of which it is a member.

For most states, we could now move on to state policy as exercised in its mission to the international organization and its delegation to assemblies and organs of the organization. However, the U.S. Congress, as we have observed, has distinct constitutional authority in shaping policy, unlike most other nations where parliaments are either controlled by the governing political party (as in Great Britain) or dominated by the top leader and party (as in authoritarian states). In addition to powerful congressional authority in appropriations of financial support to international organizations in general, Congress refuses to assist in the funding of the U.N. agencies and operations associated with SWAPO, the PLO, or the Preparatory Commission for the implementation of the 1982 Law of the Sea Treaty. Influenced by domestic sources of policy, Congress has targeted the PLO in particular as a "terrorist" organization and in no way suitable for admission to any international organization.[10] Legislation has been passed that calls for the United States to terminate its membership in any organization that evicts Israel as a member. The Congressional Black Caucus has been deeply concerned about human rights violations in nations such as Zaire, Kenya, Liberia, and the Sudan and seeks to reduce substantially military and economic aid to such nations as well as the reduction in World Bank loans to states such as Somalia and Ethiopia. All of these nations are among the more than 100 cited by the Department of State's *Country Reports on Human Rights Practices* as engaging in a national policy of gross transgressions of human rights. Senate authority to give advice and consent to all treaties negotiated by the president has been the principal reason this nation ratified so few international treaties dealing with human rights, especially the two principal U.N. covenants. Reasons for states to exercise high state authority over organizations set forth in the previous chapter help to explain this policy. But all of this is subject to change providing change is considered necessary by top leadership, governing officials, and domestic sources of policy.

All democracies members of international organizations have domestic sources of policy such as interest groups, the media, and public opinion, which can exert great influence on the states' policy to and within organizations. National nongovernmental organizations representing special interests (NGOs) are quite active in influencing state officials and especially the U.S Congress, reaching public opinion, and playing an active role in political processes and campaigns. Their goal is to encourage officials to embrace national policy that reflects their own policy position and organization goals. In the domain of human rights, the Anti-Slavery Society was a powerful force contributing to the abolishment of slavery in the nineteenth century and the 1863 International Committee of the Red Cross was (and is) a private Swiss organization that is the international pace setter for international humanitarian law. These organizations continue today as do a host of others to mobilize private support for international human rights law. Many NGOs have strong national roots and membership such as the Netherlands Institute for Human Rights, the U.S. Lawyers Committee for Human Rights, and the Human Rights Watch, with groups monitoring rights situations in Africa, Asia, and the Americas. The latter two organizations provide an annual overview of the Department of State's *Country Reports on Human Rights Practices.*

Most national organizations belong to parent international federations or confederations. They include Amnesty International, U.S.A., with the London-based Amnesty International; the United States Helsinki Watch Committee; the International Helsinki Organization; the United Nations Association/U.S.A. with the World Federation of United Nations Associations; the Australian section of the Geneva-based International Committee of Jurists; and National Councils of Churches of Christ with the World Council of Churches; along with many other national religions groups associated with their international parent organizations. We look later at the role of the nongovernmental international organizations (NGIOs) and their vital roles in the U.N. Commission on Human Rights. Both at the national and international levels, the NIGOs monitor how states carry out (or don't carry out) their obligations and commitments to the national protection of human rights and they make recommendations for international protection when national policy and action breaks down. They are particularly active in the United States in testifying before committees and subcommittees of Congress on appropriations, proposed legislation, and analysis of U.S. human rights policy.[11]

It now remains for state organizations' policy to be implemented in organizations. Policy and policy instructions go forth to the state's mission at the organization and also to the state's delegation to assemblies of members of organization. The national government must decide how much policy can be placed in the hands of people at the mission and in the delegation and, through the process of communications, how to make as certain as possible that the policy of the national government is being transmitted and effectively pursued. We now turn to this front line of state policy in international organizations.

THE MISSION OF THE STATE TO INTERNATIONAL ORGANIZATIONS

The connecting link between the state and the international organization is its mission to the organization, which is located in the city of the organization. The phone books of New York and Geneva provide the names and addresses of the missions of states members of the United Nations in New York, Geneva offices of the United Nations, and the many organizations headquartered in Geneva. Paris, Rome, and Vienna, among other prominent cities with organizations, also have states' missions. We surveyed in Chapter 1 the evolution of international diplomacy and the development of the permanent embassy of the state in the jurisdiction of other states, such as the development of bilateral diplomacy between two states. With the advent of international organizations, and especially the League of Nations, members established missions to the organizations to conduct multilateral and parliamentary diplomacy, processes of relations between and among states, which are different from and more complex than bilateral diplomacy between two states.

For many small nations, their mission to international organizations, especially in New York and Geneva, are of particular importance. Many simply cannot afford embassies and other legations in most other nations but find that their mission at the organization enables them to conduct bilateral, extra-organization diplomacy with representatives of other states at the organization headquarters. There are 159 missions in New York, the present total number of members of the United Nations and about 140 missions in Geneva. We now appraise the mission to the organization in terms of its status under international law, and then its organization and manifold operations in multilateral diplomacy. Again, our principal case study is the United States and its organizational policy in international human rights law.

Status in International Law

From the broad review of the law of diplomacy in Chapter 1, we turn to a branch of more complex diplomatic law, that of missions of nations to other nations and especially to international organizations. We have three major actors: the nation sending or establishing the mission, the international organization, and the host state. In continuing to base our case studies on the U.S. experience, we have the U.S. Mission to Organizations in Geneva, the United Nations, the specialized agencies and other organizations, and the host state, Switzerland. A web of international constitutional law of diplomacy provides the necessary legal basis for this triangular relationship.

The United States is bound by Vienna Convention on Diplomatic Relations of 1961 as the basis of its relations with the organizations and Switzerland, and the Vienna Convention on Consular Relations of 1963 would also apply if a mission performs consular functions.[12] The Convention on Relations between States and International Organizations of a Universal Character (CRISO) establishes the legal relationship between the United States and its mission and both the United Nations and the specialized agencies in Geneva. This makes possible ''the right of the member to actively participate in the decision-making process'' of the organization. This activity inside the organization is subject to the constituent act (constitution) of the organization and to its internal rules of procedure.[13]

The Headquarters Agreement between Switzerland and the United Nations of December 14, 1946, is analogous to the June 27, 1947, Headquarters Agreement between the United States and the United Nations. Both ''seat'' treaties set forth in great detail the legal relationships between the host state and the United Nations, including those between the missions of member states to the United Nations located in the host state. Switzerland has its own convention with the United Nations and other organizations in Geneva (CRISO), as well as being a signatory to the Convention on Privileges and Immunities of the United Nations (CPIUN) and the Convention on Privileges and Immunities of Specialized Agencies (CPISA). These two treaties guarantee diplomatic privileges and immunities of organizations and their personnel in the host state. All mission officials must, of course, have proper diplomatic credentials authorized by the head of government or foreign minister of their state to serve in the host state and at the organization.[14]

The United States Mission in Geneva: Organization

Because we cannot study the hundreds of missions of states to organizations in many cities, we focus on one very important mission, the United States Permanent Mission to the United Nations Office and Other International Organizations in Geneva, or U.S. Geneva Mission. The stationery of the ambassador of the mission is titled, "The Representative of the United States of America to the European Office of the United Nations, Geneva." Under the ambassador is the Deputy Chief of Mission (DCM) whose formal title is Minister Counsellor, United States Permanent Mission to the United Nations Office and the Other International Organizations in Geneva. The DCM has the principal responsibility for the day-to-day operations, relations with organizations, and the diplomacy on the floor of assemblies of organizations' members.

The organization of the mission's professional staff is as follows:

Political and Specialized Agency Affairs (PSA) with counsellors assigned to the U.N. Commission on Human Rights, the International Committee of the Red Cross, WHO, and other specialized agencies.

International Economic Affairs (IEA) with officials assigned to the Economic Commission for Europe, UNCTAD, the ITC, and others. There is a separate Geneva office for the Deputy United States Trade Representative assigned to GATT whose instructions come from the White House office of the U.S. Trade Representative and not through the mission.

Refugee and Migration Affairs (RMA) for work with the UNHCR, disaster relief, and other humanitarian activities.

Public Affairs (PA) handles all media relations and briefings, visitations by individuals and groups to the mission, publishes a daily bulletin on U.S. policy, and other activities in the domain of public diplomacy. Officers in PA are under the authority of the U.S. Information Agency (USIA) in Washington, but responsible to the ambassador.

Legal Adviser (LA). The Legal Adviser and staff work on all details requiring legal opinion and judgment as part of the extensive Washington Department of State and worldwide international lawyers in the service of the United States.

More technical sections are as follows: Administrative Affairs (ADM) in charge of logistic and administrative support for the many visiting U.S. delegations and the mission staff; International Resource Management (IRM) with officials assigned to mission and organization budget management and support systems for Mission staff; and Regional Security Office (RSO) with responsibility for all security issues inside and outside the mission and staffed in part by U.S. Marines. Officials from the United States Arms Control and Disarmament Agency have offices at the mission from which they negotiate bilateral and multilateral arms control talks. These include the negotiations with the Soviet Union in the 1980s that led to the 1987 Intermediate Nuclear Force Treaty (INF) and the multilateral talks in the United Nations Conference on Disarmament.

Officials staffing these sections have various titles, such as counsellors; first, second, or third secretary; attaches and advisers. Almost all are U.S. foreign service officers in the Department of State or foreign service information officers in PA and under the aegis of the USIA. There are also attaches from Washington executive agencies in labor (Department of Labor) and health (Department of Health and Human Services), but they also are official U.S. civil servants as are the U.S support staff. Unlike other nations, the ambassador in Geneva is not a professional foreign service officer. There have been many debates over the wisdom of the top officer being essentially a political appointment rather than a seasoned foreign service officer. A new president may enter office as did President Reagan in 1981 and the foreign service officers must follow the policy position of the new president and his ambassador at the mission even if there is a major change in policy and one that is personally opposed by one or more of the officers.[15] There are also security and military officers with their own bureaucratic base in Washington but accountable to the ambassador. Finally, there are the local employees (Swiss, of course, in Geneva) who have considerable longevity at the mission unlike other U.S. personnel who are regularly rotated to other missions or posts about every three years.

The U.S. Mission in Geneva: Operations

The mission is the conduit of policy formulated in Washington to the decision-making organs of the United Nations and other organization in Geneva. The substantial framed photographs of the president of the United States and the secretary of state in the main conference room of the mission in Geneva leave no doubt as to who is in command. As with all embassies and missions, officials first represent the United States to those with whom they conduct multilateral and bilateral diplomacy, engage in continuous communications with government officials and agencies in Washington to receive instructions and to send reports and feedbacks, and engage in diplomatic protocol and other standard embassy/mission responsibilities. Mission officials led by the Deputy Chief of Mission meet regularly with representatives of twelve other missions of major Western contributors to the United Nations and specialized agencies, nations that account for about 70 percent of the organizations' budgets. This is the "Geneva Group" that reviews all organizations' budgets and makes recommendations for budget-level reductions if and when it considers the expenditure side to be out of line with the group's judgment of cost-effectiveness and expectations for the organizations.

The mission's specific organization policy is oriented first toward the parliamentary processes and international legislation in the assemblies of member states, and second, the year-round relations with organizations in seeking to influence organizations' officials in advancing the nation's policy goals. As we shall see later in this chapter, U.S. policy in the six-week meeting of the Commission on Human Rights is advanced by attendance at daily meetings, the diplomacy of drafting resolutions, lobbying for political support before the resolution is voted on the floor, and other logistics in the politics of parliamentary diplomacy. Policy produced by organizations is the congealing of politics and diplomacy and mission officials must be experienced and agile on the floor and behind the scenes at the commission. Each day they receive sets of instructions from Washington by phone, cable, telex, or fax and, in turn, respond with reports and recommendations for new phrasing of resolutions or modest changes in policy that officials might feel should be considered given their front-line presence where the diplomacy of human rights take place. The mission has a meeting each morning of the Commission's meetings to gather officials and delegation members together to shape daily policy. The morning session also includes inputs by those present of information they may have obtained at previous evening's social activities in which officials and delegations from many other missions participate. Assembly operations also include preparations for and follow-up to the annual sessions. Mission leadership generates high performance when they promote good chemistry among the officials and pursue a sensible allocation of tasks to be performed and accounted for by mission personnel.

Second, mission officials relate throughout the year with organizations in Geneva in the protracted process of advancing policy goals through the administration of the organizations. The U.S. labor attache at the mission is well wired into appropriate officials and experts at the ILO in bilateral negotiations for effective relating of U.S. labor policy with that of the organization. The same relations and negotiations take place throughout the year between mission officials and those at organizations such as the WHO, the International Committee of the Red Cross, and the UNHCR. Mission officers attend more than 300 annual meetings in Geneva each year on a host of issues such as the crisis conference in June 1989 on the plight of Vietnamese refugees.

Studies are necessary to examine other nations' missions at international organizations and how they compare with each other and to those of the two superpowers. For instance, the mission of Colombia to international organizations in Geneva has some notable differences as compared to the U.S. mission. Its ambassador has been in Geneva for fourteen years and has seen seven U.S. ambassadors come and go. His longevity and expertise, which is paralleled by many other nations, provides an important measure of consistency and longevity that is important in mission-organization relations as well as with other missions. The staff is small but has increased over the years given the importance of the organizations such as WHO to health care in Colombia and the very vital relationship with GATT to Colombia in export of coffee, its major export resource and source of foreign exchange, drugs aside. The ambassador has a lot of rope from Bogota to make decisions on organization policy—quite unlike the U.S.

mission, which has daily instructions from Washington. Colombia works very closely with its neighbor missions in Geneva, including Venezuela, Equador, and Peru for a coherent regional policy in the organizations and for consistency in voting. The ambassadorship in Geneva is considered in Bogota to be vital for the well-being interests and goals of the foreign policy of Colombia.

THE DELEGATION OF THE STATE TO INTERNATIONAL ORGANIZATIONS

The delegation of the State to the assembly of the organization or other forum of members is the official representative and voice of the state in the decision-making processes of the assembly. Our two main areas of concern are the composition of the delegation and the logistics of its participation in the assembly.

Organization

The constitutions of international organizations prescribe the basic structure and often the composition of the delegation. Article 9, paragraph 2, of the U.N. Charter states that "Each Member shall not have more than five representatives in the General Assembly which is comprised of all members of the United Nations.[11] This is amplified by the Assembly's *Rules of Procedures* and by the convention and the previously cited CRISO, which is the case with other constitutional provisions relating to delegations. Assembly practice leaves it entirely to states to determine the five principal delegates, although they must present credentials issued to them by their head of government or the foreign minister and verified by the Credentials Committee.[16] The Rules of the General Assembly also provide for five alternative representatives and as many other advisers and specialists as the member nation may choose. Rule 16 of the Rules of the Economic and Social Council permits only one representative for each member, but as many advisers or others as is desired. These rules, of course, apply to the council's sub-organ, the Commission on Human Rights.[17]

The constitution of WHO in Article 10 states that the assembly "shall be composed of delegates representing Members," but Article 11 is more specific with respect to composition than is the U.N. Charter.

Each member shall be represented by not more than three delegates, one of whom shall be designated by the Member as the chief delegate. These delegations should be chosen from among persons most qualified by their technical competence in the field of health, preferably representing the national health administration of the Member.

Under the constitutional law of the WHO, representation from a specific governmental bureaucracy is required of member states. Article 11 does say "should be chosen" although an examination of the List of Delegations and Other Participants of the 1989 World Health Assembly reveals that all delegations are headed by top or near-top officials of national health ministries.

The constitution of the ILO has a higher level of specificity of delegation composition. Under Article 3, paragraph 1, members' delegations ''shall be composed of four representatives of each of the Members, of whom two shall be Government delegates and the two others shall be delegates representing respectively the employers and workpeople of each of the Members.'' Paragraph 5 of Article 3 carries this requirement further.

The Members undertake to nominate non-Government delegates and advisers chosen in agreement with industrial organizations, if such organizations exist, which are the most representative of employers or workpeople, as the case may be, in their respective countries.

In the United States, the U.S. Chamber of Commerce and the National Association of Manufacturers chose the annual representative of industry, while the American Federation of Labor/Congress of Industrial Organizations selects the labor representative. About all delegations are chaired by a nation's minister of labor, which is the secretary of labor for the United States. Voting in the conference is by each member of a state's delegation of four and not exclusively by one vote for the state.

Delegates from the United States to the 1989 sessions of the World Health Assembly and the International Labor Conference give us some idea of the breadth of U.S. representation and how these officials relate to and reflect the bureaus and agencies of the government in Washington. The Department of Health and Human Services is the most prominent in the delegation to the WHO, but this is no guarantee that there is agreement between and among these officials on health policy, such as WHO's concerns about tobacco and health. Are Human and Health Services offficials on the same wave length as the Department of State, which may be unhappy about a proposed U.S. policy that would conflict with the Department of State's determination of national well-being? What happens when the representative from one executive agency, Health and Human Services, receives instructions that differ from the representative from the Department of State? May these instructions differ from officials at the mission? If and where differences take place, the chief delegate is the one to reconcile policy and if this is impossible, again, back to the White House.

The composition of the U.S. delegation to the United Nations Commission on Human Rights in the 1980s reflected the Reagan administration's fairly high state authority position with respect to its international organization of human rights policy, as well as overall foreign policy priorities. The delegations in recent years had political figures as chief representatives, including Attorney General Edwin Meese, his associate E. Robert Wallach in 1987, and, as we have observed, the Cuban exile, Armando Valladares in 1988 and 1989. He required a translator as he cannot speak English. The three or four alternate faces were new each year for the most part, as were most of the fourteen to seventeen advisers. The alternates and advisers for the most part were consultants, but also with some representation from the Geneva and New York U.N. missions, and very few from the Department of State.[18] The commission's "List of Attendance" includes first the delegations of the forty-three members of the commission and then over sixty members of the United Nations who have observer delegations. The third set of participants are "non-Member States"—observer delegations including the Holy See, Republic of Korea, and Switzerland. Then came Namibia, representatives of the Office of the High Commissioner for Refugees, the ILO, UNESCO, and such intergovernmental organizations as the EC, the League of Arab States, and the Organization of African Unity (OAU). National liberation movements are on hand including the African National Congress, the PLO, the Pan Africanist Congress of Azania, and SWAPO.

Then there is a substantial number of international nongovernmental organizations recognized by the United Nations and having approval to speak on the floor of the commission upon recognition by the president. A sampler includes the following: World Association of United Nations Associations, World Confederation of Labor, World Muslim Congress, Anti-Slavery Society Coordinating Board of Jewish Organizations, International Catholic Union of the Press, International Commission of Jurists, and the International Indian Treaty Council. Almost 100 nongovernmental organizations are represented, most of which have national affiliates in many nations to coordinate national interest group activity on state governments with the international nongovernmental organizations lobbying the commission. Any annual assembly of major international organizations has this broader participation of states and nongovernmental organizations beyond the states involved in the assembly's deliberations, thus broadening the scope and significance of organizations assemblies of members.

Logistics of Delegation Participation

The principal task of the delegation and its chair by whatever title is accurately and effectively to represent and speak for the policy of the state in deliberations and voting in the assembly or forum of members. Usually the basic policy, instructions, and grand strategy are prepared in the national government and the delegation is given some rope with respect to tactics and multilateral diplomacy. Delegation members from the national government, the mission, and others must follow the nation's policy, take some initiatives in recommending modest changes in policy, and forcefully recommend policy change of a major nature. These positions depend on judgments of the political strengths of each person, of courage to object to policy if felt necessary, and considerations of consequences of marked deviation from policy. In general, delegations follow orders, but usually accompanied by subtle, yet tactical recommendations if it appears on the floor that national policy should bend somewhat. Again, these observations must be tempered with the reality of all kinds of variations in relations betwen national policy and delegation positions, given the many and varied nations in organization assemblies.

At the U.S. Mission in Geneva, the delegation to the annual Commission on Human Rights meets for an hour each morning for a review of the day's agenda and the latest instruction cable from Washington, discussion of floor tactics, assignment usually by the delegation chair to delegation members to meet with some counterparts on other delegations, especially if voting on a resolution is to take place that day, and other issues in relating the delegation's responsibilities for furthering U.S. human rights policy at the commission. Morning and afternoon sessions take place, which we discuss in more detail later, and often there are receptions and other social functions in the late afternoon or evening. Cocktail diplomacy is important and information gleaned from such gatherings is reported at the next morning's briefing session at the mission.

The substance of U.S. policy at the commission in recent years deserves note. U.S. votes were among the very few against condemnation of Israel for human rights violations in the occupied territories and votes against, in most balloting, condemnations of right-wing states with human rights violations, such as El Salvador. A key U.S. policy in commission sessions was to end the mandate of the commission's special rapporteur for El Salvador, who is assigned to review the status of human rights in that nation and report back to the commission. U.S. resolutions on this proposal had little support and thus failed. In the last several years, the principal U.S. objective at the commission was seeking support for a resolution condemning Cuban violations of human rights as evidenced by the appointment of Cuban exile, Armando Valladares, as ambassador as head of the delegation. This effort gained some steam in 1985, 1986, and 1987, irrespective of brief appearances on the delegation by former U.N. ambassador (in New York), Jeane Kirkpatrick, and the then-current ambassador, General Vernon Walters. In 1988, the commission voted to appoint a six-person mission to Cuba to gather facts and at Cuba's invitation. The ensuing report did identify human rights violations, but not with the magnitude estimated by the United States. It is anticipated that the United States will take more positive initiatives in the commission in the years to come.[19]

Finally, any survey of the structure, process, and content of policy, especially in the domain of human rights, occasionally misses the heart of essential diplomacy—people. Officials in the national government, at the missions, and on the delegations come and go, but more important, have varying qualities that affect the quality of the state's role in the organization. Cox and Jacobson put it this way.

Among the personal attributes that might enhance the individual's power [and that of the state] in the international organization are his personal charisma, ideological legitimacy, administrative competence, expert knowledge, long association with (and understanding of) the organization, negotiating ability, and ability to persist in intransigence.[20]

Cox and Jacobson also cite the official's personal status outside the organization, including election to high office, wealth, influence of others, professional achievements, and political connections.

Kaufmann, a very experienced diplomat from The Netherlands and a veteran of U.N. assemblies and conferences, sets forth a formidable list of requirements and characteristics desired of conference diplomats. Traditional requirements include truthfulness and honesty, precision, calmness, good temper, patience, modesty, zeal, adaptability, loyalty, physical and mental endurance, speed, linguistic versatility, and courage. Characteristics include the silent, the lobbyist, the orator, the procedural specialist, and the old versus the new-timers. He also makes interesting comparisons between and among delegation members who are lawyers, economists, political scientists, historians, and parliamentarians.[21] The effective official or diplomat is often overlooked in textbooks and scholarly publications on international organizations. However, whether a diplomat for a member state or an international civil servant, the person can make all the difference in the world in demonstrable movement toward goals, whatever they may be.

NOTES

1. President Carter submitted the two principal U.N. covenants on human rights for Advice and Consent in 1979 because he considered human rights the keystone of his foreign policy. President Reagan took no similar initiative.

2. Address in Geneva, June 29, 1989, Department of State Bureau of Public Affairs, Publication No. 1191.

3. Theodor Meron, ed., *Human Rights in International Law: Legal and Policy Issues* (Oxford: Clarendon Press, 1984), p. 275.

4. See John Gerard Ruggie, "The United States and the United Nations: Toward a New Realism," and Donald J. Puchala, "American Interests and the United Nations," in Paul F. Diehl, ed., *The Politics of International Organizations* (Chicago: Dorsey Press, 1989).

5. Ian Brownlie, *Basic Documents on Human Rights* (Oxford: Clarendon Press, 1981), p. 320.

6. Security assistance is to be denied to nations "which engage in a consistent pattern of gross violations of internationally recognized human rights."

7. *Country Reports on Human Rights Practices for 1990*, submitted by the Department of State to the Senate Committee on Foreign Relations and the House Committee on Foreign Affairs, February 1991, 14th annual report.

8. *Country Reports*, 1990 submitted to the Congress by Richard Schifter, Assistant Secretary of State for Human Rights and Humanitarian Affairs since 1985, contains important information on U.S. human rights policy and the procedures for submission of country human rights reports from the field.

9. *Country Reports on Human Rights Practices for 1990*, p. 3. Ironically, the annual publication of *Country Reports* appears precisely at the beginning of the annual session of the Commission on Human Rights. There is no correlation whatsoever between the

human rights condemnations in *Country Reports* and the U.S. policy at the Commission meetings in Geneva.

10. Congressional opposition to the PLO participation in international organizations led to the General Assembly's moving the December 1988 Palestine debate from New York to Geneva. The most emotional and time-consuming issue on the agenda of the WHO in June 1989 was the P.L.O. candidacy for membership in the WHO, which under U.S. leadership rejected it. About 100 states recognize the PLO as representative of the Arab Republic of Palestine, which was declared by the PLO's parliament, the Palestine National Council, in November 1988.

11. See for instance the testimony of Edward Luck, President, UNA/USA, before the Subcommittee on Human Rights and International Organizations of the House Committee on Foreign Affairs, in support of U.S. voluntary contributions to international organizations, March 2, 7, and April 12, 1989, as well as his more extended statement.

12. Louis B. Sohn, *International Organization and Integration* (Boston: Martinus Nijhoff, 1986), p. 55. The representation abroad within the framework of international diplomatic law includes 142 embassies, 71 consultates general, 26 consulates, and 11 missions, including those to the United Nations in New York and organizations in Geneva.

13. Ludwik Dembinski, *The Modern Law of Diplomacy: External Missions of States and International Organizations* (Boston: Martinus Nijhoff, 1988), p. 239. See also the extensive diplomatic bibliography, p. 263.

14. See "Delegations and Permanent Missions and Their General Characteristics," in Johan Kaufman, *Conference Diplomacy: An Introductory Analysis*, 2d ed. (Boston: Martinus Nijhoff, 1988).

15. There were important organization policy differences between Presidents Carter and Reagan that were of concern to foreign service officers at the Geneva mission. But, as the saying goes (they said), the sailors remain in the rigging even though there is a new captain of the ship.

16. Roots for credential verification in the U.N. system is found in the preamble to the U.N. Charter, "our respective Governments, through representatives assembled in the City of San Francisco, who have exhibited their full powers found to be in good and due form."

17. "What Is a Delegation?" Kaufmann, *Conference Diplomacy*, p. 114.

18. In comparing names on the commission's list of delegates in the later 1980s, it is interesting to note the basic consistency of delegates from many other nations and especially from the Soviet Union, about 70 percent of whom returned each year.

19. See *Issues Before the General Assembly*, (43rd and 44th Sessions).

20. Robert Cox and Harold Jacobson, "The Framework for Inquiry," in Diehl, *The Politics of International Organizations*, p. 109.

21. Kaufmann, *Conference Diplomacy*, p. 133.

8

THE ORGANIZATION: HUMAN RIGHTS AS A CASE STUDY

The constitution of the organization sets forth its goals; purposes; provisions for membership; organs and their functions, powers, and procedures; and many other dimensions of organization responsibility, as well as articles on amendment and ratification. This is hardly a new observation. However, the constitution is the source and the well-spring for all that follows. Each organization has its genesis, purpose, history, and record, and while studies abound about international organizations, few have produced significant analysis of a comparative nature based on important organizations' constitutions and records.

This chapter does not presume even in a general way to examine the generic organization or any one organization. It follows the basic outline presented in the introduction to Part 2 to demonstrate the separate and interdependent dimensions of sovereign states and international organizations rooted in historic development. It also continues to focus on organization for international protection of human rights as one example of the international constitutional law and practice of international organizations.

We first appraise the assembly of members as the organ delegated by members to have central authority. We then turn to the U.N. Commission on Human Rights as a case study in the assembly of nation states. The commission's parent bodies, the Economic and Social Council and the General Assembly, are partial and then full membership organs, with the council having fifty-four members and the General Assembly being composed of all members. The commission is the appropriate membership assembly to study human rights, as it has a sound geographic diversity of blocs of states in its membership, a recognition by its parent organs of its authority in human rights law establishment and implementation, and the distinction of its achievements of the past and innovations for the present and future.

We then turn to the second major foundation of the organization, the international secretariat essential for the administration of international organizations. We appraised in Chapter 5 the international civil service in the context of organization authority and we now turn to the Centre of Human Rights in the U.N. secretariat as the administrative base and arm of the commission. The officials and staff of the Centre of Human Rights must, like all international civil servants, pledge themselves to advancing the goals of the organization and to serve in their individual and expert capacity and not as officials or under orders of their home state.

Third, we turn to a case study of how organizations discharge their responsibilities and examine the pursuit of international due process to provide a day in court for people who have been victims of human rights violations by states. We also review compliance by states of their obligations to live up to the human rights commitments in the treaties they ratify. Many organizations do not have due process and compliance responsibilities, especially basically service institutions such as the WHO. However, if it is true that patterns toward high organization authority point toward more compliance by states to the treaties they voluntarily ratify, then the lessons from due process and implementation for human rights become all the more important. Finally, we briefly appraise organizations' outputs or productivity, utilization of outputs by nations, and then a note on the annual cycle of organizations' continuing to pursue their tasks and goals.

This chapter is a microcosm of our study of international organizations. It delves into the evolution of the Commission on Human Rights and the Centre for Human Rights to demonstrate the historical growth of organization authority. The same is true for the three basic due process procedures for human rights. It is naturally concerned with the enhancement of shared and progressive well-being for the enjoyment of human rights, which is a normal condition and not one of privilege. We cannot share human rights protection unless we have equality under the law and equal protection of the law and we cannot progress toward enhanced levels of protection and due process without the law and procedures of international organizations. We continue to see the issues of high state authority in some contention with high organization authority. States do not like to be accused of human rights violations because those violations are state policy and revelations and condemnations adversely impact the credit rating of the state in the international marketplace. On the other hand, the progression toward enhanced and higher organization authority in human rights law, due process, and compliance is a matter of record, especially as we witness progression toward supra-organization authority under the European Convention on Human Rights.

Finally, we describe in this chapter the advent of additional new areas of international constitutional law. We survey international procedural law and international legislation under the aegis of the Commission on Human Rights and then turn to international administrative law managed by the international civil servants in the Centre for Human Rights. International due process is also a growing field of international law as carried out by the commission and the centre. The organization and the case study of organization activity in this final chapter continues to demonstrate the thrust of Chapter 1, "The Processes of History and Patterns of Mutuality," and of Chapter 2, "International Organizations Evolution, Growth and Maturity."

THE ASSEMBLY

The assembly of member states of the international organization is the principal locus of authority and policy for the organization with the exception of provisions in the constitution of the organization that delegate bottom line authority to other organs or organizations that do not have an assembly of member states. The function and powers of the General Assembly make this point clear for the United Nations and especially Article 10. Article 18 of the constitution of the WHO states that "the functions of the World Health Assembly shall be [first] to determine the policies of the organization." The two major exceptions to the General Assembly's authority in the United Nations are the "primary responsibility for the maintenance of international peace and security" for the Security Council in Article 24 of the U.N. Charter and the fact that the International Court of Justice is the "principal judicial organ of the United Nations" in Article 92. Constitutional interpretation, the November 1950 Uniting for Peace Resolution of the General Assembly and subsequent practice of assembly authority have mitigated the centrality of the Security Council in legal security authority. The separation of authority of the Court continues to be highly respected. Members of the World Bank and the IMF have annual meetings as the board of governors. However, basic authority in both organizations is vested in the twenty-one executive directors of each organization.

The history of each assembly of each organization should be carefully studied to understand its origins, constitutional provisions, and how it has evolved in terms of practice, interpretation, and productivity, among other dimensions of organization assemblies. The structure or organization of the assembly must be appraised along with the processes, patterns, and lore of assembly diplomacy as members seek to influence others toward desirable assembly resolutions and other decisions. The international law of the assembly includes procedural law of its administration of its affairs and other procedures under the authority of "procedures" in the organization's constitution. The law also includes international legislation, which is both the making of legislation in recommendations, resolutions, and decisions and the world's different forms of civilizations.

We appraise organization, diplomacy, and international law of the Commission on Human Rights as a case study of the assembly of the international organization. We fully realize that each assembly is unique and different and each has its own constitutional authority and special attributes, as is the case of any comparative study of the dimensions of international organizations.

Assembly Organization

As we have observed, the U. N. Commission on Human Rights was the only commission of the Economic and Social Council mentioned in Article 68 of the U. N. Charter. We noted its establishment in 1946, as well as that of its major affiliate, the Subcommission on Prevention of Discrimination and Protection of Minorities. It is one of the six functional commissions operating under the authority of the Security Council and undoubtedly the most important. Although its membership is elected by the council and it reports to the council, the commission is the basic and central U. N. organ in carrying out U. N. Charter goals and commitments to international protection of human rights.[1]

The Rules of Procedure of Functional Commissions of the Economic and Social Council provide the foundations for the organization of the commission. Its forty-three members are elected by the Economic and Social Council for three year terms although the permanent members of the Security Council never rotate off commission membership. There is a geographical allocation for membership that is consistent with geographical representation policy of the entire U. N. system of organizations. Eleven are elected from Africa, nine from Asia, eight from Latin America, ten from Western Europe, and "other" (meaning the United States and Canada), and five from the socialist bloc of states. "With a view to securing a balanced representation in the various fields covered by the Commission, the Secretary-General consults with Governments selected by the Council before the representatives are finally nominated by those Governments and confirmed by the Council."[2] During the commission's annual six-week session, its members often meet in their respective geographical groups for policy discussions of items on the commission's agenda.

The first meeting of the commission each February is addressed by the chairman of the previous year's session and usually by the Assistant Secretary General for Human Rights. The five major officers are then elected by acclamation. They include the chairman, three vice-chairmen, and a rapporteur. The chair is rotated so that a representative from the developing nations, from the Western nations, and from the socialist bloc may serve for one year in a three-year cycle. A provisional agenda, which was agreed upon at the last session of the previous year, is then placed before the commission under Rule 5 of the Rules of Commissions of the Economic and Social Council and then adopted. The third meeting is usually taken with the formal organization of the commission's work.[3]

Actually, the annual meeting from early February to mid-March is preceded by much preparatory work in association with officials from the Centre for Human Rights. This is organized by the commission's secretary, John Pace, and includes the organization of dozens of studies, reports from working groups, rapporteurs and other subsidiary bodies. Although the commission formally ends its session in mid-March, its work continues throughout the year with constant consultation between the secretary, an international civil servant, and commission officers as officials from states.

The chairman of the commission presides at the podium of the commission's large assembly hall at the Palais des Nations in Geneva and is usually joined by the assistant secretary general and the secretary of the commission. The three vice-chairmen sit at designated posts on the floor along with the delegations. The observer at commission sessions always finds it of great interest to survey the working relationships between officials from states and international civil servants organizing the work of the assembly. Often the international civil servants guide the deliberations and press forward with meeting the demands of the agenda, but they always realize that this is a gathering of representatives from states and take caution that their initiatives and diplomacy never offend the sensitivities and responsibilities of member states' officials.

In the formal establishment of the commission by the Economic and Social Council on June 21, 1946, provision was made in the constitutent resolution for the commission "to call in ad hoc working groups of nongovernmental experts in specialized fields or individual experts." The first such body was the Ad Hoc Working Group of Experts on Human Rights in South Africa established in 1967, as we have noted, and this group continues its important activities today.[4] This pioneering group was followed in 1970 by the Working Group on Situations— situations which may appear to reveal a consistent pattern of gross violations of human rights in the wording of Economic and Social Council Resolution 1503. Others have included the 1980 Working Group on Enforced or Involuntary Disappearances; the Working Group on Governmental Experts on the Right to Development, 1981; and working groups to draft conventions including the Convention on the Rights of the Child, which was approved by the General Assembly in 1989.

The Commission has also appointed special rapporteurs, representatives, and envoys to examine both human rights issues and violations in specific countries and with respect to themes or subject areas of human rights violations. The first special rapporteur was appointed by the commission in 1967 to review and report on apartheid and racial discrimination in Southern Africa. Other experts were named in rough chronological order to look into specific countries including Chile, Bolivia, El Salvador, Guatemala, Afghanistan, and Iran, while others were appointed to specific themes including Summary and Arbitrary Executions, Torture, and Religious Intolerance. We review the work of these experts later in this chapter under international procedural and due process of the law.

The Subcommission on Prevention of Discrimination is also governed by the Rules of Procedure of the Economic and Social Council and today meets for the month of August in Geneva. Members are nominated by governments, but serve as experts in human rights in a personal capacity and not under government instruction. Since 1982, each member of the subcommission is to be joined by an expert who may also serve as an alternate to the representative. The subcommittee elects its own chairman, three vice-chairmen, and rapporteur.[5]

The subcommittee was charged by the Economic and Social Council in the constitutive resolution of June 1946

1. to undertake studies . . . and to make recommendations to the Commission on Human Rights concerning the prevention of discrimination of any kind relating to human rights and fundamental freedoms and the protection of racial, national, religious, and linguistic minorities;

2. to perform any other function which may be entrusted to it by the Economic and Social Council or the Commission on Human Rights.

The subcommittee has made many important studies, taken a number of initiatives leading to recommendations to the commission, and was delegated the very important responsibility by the council in 1970 to be the prime agency for receiving complaints about consistent patterns of gross violations of human rights under the Resolution 1503 process. A Working Group on Communications was established by the subcommission in 1971 to receive, process, and consider for admissibility all communications with complaints under Economic and Social Council resolutions and especially Resolution 1503. The five members of this working group are members of the subcommission and selected on a geographically representative basis. There are also subcommission working groups on slavery, indigenous populations, and mental health detainees.

Tensions have always existed between the commission of sovereign state representation and the subcommission of experts. Over the decades, there have been subcommission members who voiced more their nation's interests than expert advice but, as we have seen, the commission of states has progressively placed more authority in members of the secretariat, the working groups, and rapporteurs, who are themselves experts. By the mid–1970s, the commission was evolving into an organ of increased authority while the subcommission tended to view itself as a think tank and was somewhat ignored by the commission, except for the important Resolution 1503 procedures. The relationship between the two bodies continues to be somewhat contentious.

Assembly Diplomacy

A member state seeks in assembly diplomacy an outcome as congenial as possible to the state's goals of any requirements for its security and well-being. Conversely, a member state will oppose or seek defeat of an outcome such as a resolution if it is far from being in harmony with the state's goals. The goals of international organizations for the most part are ones of shared security and shared and progressive well-being. In many and varied ways, outcomes of assembly diplomacy reflect compromise of the goals of states in the assembly and the organization's goals as set forth in its constitution.

Professor Kaufmann has prepared a list of steps in the preparation, discussion and adoption of a resolution by states in the assembly of an organization. They are as follows:

Preparation, Discussion and Adoption of a Resolution

1. Preparation of text
    a. In capitals (consultation with other governments)
    b. At conference site (consultation with other delegates and/or with secretariat)
2. Informal circulation of text
    a. Among selected delegations
    b. Among groups
    c. Possible revision of text
    d. Constitution of group of sponsors
3. Deposit of draft resolution with secretariat
4. Official conference circulation in working languages
5. Oral introduction by one or more sponsors
6. Debate (statements by other delegations)
7. Introductions of amendments
8. Debate on amendments
9. Sponsors decide whether amendments are acceptable
10. President may constitute negotiating group
11. Possible deposit of revised draft resolution
12. Debate on revised draft
13. Voting on sub-amendments
14. Voting on amendments
15. Explanations of vote
16. Voting on draft resolution
17. Explanations of vote

Note: This example assumes a certain amount of controversy and hence negotiation. Many draft resolutions are adopted without efforts to amend and without a vote.[6]

In the lexicon of most international organizations, an outcome or product of the assembly is a recommendation, a proposal to members for their taking individual action, a resolution that calls for action by the assembly or organization, a declaration or a policy statement that may include proposals for action and/or a decision that is a clarion call for action by the organization. Frequently, a proposal from an assembly will include several of these desired outcomes. In the legislative history of the Convention on the Rights of the Child adopted by the General Assembly in 1989, the Commission on Human Rights at the 55th meeting of its 43rd session in 1987 framed a proposal that concluded with three paragraphs, each one headed by a specific word "decides," "requests," or "recommends the following draft resolution to the Economic and Social Council."[7]

The process of assembly diplomacy is geared to getting to yes, a vote shipping off a specific outcome on to the Economic and Social Council and then the

General Assembly. It is an intense political process because states compete for an outcome generally favorable to their goals. Given the array of states in any U.N. assembly including the Commission on Human Rights, there obviously is a wide divergency in goals of security and well-being and requirements for those goals. Nevertheless, the productivity of the commission and other organizations in the U.N. system clearly demonstrate extensive compromise and then agreement in international laws and other outcomes for shared security and shared and progressive well-being. The extensive inventory of covenants of international human rights law at the end of this chapter is testimony to assembly diplomacy and "getting to yes."

Kaufmann's taxonomy of the steps in passing a resolution in the assembly such as the commission has little of the exciting dialectics of assembly diplomacy. However, such was not his intent in laying down the formal procedures. Chapter 10 of his important and expert study on conference diplomacy is entitled "Tactics, Instructions, Speeches and Conciliation in Conference."[8] This provides the student of assemblies of international organizations with keen insights on the congealing of member politics through diplomacy (and other means) to get to yes. Kaufmann's tactics include getting a proposal adopted or defeated if there is momentum toward not getting to yes. A case study the author examined at some length in Geneva in May 1989 was the U.S. leadership in defeating on the floor of the World Health Assembly a proposal to invite the PLO to membership in the WHO. In Kaufmann's words, the "intellectual [and other] arguments, promises, over-asking and under-offering and threats and warnings" were explicit and implicit in the lobbying and marshalling of support to defeat the proposal.

For all members, the policy marching orders or instructions come from the home government as we observed in the previous chapter. How much rope a mission and its delegation to the assembly is given varies from state to state. In general, state participants in conference diplomacy give their diplomats at the assembly considerable rope if they have served as delegates for many years and have a high level of expertise in the subject matter, neither of which is generally true of the U.S. representation at the Commission on Human Rights. The rope gets shorter for the democracies, which must heed the policy proposals of domestic sources of policy and especially interest groups devoted to the specific topics before the assembly. The United States as we have seen also has the interests of Congress and its constituencies as inputs into instructions. Washington sets the broad human rights strategy but mission officials do say they have much area for logistical maneuvers and tactics in assembly diplomacy. Again, the broad umbrella for Washington and its representation in Geneva on human rights or any other policy area is assembly output that is as congenial as possible to the U.S. goals of security and well-being.

As in all political bodies, the power of the actors has a direct correlation with the assembly's political processes. The United States and the Soviet Union in U.N. assemblies are thus key actors for obvious reasons, followed by their respective blocs of allies and friends. Any study of bloc voting in international assemblies demonstrates this construction of power and the diplomatic logistics in marshalling for the vote on a resolution or decision.[9] A review of the size of delegations to the annual sessions of the Commission on Human Rights is one way to quantify the power sought by the superpowers and then the states with high level power such as U.S. allies in Western Europe and Japan. Another factor is the very small delegations from most developing nations with only one or two representatives and scarce resources at their missions and in home states to provide seasoned diplomats for service in missions and on delegations. However, each member has one vote and thus their favor is curried most actively by the states with more power.

The politics and assembly diplomacy take place in the working groups and other smaller gatherings of delegates, on the floor of the assembly, with much scurrying around prior to taking votes or motions for adoptions of resolutions, in the delegates' lounges, at receptions given by missions and other social gatherings, or cocktail diplomacy, and in the bistros of New York and Geneva where diplomats can meet and talk. As we observed in appraising Article 1, paragraph 4, of the U.N. Charter—the United Nations as a place to harmonize interests— the annual gathering of representatives of states provides even those hostile to each other to meet and talk on a neutral ground with no fear of recrimination. Add to all of this the role of the international civil servants. They provide the manpower for assembly diplomacy, often are asked to serve as mediators between and among delegations, take initiatives on the wording of resolutions if and when the opportunity arises, possess the institutional memory of the assembly and organization, and carry on the work of the organization after the assembly brings its annual sessions to a conclusion. Organizations are those of sovereign states but, as we have observed many times, their central machinery is managed by international civil servants who play indispensible roles in translating assembly outputs to international policy and law. Finally, there are the many international nongovernmental organizations active in the assembly corridors, at briefing sessions, at other meetings, and in sessions with delegations to press the cause of their interests. Under the Rules of the Commissions of the Economic and Social Council, they may even speak on the floor of the Commission of Human Rights and many are considered vital sources of information and influence, such as Amnesty International.[10]

International Law

The assembly of the organization constantly adds to the body of treaty law, customary international law, principles as law, and a steady expansion on the sources of international law as set forth in Article 38 of the covenant of the International Court of Justice. The assembly itself has become a source and may be by amendment of the statute recognized as a significant source of international law. We demonstrate in this Chapter 5 important areas of assembly-generated international law. We now turn to international procedural law and then to international legislation. Then we appraise international administrative law with particular emphasis on the managerial responsibilities of the U.N. Centre for Human Rights. Finally, we view the role of both the Commission on Human Rights and affiliated agencies it helped to create and also the Centre in the rapidly growing area of international due process law. All of this is in addition to the fairly new bodies of international law, such as international criminal law.

International Procedural Law

This area of law deals with procedures of assemblies and other organs of organizations established by states. Constitutions of organizations as we have observed include specific articles dealing with procedures. "Procedure" for the General Assembly is to be found in Articles 20, 21, and 22 of the U.N. Charter. Articles 28 through 32 are Security Council procedural law, Articles 68 through 72 for the Economic and Social Council, and Articles 90 and 91 as "procedure" for the Trusteeship Council. Chapter 3 of the Statute of the International Court is entitled "Procedure." Second, constitutions of organizations as we have observed include provisions for the organs to establish their own rules of procedure that are not only written rules of law, but also customary law that constantly accumulates with each annual assembly as legal guidelines for the deliberations of the assemblies and other organs. Third, procedures include constitution provisions for voting, such as Article 18 of the Charter for the General Assembly and financial arrangements in Article 19.

International procedural law in the domain of human rights is impressive. First, the U.N. Charter authorizes the Economic and Social Council in Article 72, paragraph 1, to "adopt its own rules of procedure." Article 68 provides for the council to establish commissions "for the promotion of human rights" among other bodies, and, with the establishment of the Commission on Human Rights, the council drew up Rules of Procedure for Functional Commissions of the Economic and Social Council so that these bodies might have their own procedural law. The Subcommission on Prevention of Discrimination and Protection of Minorities was established by the Council in June 1946. As a subsidiary body of the commission, it is bound by the Rules of Procedure for Functional Commissions under Rule 24.

Chapter 5 of the commission's Rules of Procedure permits the commissions to organize committees and working groups with experts serving in their personal capacity to be appointed by the commission chairman and with approval of the commission. The many working groups and special experts named by both the commission and subcommission find legal status in this chapter. The progression continues. Article 62, paragraph 3, of the U.N. Charter states that the council may prepare draft conventions for submission to the General Assembly. We turn to international legislation shortly to amplify on that provision. One of the conventions produced by the Commission on Human Rights, presented to the council, and approved by the General Assembly in 1966 is the International Covenant of Civil and Political Rights. This covenant authorizes under Part 4, and especially Article 28, the establishment of a Human Rights Committee as part of the international due process law of the threaty. Article 39, paragraph 2, enables the committee to set up its rules of procedure. Further, the committee may appoint in Article 42 a Conciliation Commission, which is authorized to write its rules of procedure in paragraph 3 of that article.

Procedural law for human rights is to be found in the other six "treaty bodies" created by human rights treaties such as the Human Rights Committee of the Civil and Political Covenant. Procedures for the Commission on Human Rights constantly expand with the establishment of due process mechanisms and personal, much of which stems from the 1970 Procedure for Dealing with Communications Relating to Violations of Human Rights, the famous Resolution 1503. The many important studies undertaken by the subcommission of the commission are important procedures that have generated much subsequent commission policy.[11] The extensive activity of officers of the Commission on Human Rights and staff from the Centre on Human Rights prepares for the annual meeting of the commission and for its extensive follow-up activity in moving commission output on to the Economic and Social Council and the fall session of the General Assembly. Then the February opening of the commission is practically at hand in the annual cycle of the commission's work and compliance with procedural law, which is its mandate from the Council and which it also generates. Finally, if we add the international procedural law of organizations in economics and trade, such as the World Bank and GATT, procedural law in all the specialized agencies and their suborgans, the total body of this area of law is enormous and constantly growing.[12]

International Legislation

Assemblies of all international organizations churn out recommendations, resolutions, declarations, and decisions that comprise the collectivity of the organizations policies for implementation around the world. Many, as we noted in the case study of the IMO at the end of Chapter 3, have provisions for producing conventions or the international laws for their specific responsibilities. We saw in Chapter 2 that even before its creation in 1919, the ILO evolved out of proposals to establish an organization that could produce its international laws. The ILO since 1919 has, through its conference or annual assembly of its members, produced through assembly diplomacy about 170 conventions, which collectively is an enormous body of international labor law. The body of international human rights law we set forth at the end of this chapter has been produced in large part by the Commission on Human Rights, a phenomenon that never could have been foreseen in its creation in 1946.

The goal of international legislation for the commission is primarily to produce international human rights laws that signatories to the treaties will domesticate into their own municipal law. As such, commission legislation is high organization authority because not only are parties to treaties called upon to domesticate the rules, but also to report to and comply with the rules of the treaty bodies such as the Human Rights Committee under the International Covenant of Civil and Political Rights. This is more than the organization-partnership relationship; it does apply to commission members such as the United States that have not ratified most of the human rights covenants. It is also not supra-organization authority as exemplified by the European Convention on Human Rights.

We have observed before the flow from words in speeches to arduous negotiations for standards such as the 1948 Declaration of Human Rights and then to the two international covenants on human rights of 1966, which have then inspired further treaties in elaboration on the basic laws of civil, political, economic, social, and cultural rights of those two historic treaties. We also traced the progression of right to life through to the Convention Against Torture of 1984 and beyond. We now turn to the legislative history of the 1989 Convention on the Rights of the Child as a case study of assembly diplomacy producing international human rights law.

The forty-fifth session of the Commission on Human Rights in 1989 completed its years of negotiation of the final draft of the Convention on the Rights of the Child and this will provide us with a case study of international legislation. We are all familiar with Oliver Twist and the writings of Charles Dickens and others on the exploitation and tribulations of children, especially those trapped in poverty. This led in part to step-by-step legislation in many nations providing for various kinds of safeguards to protect children, especially those in the factories and other workplaces. Protective legislation moved to international laws under conventions produced by the ILO after its inception in 1919, which was a global stimulus for additional national legislation. Furthermore, the League of Nations' Assembly produced its own Declaration of the Rights of the Child in 1924.

The 1948 Universal Declaration of Human Rights stated in Article 25 that "Motherhood and childhood are entitled to special care and assistance" and certainly the "everyone" in about all the articles of the Declaration included children. In the same year, the American (Latin America) Declaration of the Rights and Duties of Man in Articles 7 and 30 stated respectively that "all children shall have the right to special protection, care and aid" and "it is the duty of every person to aid, support, educate and protect his minor children." These declarations flowed into the international law of the 1969 American Covenant and Articles 17 and 19 with "every minor child [having] the right to measures of protection." The 1966 International Covenant on Civic and Political Rights has extensive provisions for children in Article 24.

The other principal U.N. Covenant on Economic, Social and Cultural Rights has detailed provisions in Article 10. The European Social Charter of 1961 has the most extensive coverage of rights and protection of children of any of these covenants and Article 18 of the African Charter on Human Peoples' Rights declares that the "State shall . . . ensure the protection of the rights of the women and the child as stipulated in international declarations and conventions."

With a view that further international declarations leading to law are necessary, the General Assembly adopted the "Declaration of the Child" in 1959.[13] In

1978, the Economic and Social Council called on its Commission on Human Rights to begin to draft a convention, which it did in 1979. In the same year, the subcommission also placed on its annual agenda the issue of exploitation of child labor.[14] The commission began negotiations on the basis of a draft treaty submitted by Poland, which continued throughout the 1980s. Most of the development of the covenant took place in the Working Group on the Rights of the Child. Many delegations submitted draft provisions as did more than fifty nongovernmental organizations, especially those with specific interests in the welfare and protection of children. UNICEF made many contributions and was extensively consulted.

Each year since 1978, the General Assembly and the Economic and Social Council have passed resolutions that call on the commission to work diligently and that negotiations for the convention had a very high priority. Each year the commission itself has voted on a decision to continue and accelerate its work, which basically was completed in 1988. The convention finally received the approval of the Commission at its forty-fifth session in 1989.

All outputs of the commission are forwarded to its parent body, the Economic and Social Council, for review and approval and then to the General Assembly in New York. They are first processed by the Assembly's Third Committee (Social, Humanitarian, and Cultural) composed of all members of the United Nations. However, the annual report of the Special Committee to Investigate Israel Practices Affecting Human Rights of the Population of the Occupied Territories goes to the Special Political Committee for consideration. Then this output goes on to plenary sessions of the Assembly. Because the Commission is viewed as the heart and source of the evolution of international human rights law, its output is rarely changed or amended by these higher stages of U.N. organization.[15] Thus the Convention on the Rights of the Child was approved by the General Assembly in November 1989 after ten years of negotiations and conference diplomacy and is now open for adoption by states. It goes into force upon the ratification of twenty states as provided for in the convention. Such is the legislative history of the Convention on the Rights of the Child.[16]

Assembly diplomacy has many concerns in devising and orchestrating the words that go into outputs from recommendations to conventions. There is some feeling that the commission has engaged in too much standard setting and convention formulation. The forty-fifth session in 1989 reported that it was working on three more draft conventions: freedom of expression and assembly, rights of minorities, and rights of the medically handicapped. If these drafts evolve into conventions and international law, they, like those before, place many obligations on states signing on to the conventions, as was and is the case with the Convention of the Rights of the Child. Do the contents and substance lend themselves for domestication into municipal law by treaty adherents? The United States has a difficult time with domestication for some of the reasons concerning high state authority we explored in Chapter 5. It is fairly comfortable with the U.N. conventions it has ratified, including genocide and torture. It is not uncomfortable with the U.N. Covenant on Civil and Political Rights, a "first generation" set of rights rooted in the constitutional history of the democratic nations, even though it has not ratified this covenant. It is not supportive of the Covenant of Economic, Social, and Cultural Rights, those of the "second generation of twentieth century liberalism and high state activity including regulation." It definitely is not embracing the third generation of collective rights such as those of the New International Economic Order and especially the "Right to Development," which has been pecking at the Commission for a number of years.[17] In brief, can these standards as they evolve into international law really be domesticated in a manner that is acceptable as viable municipal law of human rights?[18]

Further, the large body of international human rights treaties establish their own treaty bodies that have authority to monitor states' adherence to the treaties, are the recipients of signatories' reporting on their progress under the specific treaty, and may be involved in compliance or enforcement under international due process to which we turn shortly. The reporting process, in particular, places many administrative burdens on states, many of which do not have the resources or expertise to participate in this international procedural law. Others point out that many of the treaties lack the precision required by any definition of law because they are the product of an assembly of sovereign states.

ADMINISTRATION OF INTERNATIONAL ORGANIZATIONS

International civil servants are charged with the administration of international organizations within the framework of authority conferred to them by assemblies of international organizations. It is their responsibility to strive for cooperation in state-organization partnership, high organization authority in delegated areas, and in supra-organization authority if such is their mandate. In the longer run, they and officials from states seek shared security and shared and progressive well-being in a cooperative endeavor to enhance both goals of the organization as set forth in its constitution and a blending of state goals into organization goals as the long term objective. In the wording of Article 1, paragraph 4, of the U.N. Charter, a major purpose of the organization is "to be a centre for harmonizing the actions of nations" in the attainment of the goals set forth in the first three paragraphs of this article, shared or collective security, and shared and progressive well-being.

Such is the ideal. The reality is that such exercise of high state authority for reasons we cited in Chapter 5 renders even the state-organization partnership role difficult. But the progression toward "harmonizing the actions of states" has been remarkable in the forty-five years of the U.N. organizations and even more so in high organization and supra-organization authority, such as is found in the EC and the European organs for protection of human rights.

The central responsibility for organization administration falls on the chief executive officer, especially the secretary general of the United Nations and member states mandate to him or her in Chapter 15 of the U.N. Charter. In the EC, the commission and the international bureaucracy of the EC have very high levels of authority in making and implementing decisions on policy that become community law and in other areas of organization administration such as personnel, finance, organization of meetings of member states, administration of the laws of the EC, and relations with member states, nonmember states, and all kinds of international organizations. The constitutional foundations for management in organizations' constitutions such as Chapter 15 of the U.N. Charter, the rules and norms emanating from the wording of the constitutions, the accumulations of written mandates to organization management and civil servants, precedents, court decisions dealing with managerial issues and responsibilities all are part of the ever-growing body of international administrative law.[19]

International administration is therefore grounded in international administrative law, which is not to be found in any one place, but rather in all the sources cited above. The managers are the international civil servants who, as we have earlier observed, are legally committed to serving the organization and its goals, not their national states or any others. It is far beyond the scope of this study to explore the many dimensions of international management and administrative law. It is, however, appropriate to return to our case study of international human rights and thus the administrative law of this segment of the United Nations.

The United Nations is a political organization of member states and its primary organ of human rights responsibilities is the forty-three–member commission, although all policy and legislation ultimately has to be the product of General Assembly resolutions. Thus the organization chart of the United Nations generally shows organs and suborgans, such as the Economic and Social Council and the Commission on Human Rights. In tandem with the members' organs is a bureaucratic organizational chart of the secretariat of the United Nations with offices and officials corresponding to the organs and suborgans. For human rights, the members' organs are the Economic and Social Council and the Commission on Human Rights, while the bureaucracy has corresponding bureaucratic titles for the Council and its component parts, and then the Centre for Human Rights in Geneva to serve with the commission, subcommission, and other human rights bodies, such as the Human Rights Committee established by the 1966 Covenant on Civil and Political Rights.

The reader may question the "serve with" in the previous sentence. Are not the international civil servants just that—servants of member states of the political organization of sovereign states? A pure model of high state authority would leave out the "with" while the partnership might approve of the "with," providing it is made clear that member states individually or collectively can leave the partnership—as the United States currently is doing with UNESCO. The international bureaucrats in Brussels in some areas serve "over" the members and so the model and pattern will vary in time, place, and organization. It is a delicate situation for analysis in scholarship and in the real world, say on the floor of the Commission on Human Rights each year in Geneva. A practiced observer can often detect the civil servant as a prime mover and/or a policy piper for some member states to follow. Key officials in the Centre for Human Rights have the longevity, experience, credibility, and institutional memory that delegations of states lack. Delegations and their members come and go, but the international civil servants remain. Further, assemblies of members states come and go each year, but the other eleven months find the international bureaucrats in charge.

This, of course, is not entirely accurate because most international organizations have executive or governing boards that remain at the seat of the organization to work with the bureaucracy in carrying out the mandates and resolutions of the assemblies of member states. The United Nations has no such executive board. The IMO, which we studied in Chapter 2, has an executive council of thirty-two members, the ILO a governing body of fifty-six, GATT a consultative group of eighteen, and the IAEA a board of governors of thirty-five. However, these quasi-executive agencies of member states—usually made up of officials intelligent in the goals and policies of the organization—meet at best three times a year, and many are rotated off the board after three years to provide opportunities for new representatives. Again, the international secretariat remains with its experience, credibility, and recognition in areas reached by the organization throught the world, and especially institutional memory or an in-depth knowledge of how the organization evolved, problems and crises, successes and failures, and relating the past experiences to the shaping of policy for today and tomorrow.[20]

We have observed in Chapter 5 some issues relating to the administration of the U.N. system within the context of the United States demonstrating high state authority in using the lever of contributions to bring about administrative change. We have cited many problems and issues of international organization administration in Chapter 5 and are aware of bureaucratic problems in any international organization. Pitt and Weiss in their excellent study marshall two case studies of severe problems in the management of UNCTAD and UNESCO. Their concluding chapter is entitled, "The United Nations: Unhappy Family," by Paul Streeten. Perfection, or near-perfection, is not an attribute of any bureaucracy, whether an international organization, the Commonwealth of Massachusetts, or a university. However, if the goals and missions of organizations are accepted by member governments as necessary and vital to their own goals of security and well-being, the policy choices and options are to face the problems and issues and correct them as much as possible. The solution is not the reversal of the progression of international constitutional law to make this small planet a better place.

It is a better place because of the administration of the enhancement of human rights and fundamental freedoms. Much of this good report is due to the international civil servants with the mandate to implement the policy and laws of the commission, the council, and the assembly of member states.

Evolution of International Administration of Human Rights Policy and Law

The central administrative organ for human rights is the Centre for Human Rights in Geneva with a small office at the U.N. headquarters in New York. Like all other U.N. bureaucracies, the Centre functions under the authority of the secretary general, who is the "chief administrative officer" of the organization in Article 97 of the U.N. Charter. Under Article 98, the "Secretary-General shall act in that capacity in all meetings of the . . . Economic and Social Council," along with the other major organs. Clearly, the secretary-general is in charge of international administration of human rights law, which basically is under the authority of the council. Article 100, paragraph 2, states that "Each member of the United Nations undertakes to respect the exclusively international character of the responsibilities of the Secretary-General and the staff." The General Assembly in 1979 stressed the important role of the Secretary-General in "taking effective action . . . against mass and flagrant violations of human rights." The Commission on Human Rights in 1980 "requested the Secretary-General to continue and intensify the good offices envisaged in the Charter of the United Nations in the field of human rights."[21] Thus the secretary-general and especially Secretary-General Javier Perez de Cuellar, has been mandated and has taken on increased responsibilities in the international administration of human rights policy and law.

At the beginning in 1946, the new Division of Human Rights was under the aegis of the Department of Social Affairs in the U.N. bureaucracy. The department was subsequently moved on the organization chart to operate under the Office of the Under Secretary-General for Special Political Affairs and then the Office of the Under Secretary-General for Political and General Assembly Affairs. Momentum between 1979 and 1982 for a more solid structure and with General Assembly backing led the secretary-general to establish the current Centre for Human Rights in 1982. In 1986, a further structural change took place with the Centre now coming under the administration of the new Under Secretary-General for Human Rights, Jan Martenson, who also is the Director-General of the U.N. office in Geneva. The combining of these two high posts reflects a distinct move toward high organization authority for the administration of human rights policy and law with a consolidation in Geneva of both member states assembly, the Commission on Human Rights, and the accompanying administrative operations

Organization of the Centre for Human Rights

Under the authority of the Secretary-General of the United Nations, the Under Secretary-General for Human Rights adminsters the central secretariat and international civil service for human rights. He or she is assisted by a Deputy

Director, an Executive Assistant, an adminsitrative officer, and administrative assistant. The six sections of the Centre with their respective chiefs and staff are as follows.

International Instruments Section

Carries out functions and responsibilities relating to the implementation of international human rights treaties, such as the International Covenant on Civil and Political Rights; the International Covenant on Economic, Social, and Cultural Rights; the International Convention on the Elimination of All Forms of Racial Discrimination; the International Convention on the Suppression and Punishment of the Crime of Apartheid; and the Convention Against Torture and Other Cruel, Inhuman, or Degrading Treatment or Punishment. Provides technical and substantive servicing for the human rights supervisory organs functioning under the above-mentioned international instruments; provides technical and substantive servicing for the meetings of states' parties to the above-mentioned international instruments.

Communications Section

Processes communications concerning allegations of violations of human rights under existing confidential procedures, such as the procedure governed under Economic and Social Council Resolutions 728 F(XXVIII) and 1503 (XLVIII); the Optional Protocol to the International Covenant on Civil and Political Rights; Article 14 of the International Convention on the Elimination of All Forms of Racial Discrimination; and Article 22 of the Convention Against Torture.

Services the various human rights organs concerned with the implementation of the above-mentioned procedures, including the Commission on Human Rights and its Working Group on Situations; the Subcommission on Prevention of Discrimination and Protection of Minorities and its Working Group on Communications; the Human Rights Committee and its Working Group on Communications; the Committee on the Elimination of Racial Discrimination; and the Committee Against Torture.

Provides secretariat services for specific direct contact missions authorized by the Commission on Human Rights.

Special Procedures Section

Provides substantive services to ad hoc or extraconventional activities decided upon by the General Assembly, the Economic and Social Council, and the Commission on Human Rights consisting of special or ad hoc working groups and/or special rapporteurs, representatives, or other nominees mandated in regard to situations of human rights in particular countries or in regard to specific questions.

Research, Studies, and Prevention of Discrimination Section

Prepares studies and reports on the promotion and protection of human rights requested by human rights organs; assists in the drafting of international instruments on human rights being discussed by human rights organs; services the Subcommission on Prevention of Discrimination and Protection of Minorities and pre-sessional Working Groups on Slavery-Like Practices and on Indigenous Populations established by it to deal with those questions. Prepares studies and reports on the Prevention of Discrimination and the Protection of Minorities; carries out work on slavery and studies on discrimination, minorities, indigenous populations, rights of detainees, human rights in states of emergencies and economic, social and cultural rights; implements the program for the Second Decade of Action to combat Racism and Racial Discrimination; carries out research, analyses reports from governments and prepares studies relevant to the decade and maintains coordination with governments, intergovernmental organizations, the specialized agencies, nongovernmental organizations, and others concerned.

Advisory Services Section

Administers the program of advisory services and technical assistance in the field of human rights; prepares international seminars and training courses in all regions of the world on major human rights questions; supervises the yearly program of fellowships in the field of human rights for governmental offices dealing with specific issues of human rights; supervises the yearly program of internship for graduate students; responsible for the program of promoting regional institutions for the promotion and protection of human rights; maintains reference library of the Centre for Human Rights.

External Relations, Publications and Documentation Section

Responsible for ensuring the effective functioning of the external relations aspects of U.N. human rights programs and policies, liaises with nongovernmental organizations, academic and research institutions, press and national institutions, and manages public affairs and public relations; arranges for the publication of the Yearbook on Human Rights and other publications in the field of human rights; supervises, follows up, and coordinates the handling of documentation for the Centre and responds to general inquiries concerning the activity of the United Nations in the field of human rights; deals with public inquiries and the informational activities of the Centre for Human Rights concerning the U.N. human rights program.[22]

International Administrative Procedures and Law

Under the office of the Under Secretary-General, international civil servants assigned to human rights responsibilities

provide secretariat services required by the Third Committee of the General Assembly, the Second Social Committee of the Economic and Social Council, and their subsidiary bodies when they deal with human rights questions. [They] provide the secretariat services required by the Commission on Human Rights, the Subcommission, and their subsidiary bodies. [They also] provide the secretariat services required by international conferences and seminars in the field of human rights.[23]

Further, they also staff the treaty bodies of international covenants such as the Human Rights Committee under the aegis of the Covenant on Civil and Political Rights. In addition, the Centre staff provides services to the working groups of the commission and the subcommission and in particular deals with the inflow of urgent communications and crises situations to which no member state representative can respond, but only the international civil servant at his or her post. Centre officials service in the New York office during the annual sessions of the General Assembly, steer commission resolutions adopted by the Security Council through General Assembly committees and assembly diplomacy, and work intensely with international nongovernmental organizations and a collection of experts and observers all concerned with international human rights legislation. All of this is international administrative law and policy and it is a substantial and impressive undertaking.

At its 47th session in 1991, the commission devoted many hours and much discussion to an old problem—the assembly of nations in the international organization making decisions, passing resolutions, and enacting policy which it expects the secretariat of the organization to implement without any adequate measure of the total amount of administration and output required to translate orders of nations into concrete policy by the international civil service. However, the commission members in the role of assembly of sovereign states recognized the burden they asked the Centre on Human Rights to undertake with its limitations of staff, financing, and clarity of orders given by nations to their international staff. Servicing the commission and bearing responsibility for seeing commission decisions carried out, servicing all the staff, experts, and legal bodies responsible for international human rights due process, engaging in fact-finding throughout the world, and providing information and education for humans to understand and enjoy their rights among other delegated tasks and duties have overloaded the Centre and staff. Although the commission and the Centre continue to seek partial solutions to this long-standing problem, the issue of the efficiency of international administrative law and productivity requires intense consideration and solutions in the 1990s.

INTERNATIONAL DUE PROCESS

International due process of the law for protection of human rights—if that protection is not upheld within or by a sovereign state—began with the advent of international humanitarian law and the International Committee of the Red Cross in 1863 and 1984. It was broadened under procedures and guarantees for minorities and people in the mandated territories under the League of Nations, as we have observed, as well as significant processes for rights of labor in the

ILO. The Nuremburg charter, indictment, and trials added to the expanding scope of international due process but the provisions in the 1948 Universal Declaration of Human Rights consolidated international due process, especially in Articles 7 through 12, which essentially internationalized the basic features of due process in the constitutional systems of many states. These rights then flowed into concrete international law in the Civil and Political Rights Covenant of 1966 with the guarantee of rights and then due process procedures at the international level in Part 4. The same is the case with the Economic and Social Covenant for economic and social rights and international due process procedures also in Part 4. All treaties guaranteeing human rights contain due process procedures for protecting and enriching those rights irrespective of the realities of human rights violations in all areas of the world.

In our study of international due process, we turn first to "Track One," or the Resolution 1503 procedures under the aegis of the Commission on Human Rights and its Subcommittee on Prevention of Discrimination and Protection of Minorities. Then we appraise "Track Two," due process under the treaty bodies such as the Human Rights Committee under the Covenant on Civil and Political Rights. We then turn to "Track Three," due process of "extra-convention" procedures by working groups and experts appointed by and responsible to the Commission on Human Rights. State compliance to the requirements of protection of rights and due process is appraised, followed by an overview of this essential component of international human rights law.

Track One: Resolution 1503 Due Process

The Resolution 1503 procedure of international rights due process was appraised within the context of its evolution earlier in Chapter 6. From its inception in 1970, Resolution 1503 has constantly expanded, has generated its champions and critics, but has also brought forth new and unprecedented mechanisms for international due process, which we study in an upcoming section.

Communications

Hundreds of thousands of communications containing allegations of gross violations of human rights pour into the Centre for Human Rights in Geneva each year.[24] They take many forms and arrive in varied stages of literacy. They come from individuals as well as nongovernmental organizations, such as Amnesty International, on behalf of victims unable to send their own communications. The NGO communications are particularly important because they usually attest to direct and reliable evidence of a "consistent pattern of gross and reliably attested violations of human rights" as required by Resolution 1503.

Screening for Admissibility

Centre staff examine the communications for "admissibility" to make certain they are "reliably attested." The violations must be by a specific government and not by nongovernmental actors. The complaint is not admissible if it is anonomous, vague, contains abusive language, or is obviously politically motivated. There must be evidence that domestic remedies were sought and exhausted to qualify for international due process. It is not always an easy task to judge the evidence accompanying the complaint and decisions must be made to see whether the communication fits into a "consistent pattern" and is not just an ad hoc complaint.

Processing of Complaints

Communications are sent to the Communications Section of the Centre for Human Rights at the Palace of Nations in Geneva. The process now becomes fully confidential and closed to any public scrutiny or media examination. Each communication is readied by a staff of about fifteen people, usually aided by interns. Under the direction and policy of the section chief, they are reviewed carefully, summarized, and placed on cards with the concise information. All communications are filed, even those that are, as one staff member put it, "off the wall." Form letters are usually sent to the author that acknowledge receipt of the communication and a statement as to why or why not the communication will be further processed. All of this takes much time with delays in processing. Response is made more difficult because the office may receive complaints under other treaties and their procedures. Financial constraints, thus far, have not enabled the Centre to put this process on computers, which would vastly reduce delays, avoid many duplications, and provide for much more orderly screening.

Under the guidance of the section chief, communications that are genuinely admissible according to the criteria outlined above proceed to the subcommission and to a five-person working group. Actually only a fraction of the original batch of communications proceed in this manner and these are very well documented and appear to comprise a "consistent pattern." The working group conducts its review directly before the annual meeting of the subcommission each August and then sifts the group of communications before passing them on to the subcommission. In the meantime, governments alleged to have committed violations of human rights are initially contacted to gather whatever response they would like to submit.

The subcommission then submits its fully processed ten to twenty communications to the Commission on Human Rights that in its judgment comprise a solid and reliable body of complaints. Another working committee of five commission members makes still another examination before they are taken up in a very confidential set of sessions by the commission. It is at this point that the actual processing of complaints comes to an end as the commission now makes determinations on specific courses of action concerning states provisionally found to be a violation of their responsibilities for protecting the human rights of those admitting "reliably attested" communications.

Dialogue with Governments

By the mid-1980s, the complaints fall into two categories: those patterns of gross violations by specific governments, and those patterns that cluster around a particular theme, such as enforced or involuntary disappearances as the result of policy by several governments. A commission Working Group on Communications reviews the file of each category and the responses of governments that have been contacted requesting responses to the allegations of violations. The working group conveys recommendations on options for commission action, again in confidence.

In approaching decisions on action with respect to the targeted government, the closed commission discussion and debate is often intense and confrontational due to political interests and defenses with respect to accusations of governments that have friends on the commission. As always, human rights violations are committed by governments and accusations are found to be very offensive by targeted governments. Representatives of such nations are invited orally to respond to the allegations although the authors of communications are not.

The commission may, after the discussion of specific cases, decide to proceed to further on the basis of incomplete information, or because the accused government has successfully persuaded the commission that the complaint is not part of a pattern, or that the substance of the complaint has been addressed and eliminated. The commission may also decide that the complaint may require a continuation of monitoring of the situation, and thus it decides to table the issue for the particular year. The commission may decide to conduct a further thorough study of the specific case—a targeted country or the "theme"—or to make a thorough investigation of the situation in the target nation, which requires approval by that nation of such a process. Furthermore, as this process evolved in the 1980s, the commission may decide to establish a special working group of its members or a special rapporteur or representative to advance the due process and report back to the commission. This option we may term "extra-convention law" or Track Three of due process procedures. This procedure is not based on Resolution 1503 or specific conventions such as the Convention on Civil and Political Rights and represents a further evolution of due process to which we will turn shortly.

Resolution 1503 is yet another case study of member state-organization relationship. Many targeted governments take the high state authority position in denying allegations, claiming the communications never should have been admitted for screening, or that communication information is now out of date. Another position is that national security and public order have a higher priority over protection of human rights if the government can make a case for the security defense. A milder response, but yet high state authority, is to cooperate formally with the commission but stretch out the process as long as possible to avoid any public condemnation. Paraguay has been monitored by the commission for about ten years, but there has been no public report. The accused state may choose to dazzle commission members or other officials invited to enter the state for investigation purposes and seek to smooth and sooth with the aim of demonstrating that nothing is wrong. However, the Resolution 1503 process increasingly produces positive responses from targeted states that almost always do not hide under the security blanket of domestic jurisdiction in Article 2, paragraph 7, of the U.N. Charter. Targeted states earnestly seek to avoid any public revelation of commission investigations, work hard to negotiate any written statement with respect to their situation, and generally cooperate with the commission and Resolution 1503 procedures to avoid losing face before the international community.

The entire Resolution 1503 process thus far is confidential. The commission did decide in 1978, after prodding from a number of governments, to at least announce the names of states on its list of investigations, either those it continues to probe and monitor and those it had removed from its list. The few publicly announced states grew to a list of forty-four targeted states in 1988. Because of confidentiality, we do not have hard data on the degrees of success or failure for due process under Resolution 1503 but if the procedures were not producing significant results, it still would not be in operation in the early 1990s. Some argue there is too much confidentiality and that there should be more "transparency" or openness of the process. This would produce more public understanding of the process and thus would enhance education about avenues for the redress of human rights violations. Others contend that confidentiality is essential to governments complying with the procedures and that much can be accomplished in private than in public.[25]

Evaluation

Resolution 1503 has elicited many pro and con arguments over the past twenty years. Perhaps the main attribute of Resolution 1503 due process is that it applies to all nations and not just to those that sign human rights covenants. Nonsignatories that respond to commission inquiries about alleged human rights violations legitimize the entire process, which adds to the accumulation of international procedural and due process law. It is an important supplement to the due process of Track Two or the activities of working groups and rapporteurs assigned to specific countries or themes of human rights violations. Cross references, accumulation of evidence, and different approaches to alleged violations of human rights law all add to the edifice of the total due process structure under organizations in the U.N. system. Resolution 1503 deals with patterns and is not designed to respond to specific individual pleas for help. It provides for no quick relief, but this has become a mission of the Track Three working groups and special rapporteurs working with the staff of the Centre for Human Rights. It also enables nongovernmental organizations to play key roles in submitting communications and evidence of violations. Resolution 1503 improves with each passing year and, we trust, is proving its value.

Track Two: Treaty Due Process

Treaty or covenant due process is administered by "treaty bodies" or committeess established in a number of human rights covenants to monitor compliance by signatories to the treaties and to provide avenues for due process for those alleging treaty violations by governments. Treaty bodies flow from the progression of international constitutional law. The U.N. Charter provides in Article 68 the establishment of Economic and Social Council commissions such as in human rights, and in Article 62, paragraph 3, the authority for the council to present draft conventions to the General Assembly for adoption by states. The commission once established in 1946 wrote the Universal Declaration on Human Rights in 1948, which flowed into the two basic covenants on civil and political and on economic, social, and cultural rights in 1966. These covenants provide for state compliance and due process in Part 4 of each and the Civil and Political Covenant contains provisions for its treaty body, the Human Rights Committee. This structure for organization-generated international human rights law drew heavily from the 1919 constitution of the ILO, which has its own agencies or treaty bodies for monitoring state compliance and for due process dealing with violations of the treaty rights of the working place.

Human Rights Treaties and Treaty Bodies

Convention on the Prevention and Punishment of the Crime of Genocide of 1948 has no treaty body but calls on parties in Article 8 to address "the competent organs of the United Nations" to take "appropriate action for the suppression and prevention of the crime of genocide." The International Convention on the Elimination of All Forms of Racial Discrimination of 1965 contains in Article 8 the Committee on Racial Discrimination, with monitoring and due process procedures in Part 2. The International Covenant on Civil and Political Rights of 1966 provides in Part 4 for the Human Rights Committee and monitoring and due process procedures, while its First Protocol has similar procedures for complaints by individuals. The Covenant's Second Protocol was approved by the General Assembly in 1989 and provides for the abolition of the death penalty. The companion Covenant on Economic, Social, and Cultural Rights finally attained in 1985 the Committee on Economic, Social, and Cultural Rights, after intermediate agencies handled due process in Part 4.[26]

The International Convention on the Suppression and Punishment of the Crime of Apartheid of 1973 has as its treaty body the "Group of Three," members of the Commission on Human Rights to monitor the treaty. The 1979 Convention on the Elimination of All Forms of Discrimination Against Women provides in Article 17 its monitoring and due process committee and works closely with the Commission on the Status of Women, established by the council in 1946. The 1984 Convention Against Torture and Other Cruel, Inhuman, or Degrading Treatment or Punishment has as its treaty body the Committee Against Torture in Part 2 and especially Article 17. Provisions in Article 21 and 22, which are optional to signatories, provide for due process for a state complaining against another state and for individual complaints respectively.[27] Finally, the 1989 Convention on the Rights of the Child also has a treaty body in Article 43, the Committee on the Rights of the Child.

Each treaty body has essentially the same criteria for the experts that comprise treaty body membership. They must have "recognized competence in the field of human rights" with a desirable background of "legal experience," be of "high moral character," and serve in their personal and not their national capacity according to provisions in the International Covenant for Civil and Political Rights. They are nominated by states signatory to the treaty and elected by secret ballot by those states. There must be "equitable distribution of membership" and representation of "different forms of civilizations and the principal legal systems."

Each treaty body is grounded in the constitutional provisions of its treaty and each has developed its own rules of procedure, procedural law, and machinery for monitoring compliance in receiving and commenting on reports from member states. These reports "serve as a means of (1) shedding light on the normative implications of particular rights; (2) identifying effective implementation of techniques which might be adopted by other states; and (3) promoting public accountability on the part of states."[28] Each treaty body has its own record of monitoring treaty members and pursuing compliance and its own record in due process. Each has a well-documented history. A comparative study of all treaty body operations and achievements would be of great value.[29]

The Human Rights Committee

The Human Rights Committee was constituted in 1976 after its parent treaty, the International Convention on Civil and Political Rights, entered into force on March 26, 1976. The constitutional provisions for the committee's establishment are in Part 4 of the covenant and Article 29.2 authorizes the committee to establish its rules of procedure. The rules establish the method of operations for the committee including sessions, agenda, committee members and officers, secretariat, languages, public or private meetings, records, conduct of business including voting, and especially procedures for receiving and considering reports from treaty signatories. The committee normally meets twice a year and adopts an agenda at the beginning of each session that has been drafted by the office of the secretary general. It submits its annual report each year to the General Assembly through the Economic and Social Council.[30]

The convention and its two optional protocols impose on the committee three basic responsibilities: receiving and responding to reports from states party to the convention on measures of compliance with the convention, optional receipt of communications from one state alleging human rights violations by another state (Articles 41 through 43) of the convention, and receipt of communications by individuals claiming that they are victims of human rights violations by the state under whose jurisdiction they are located. The second and third functions deal with specific due process procedures but can be placed in motion only upon authorization of states parties to the convention and/or protocol. The chart on the next page outlines the basic steps undertaken by the committee in its exercise of its constitutional responsibilities delegated to it by the convention and protocol.

Evaluation

The collectivity of the discrete treaty bodies and their productivity thus far has produced a "solid body of legal jurisprudence for the interpretation of different treaty provisions and in developing a framework for systematic review of country performance. It was also seen as important in providing a basis for criticism by a state of its peers."[31] The "legal jurisprudence" includes incremental international procedural law and international due process law, which will only gather more experience and effectiveness with the passing of time.

However, problems abound. Reporting procedures mandated on states makes many demands on state bureaucracies composing the reports. Many states lack competent civil servants for such requirements for reporting. Delays in reporting produce backlogs and render deadlines meaningless in many cases. Reservations states attach to their ratifications of the covenants likewise add confusion and reduce coherency of the entire procedure.[32] The United States has ratified only one treaty with a treaty body, the Convention Against Torture, which impairs the theory and practice of the broader treaty body due process.

Secretary General Perez de Cuellar convened a session of the chairpersons of the treaty bodies in 1988 and 1990 to examine some of these problems. These experts reviewed problems of reporting by states and especially the preparation, submission, and feedbacks concerning the monitoring process. This process of comparative studies of treaty body monitoring and due process will continue along with seeking a more unified process to reporting and greater assistance by the staff of the Centre on Human Rights to states that are genuinely burdened with the proliferation of reports, monitoring mechanisms, and responses to allegations of human rights violations.

Track Three: Extra-Convention Procedures and Due Process

Distinct from the Resolution 1503 process and treaty bodies are the experts or rapporteurs and working parties appointed by the Commission on Human Rights and operating on the basis of commission mandates and not within the constraints of human rights conventions. These "extra-convention" experts are mandated to investigate human rights violations in a specific country such as Iran or a "theme" such as torture that may be practiced by a number of states. Extra-convention commission procedures evolved in the late 1960s, as we observed in Chapter 6. As of 1990, the four themes were disappearances, torture, summary and arbitrary executions, and religious intolerance. Targeted countries included Iran, El Salvador, Afghanistan, Republic of South Africa, Israel, Rumania, Guatemala, Haiti, Cuba, Albania, China, and Iraq.

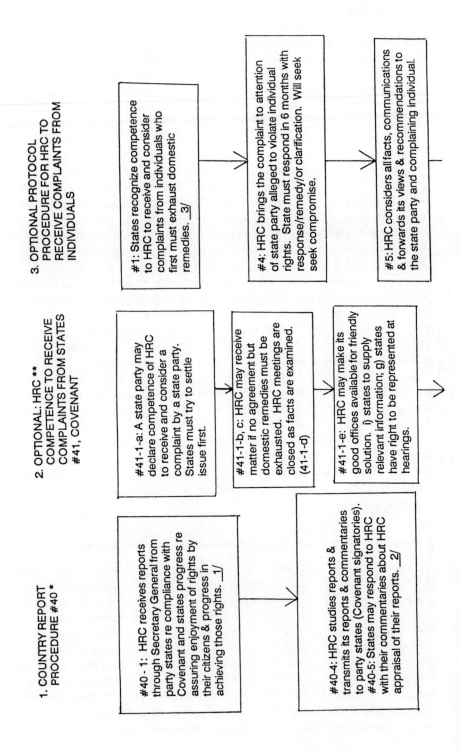

1. COUNTRY REPORT
   PROCEDURE #40 *

2. OPTIONAL: HRC **
   COMPETENCE TO RECEIVE
   COMPLAINTS FROM STATES
   #41, COVENANT

3. OPTIONAL PROTOCOL
   PROCEDURE FOR HRC TO
   RECEIVE COMPLAINTS FROM
   INDIVIDUALS

#40 - 1: HRC receives reports through Secretary General from party states re compliance with Covenant and states progress re assuring enjoyment of rights by their citizens & progress in achieving those rights. _1/

#40-4: HRC studies reports & transmits its reports & commentaries to party states (Covenant signatories). #40-5: States may respond to HRC with their commentaries about HRC appraisal of their reports. _2/

#41-1-a: A state party may declare competence of HRC to receive and consider a complaint by a state party. States must try to settle issue first.

#41-1-b, c: HRC may receive matter if no agreement but domestic remedies must be exhausted. HRC meetings are closed as facts are examined. (41-1-d)

#41-1-e: HRC may make its good offices available for friendly solution. f) states to supply relevant information; g) states have right to be represented at hearings.

#1: States recognize competence to HRC to receive and consider complaints from individuals who first must exhaust domestic remedies. _3/

#4: HRC brings the complaint to attention of state party alleged to violate individual rights. State must respond in 6 months with response/remedy/or clarification. Will seek compromise.

#5: HRC considers all facts, communications & forwards its views & recommendations to the state party and complaining individual.

#6: HRC incorporates in its annual report a summary of its activities and thus a public statement of matter if it is not resolved.

#41-1-h: HRC has 12 months to submit a re-report. Brief statement if solution or not... & report to states parties.

#42: If no solution, HRC appoints an _ad hoc_ Conciliation Commission to study, make recommendations, report to states which must reply.

INTERNATIONAL COVENANT OF CIVIL AND POLITICAL RIGHTS - 1976

Human Rights Committee (HRC), #28 - 39; organization, members, officers, meetings, rules. Annual reports to the General Assembly.

* #40 = Article 40 of Covenant of Civil & Political Rights

** HRC is Human Rights Committee

1/ Secretary, General may submit reports to appropriate specialized agencies

2/ HRC may submit reports with its commentary Economic & Social Council

3/ #3 &5 of Optional Protocol deal with admissibility of communications

Formation and Access

A special rapporteur (or representative or envoy) or a working group is established by the commission when the Resolution 1503 procedure identifies a definite and "consistent pattern of gross and reliably attested violation of human rights" in a specific country or transnational thematic violation. The commission might also launch an extra-convention working group or rapporteur on the recommendation of the subcommission or on the basis of verifiable facts submitted to it by a nongovernmental organization such as Amnesty International. Experts are selected on the basis of their nomination by their nation and within the criteria established for treaty bodies. The one or two year mandate to the group or person should be as specific as possible as formulated by the commission with the approval of the Economic and Social Council and the General Assembly.

The central mandate is to find the facts with respect to communications alleging human rights violations and to report back to the commission for further action including possible due process for victims of violations.

Facts and evidence are gained by visits by the rapporteurs or working parties to the targeted countries. The Republic of South Africa has never permitted any U.N. investigation in its jurisdiction and Israel has consistently closed its borders to the Special Commission to Investigate Human Rights Practices in the Occupied Territories.[33] In both cases, officials of the Commission on the Special Committee and Human Rights Centre staff travel to nations neighboring on these two states where they receive testimony from those able to provide information in addition to gaining evidence from many other sources on human rights violations. President Pinochet for years refused to permit commission entry into Chile for fact finding until negotiations between both parties enabled the group to enter Chile in 1986, an important step toward democracy for Chile in 1989. Iran finally permitted Special Representative Galindo Pohl to visit Iran early in 1990 and to the surprise of many, Cuba invited a working party to visit in 1988.[34]

There is much give and take on the experts gaining access to targeted nations. Requests for visits are preceded by negotiations to establish conditions for the visit. Generally the experts under the authority of the commission want full rights to enter, to make inquiries unfettered by government surveillance, interview anyone it seeks out, to examine government documents and procedures, and otherwise to find the facts and evidence with respect to alleged violations of human rights. The accused government, never thrilled at the prospect of an investigation of its policy and practice, wants to limit access and channel the experts into inquiries and information the government feels is all the experts should be exposed to on the visit. Access is enhanced if there are strong domestic sources of policy backing the commission's inquiry, if the procedure has the obvious strong and emphatic backing of the commission as well as nations friendly or allied with the accused nation, or other power bases that make it difficult for the accused nation top leadership to say no or place limitations on commission inquiry. This is why for the most part General Pinochet permitted the commission fairly full access in 1986 and why, therefore, subsequent events led to his departure from top leadership. Rapporteur and working party annual reports have much information on the dynamics of access.

Fact Finding and Action

The confidential reports of the rapporteurs and working parties are submitted to the commission each year and after closed-door examination, the commission usually permits reports to be printed, made public, and considered in detail in open sessions by the commission at its annual session. The experts are usually congratulated, their mandate extended for one or two years, and then the reports are sent on for subsequent consideration by the Economic and Social Council and then the General Assembly in its annual fall session in New York. In this chain of consideration of reports from time to time there are concerns expressed by commission members of protracted negotiations between the experts and officials of targeted countries to produce a report which may be compromised in varying degrees. Nongovernmental organizations politely accuse the experts of not being as firm as they should and caving in to government appeals for moderation. Others note that some information and light on a human rights problem are better than none and that in some cases, compromise is essential to gain access and tell the world at least part of the story.[35]

Hard core facts are the bottom line. People and groups within the targeted state point to the facts as presented in the agents' annual reports as justification for their opposition to the regime. Others who have submitted complaints from outside the targeted nation base their own credibility on the agents' finding and reporting on facts that were included in the complaints in the first place. Flawed or incorrect facts thus undermine internal opposition and external sources of complaint communications.

Perhaps one of the most experienced statespersons in international human rights law is Professor P. H. Kooijmans of the University of Leiden who observes that

In the international machinery for the protection of human rights, fact-finding is probably one of the most essential elements. From my own experience as head of the Netherlands delegation to the Commission of Human Rights (1982–1985), as Chairman of this Commission in 1984, and as its Special Rapporteur on Torture [since 1985], I know that at almost every stage of the proceedings, one is confronted with the question of how to determine the often disputed facts.[36]

Reports name names, expose violations of specific human rights set forth in the Covenant on Civil and Political Rights in particular, and make recommendations for various kinds of action including condemnations—which we review in the next section under compliance. The political equation is ever present—that of governments on the commission voting to condemn human rights practices by other governments on the basis of the evidence submitted by experts acting on their personal authority. But the extra-convention process grows ever stronger and more embracing of targeted countries and themes of violations.

Due process can emanate from extra-convention procedures during the course of working group or rapporteur fact finding in the field. The agent, on not a few occasions, has come across hard evidence of a specific human rights violation, such as torture by the targeted government or a summary execution. These violations are also denial of due process to victims that the government has committed itself to in ratifying a human rights covenant, or even if it has not because due process is ingrained in customary international law as well as treaty international law. Intervention by the agent has produced an ''international ha- beus corpus'' or rapid response intervention, causing the government either to cease and desist from the violation, or in the case of habeus corpus, explaining to a victim of violation the legal basis for accusation or detention. Another procedure is to communicate directly to an official at the Centre for Human Rights in Geneva with the facts of the specific violation and a plea for official intervention to the violating government. It is not possible to document such due process procedures, many of which have saved lives and provided release from detention, but the reader may be assured that such procedures have indeed achieved results.[37]

Finally, the commission makes annual decisions with respect to identifying new countries for targeting, continuing the mandate or the country or theme, or terminating this procedure in view of significant improvements in human rights protection in a targeted country. Many have come off the country list, including Argentina, Uganda, and Uruguay, to name a few. The reports are on file and provide a significant reservoir of evidence of human rights violations that, as we shall see, is important to the next step, compliance.

Evaluation

The extra-convention procedures are vital to fact finding and seeking the essential evidence that convention human rights have not been protected and that many have been violated. International procedural law has been the incre- mental product of extra-convention processes. These procedures are important supplements to Resolution 1503 and to treaty-body due process. In the theme of torture, as we have noted, there is both a special rapporteur and a treaty body, the Committee Against Torture. Each has a different legal foundation and thus different responsibilities and a different accountability. The main difference is that the special rapporteur can operate much more quickly and directly if there is hard evidence of official state torture or cruel punishment, while the treaty body has a treaty mandate to operate in a more indirect manner. It remains to be seen if this two track approach to a major human rights violation is less or more effective than the other more discrete processes. Extra-convention proce- dures have resulted in innovative and creditable approaches to identifying human rights violations, especially in penetrating sovereign domains and in gaining a rapid response to accusations of violations. These procedures have basically removed the recommendations by many in the early 1980s that there should be a high commissioner for human rights with intervention authority and legal responsibility similar to that of the UNHCR. That office may well evolve but for the present, extra-convention procedures and experts are charting new courses for international human rights law and respect for that law.

Compliance

The principal criticism and source of cynicism with respect to international law is that unlike municipal law, it has no means of gaining compliance by governments alleged to violate that law and no mechanisms of enforcement such as an international police force, an international court for compulsory jurisdiction, and no firm methods of punishment of the transgressor state and/or its officials. This criticism and cynicism miss the mark. Von Glahn observes that states comply far more with international law than they violate because the law that states themselves constructed is essential to stability in international relations and transactions. This in turn is essential to states' pursuit of resources and conditions in the international marketplace that are vital to their requirements for security and well-being. Compliance, further, is important for the state's credibility, its standing in world public opinion, its need for approval by other states, and its avoidance of the costs of noncompliance. Compliance becomes a habit of relations with other states but regrettably, noncompliance, threats, and uses of force dominate attention and the media rather than the standard acts of compliance, which are over 90 percent of states' relations with others in the international marketplace.[38]

State compliance is rooted in their domestication of international treaties, as we noted in Chapter 5. They are expected to comply with international custom and principles as in the 1948 Universal Declaration of Human Rights and under the Martens clause in international humanitarian law, which obliges states to comply, treaty or not, given the "principles of law of nations, as they result from usages established among civilized peoples, from the laws of humanity, and the dictates of public conscience." The Resolution 1503 procedure of due process applies to all states. The imperative of states' compliance to the human rights laws they wrote or should observe is without question, and the spectrum of compliance runs from quiet diplomacy and obedience to mechanisms for deprivations and punishment.

Quiet Diplomacy

The confidential, quiet diplomacy of the three main due process procedures have been very effective in bringing about compliance because diplomatic pressure is present as the working groups, rapporteurs, and experts, along with the international civil service represent the directives of the Commission on Human Rights and signatories to treaties. When the facts are certain and the possibility of public exposure is possible, states often submit to the diplomatically crafted commands for compliance. This is the mode of compliance traditional to the procedures of the International Committee of the Red Cross in the implementation of international humanitarian law. The more than 100-year record of the committee on compliance speaks for itself. We cannot ever measure compliance achieved by the quiet and confidential processes emanating from due process procedures, but must be assured that this main mode for compliance is quite successful. Finally, it is important to note the good offices of the secretary-general in the pursuit of compliance by highly confidential procedures. Often it is the person at the top who can call the head of government or other top leaders and urge compliance, request the cease and desist of a human rights violation, or even a stronger statement if required.[39]

Public Condemnation

When private and confidential diplomacy does not work, names are named. The Commission on Human Rights each year names nations being appraised under Resolution 1503 procedures, treaty bodies in their annual reports name states in violation if confidential procedures do not work, and the commission decides upon recommendation of working parties and rapporteurs as to which countries are targeted and merit public condemnation, as well as those nations on the theme list such as torture. In August 1989, the Peoples Republic of China became the first permanent member of the Security Council to be condemned by the subcommission for its violation of students' rights and lives in the June 1989 uprising in Beijing.

Public condemnation of a targeted state is a mobilization of shame determined by other states in a vote or resolution in an assembly of states such as the Commission on Human Rights. The more certain the facts and evidence and the larger the majority in support of the condemnation, the more authoritative and creditable is the accusation. Few are aware of the extent targeted states go in the commission, the Economic and Social Council, the Third Committee, and the General Assembly itself to tone down the condemnation resolution accompanied by promises of compliance.[40]

Public condemnation is not a shallow mode for compliance. It is feared by people as well as nations and especially in the domain of human rights. It emphasizes the damaging of human beings and thus stains the credibility and public image of the state and its leadership, it highlights the violation of solemn commitments to treaties, and lowers the overall credit rating of the state in the esteem of others. It impairs that essential ingredient in the second purpose of the U.N. Charter in Article 1, "friendly relations," without which states have difficulty in the pursuit of their requirements for security and well-being in the international marketplace.

Condemnation by international governmental assemblies is the voice of the global community and the international human rights law it generated. It is based on strong factual evidence as judged by sovereign states in voting to comdemn. As such, it lends political support to domestic sources of policy within the state in opposition to governance causing violations of human rights as well as to opposition abroad. Condemnation by the United Nations thus was a powerful force in toppling the rule of the generals in Argentina in 1982 as well as helping to cause governmental change in Uruguay and Uganda. Furthermore, evidence on Argentina's repression of human rights gathered by the Commission on Human Rights was used in the subsequent trials of the generals. A principal witness for the prosecution was the former director of the U.N. Office of Human Rights, Professor van Boven, who provided evidence of impeccable credibility and was verified by many sources. Top leaders and governance engaged in human rights violations must know that at some time in the future commission evidence might be presented in their own courts and against them.

The European and Inter-American Commissions and Courts of Human Rights have produced compliance through administrative orders by the commissions and decisions by the courts. There is optimism with the winding down of the cold war that the two superpowers will pave the way for a more active role by the International Court of Justice in human rights law through treaty review and interpretation, judgments with increasing Court jurisdiction, and advisory opinions as well. A chamber of five judges of the Court might be organized in time to serve as an international criminal court or "international penal tribunal" as anticipated in Article 6 of the 1948 genocide treaty for individuals alleged of commiting international crimes if and when the Court's statute is amended to address crimes of individuals as well as states.

Deprivation

If private diplomacy and public condemnation do not result in calling upon a state to cease and desist violations of human rights law and redressing the grievances of the wounded individuals, compliance by a specific deprivation may be the next step. In national law, a person may be deprived of financial resources through a fine, liberty through a sentence in jail, or even his or her life for the most serious of crimes. International deprivation cannot take a state to jail but there are many means to deprive the state of resources or conditions it requires for its security and well-being. They include a severance of diplomatic relations, blockade, embargo, quarantine, denial of trade rights, and other kinds of sanctions. A number of treaties permit states capturing criminals in the areas of genocide, torture, or terrorism to try international culprits on behalf of the international community irrespective of the jurisdiction of the crime. This follows the 1945–1946 Nuremburg precedent of trying and depriving the leading Nazi war criminals of their lives, which was endorsed by and on behalf of the United Nations in 1946.

The Security Council, if it has the unanimity of the five permanent members and four other affirmitive votes, can take action under Chapter 7 of the U.N. Charter against states in violation of international law and treaties including the sanctions set forth in Article 41. The Security Council voted for sanctions against the white supremacist regime of Rhodesia in 1966, an arms embargo sanction against the Republic of South Africa in 1977, and firm condemnation and economic sanctions against Iraq in August 1990. At the Security Council, the United States and the United Kingdom have constantly voted against economic sanctions against the Republic of South Africa, which has raised the question of priorities between the profound violations of human rights in South Africa and economic interest.

On the other hand, the U.S. Congress passed over President Reagan's veto of the Anti-Apartheid Act of 1986 that halted new U.S. investment and airline concessions and also demonstrated the moral will of U.S. policy as fashioned by the Congress to pressure for change in apartheid policy. This is a classic case of U.S. separation of power and the victory of sanctions over support for the white regime in the Republic of South Africa by the executive branch. It was also a victory for domestic sources of policy in the United States, including human rights nongovernmental organizations and anti-apartheid policies of cities, states, universities, corporations, and others. The new government of President F. W. de Klerk acknowledged the damage caused by the governmental and private sector economic sanctions, which were a major reason for his dramatic alteration of the course of apartheid in 1989 and 1990 and the release from prison of the African National Congress leader, Nelson Mandela. The nation could no longer pay the high price of apartheid.[41] In any event, the machinery for severe economic and other kinds of deprivations mandated by the Security Council is in place for action against violations of human rights law and ready for implementation if there is the political will to do so. Finally, under Article 94, paragraph 2, any state not complying with the judgment of the International Court of Justice may lead to a Security Council decision to "decide on measures to be taken to give effect to the judgment." This provision links compliance with enforcement, a linkage not found in the U.S. Constitution.[42]

Nongovernmental International Organizations (NGIOs)

A vital but often overlooked force for compliance are the NGIOs dedicated to protection of human rights and compliance to human rights law. The list of NGIOs attending the annual sessions of the Commission on Human Rights is an impressive overview of the many and varied human rights interest groups accredited to the Economic and Social Council under Article 71 of the U.N. Charter, and subsequent policy and rules for the consultative status of these organizations. The council's Committee on Nongovernmental Organizations has held over 500 meetings as the member-state policy body for these groups that have their own Conference of Nongovernmental Organizations in Consultative Status with the Economic and Social Council. We observed earlier in the study by Thoolen and Verstappen entitled *Human Rights Mission* the most important role of these organizations, that of fact-finding and verifying the reliability of information on deprivations of human rights by specific states. Other functions include consultation between the private sector and governmental human rights organizations, education, mediation, such as the International Committee of the

Red Cross performs between prisoners and detaining states, participation in the sessions of the Commission on Human Rights, providing legal services, and serving as initiators for enhanced international procedural law, international legislation, due process, and compliance for the international protection of human rights.[43] The Geneva-based International Commission of Jurists and its many national affiliates have panels of lawyers and jurists who observe trials in many nations of people whose rights have been denied or violated in some manner by the state having jurisdiction over them. The observers make public, as well as private, reports of due process or lack of it and, in particular, review fairness of the trial and the relation between the punishment and the alleged infraction of state law such as a protest or antigovernment publication. Their presence in court elevates the morale of the accused and the opposition to a government violating human rights. Furthermore, the lawyers relate to the lawyers in the country of the trial and judges to their fellow judges in that country. This transnational, professional fellowship can and does render due process more in line with the international standards of the International Covenant on Civil and Political Rights and less in conformity with a government command that its repressive policy is to have priority over international law. National affiliates of the NGIOs play key roles in influencing their governments to comply with international human rights law and to make public reports of noncompliance. The network of national and international nongovernmental organizations not only is a key source for evidence for human rights violations, but they also light the fires all over the world to cast light on violations and to make demands for redress of profound human rights grievances.

Compliance by states to their commitments to international human rights law in the treaties they ratify and to their nonconvention commitments under international customary law and to the U.N. Charter is much more concrete and respected now than it was only ten years ago. New modes for compliance are evolving slowly but surely and is evidenced in particular by the extra-convention due process procedures under the authority of the working groups and special rapporteurs of the Human Rights Commission. It will always confront forces under high state authority—studied in Chapter 5—that resist intrusions into sovereign domains, but any high state authority claims for exclusiveness of its domestic jurisdiction in light of factual and verifiable human rights violations no longer is acceptable. We still must view with heartbreaking sorrow the gross violations of human rights in many places on our small planet and the frustration of the limitations due to high state authority of due process, compliance, and official international legal deprivation. But change is in the wind as is evidenced by the massive transformations in the Soviet Union and Eastern Europe in the late 1980s and early 1990s. With political will in governments supported by organizations, individual activities, and public opinion, change toward enjoyment of human rights on increasing scales will continue.[44]

This was evidenced in August 1990 with the unprecedented decisions by the Security Council with respect to the Iraqi invasion of Kuwait. The Security

Council voted on August 2, 14 to 0, to condemn the invasion and to demand Iraq withdraw its forces from that internationally recognized sovereign nation. The Security Council, by a vote of 13 to 0 on August 6, called for a trade and financial boycott of Iraq and Kuwait, and on August 9 voted 15 to 0 to declare that Iraq's annexation of Kuwait was a violation of international law. On August 18 the Security Council voted 15 to 0 to call on Iraq to release all detained foreigners—also a violation of international law. By a vote of 13 to 0 on August 25, the Security Council affirmed the right of nations to enforce the economic embargo, by military means if necessary. The five permanent members certainly had the political will to vote unanimously. On the fourteen-member vote, Yemen abstained and on the 13 to 0 votes, Yemen and Cuba abstained. The main point is that the Security Council took firm measures in the manner anticipated by the U.N. Charter's authors in 1945—to possess the "primary responsibility for the maintenance of international peace and security" under Article 25.

PRODUCTIVITY AND UTILIZATION OF OUTPUTS

Our study of the organization for protection of human rights has covered to a large extent the productivity of the Commission on Human Rights and the Centre for Human Rights as well, and how productivity or output has been utilized by people and nations within the framework of the organizational chart for Part 2. The overall plan of this book is that its organization and approach are designed in part as a guide for other studies of organizations' evolution, goals and means to goals, the spectrum of state to organization authority, and a depth analysis of an important area of organization activity, such as our case study in human rights. We therefore conclude our study with a brief examination of the structure of organization productivity and utilization of outputs by referring not to human rights, but to the work of many other kinds of international organizations.

Most studies of organizations deal with outputs or what organizations do rather than put much emphasis on the inputs by member states and the processes of decision making within the organization. Therefore, material and studies are abundant on outputs, but less on how the beneficiaries of those outputs utilize the productivity and how organization personnel seek to guide state beneficiaries toward using the outputs in the manner intended by the organization and especially its assembly of states. This latter point is particularly important if we are to place emphasis on a high correlation between organization goals of shared and progressive well-being and how states define their own goals of security and well-being.

Outputs of Organizations

The productivity of the Commission on Human Rights and the Centre for Human Rights in advancing their constitutional obligations for the enhancement of human rights falls in all the categories of outputs to which we now turn. For instance, if the first output we examine is services, we find extensive and increasing work by the Centre for Human Rights in advisory services and technical assistance. This output is extremely important so as to assist the police and military in many developing countries to understand the basic national and international human rights laws that their governments have legally committed themselves to in international human rights covenants and obligations to domesticate those commitments.[45] We now turn to the outputs of a wide variety of other organizations beyond the productivity of the main organs of the United Nations such as peacekeeping and outputs in the ecnomic and social areas, work of the Secretariat, and decisions of the International Court of Justice.

Services

PROTECTION. The UNEP has responsibilities for environmental protection and the IMO for protection against oil spills and maritime pollution.

LEGAL. Outputs of GATT emphasize the basic rules of international trade relations, and the UNHCR has legal responsibilities for protection of, aid for, and resettlement of over 10 million refugees.

FINANCIAL. The World Bank and the IMF provide extensive financial services to developing nations, as do the four regional development banks.

PREVENTIVE. The WHO is deeply involved in outputs of preventive medical service and the ILO of preventive services and laws dealing with child labor and adverse labor conditions.

TECHNICAL ASSISTANCE. The U. N. Development Program provides funding for development programs and the IFAD is particularly concerned with assisting farmers in developing countries in agriculture and irrigation among other technical services to expand food growth and production.

TRAINING. The ITC is charged with the training of men and women in developing states on how to market their products—including packaging, advertising, and competing in the international marketplace—as an important step toward economic diversification and reliance on the export of a primary product such as coffee or phosphate. Similarly, UNIDO trains people to move toward industrialization in all of its dimensions and also to diversify the economy of the developing state.

ADVISORY. Advisory services are important outputs of UNCTAD and the FAO in assisting states in many ways to improve their government bureaucracies in trade, development, and food administration.

RESEARCH AND EDUCATION. The U. N. Institute for Training and Research sponsored many studies used in the writing of this book. UNESCO provides important fundamental education programs in many developing nations in addition to the extensive productivity in many other areas.

Standards

The WIPO is concerned with standards registration, promotion of patents, copyrights, trademarks, and other forms of intellectual, industrial, literary, and artistic works. The WMO, among other purposes, promotes the standardization of meterological and related observations to ensure the uniform publication of observations and statistics.

Regulation and Compliance

Members of organizations, through the founding constitution or resolutions and decisions of the assembly of members, delegate authority to the organizations to regulate or administer the standards and rules established by the organization. This regulatory activity is for shared well-being to advance the goals of states and not to establish regulatory mechanisms for any ideological or controlling purpose. The first specialized agency of the United Nations, the ITU, has extensive regulatory authority in many areas of communications including satellites, and the next oldest agency, the Universal Postal Union, has only one jurisdiction for its rules and regulations, the world. The obvious necessity for regulations of their functional areas by the IAEA and the ICAO prevents unacceptable and illegal nuclear proliferation and collisions of airplanes at international airports among their many responsibilities. All these and other organizations with rule-making authority are based on constitutions that call for compliance by member states to those rules or laws. Thus widespread domestication of the law of the organization is an integral part of compliance to the law and to regulations.

Law

As we have observed many times in our study, constitutions of many organizations provide for the organization to generate its own laws. The prime authority is in Article 13 of the U. N. Charter, as we have noted, which calls on the General Assembly to encourage "the progressive development of international law and its codification" (in terms of treaties and other instruments).

This is only a brief inventory of outputs or productivity of international organizations. Each of the agencies cited above works in many other areas of outputs, such as WHO. It is concerned not only with preventive services cited above, but also with protecting people against epidemics, providing quasi-legal services (such as voluntary codes against unauthorized marketing of milk-substitute products), training of midwives, advisory services to health bureaucracies in developing nations, and certainly with research and education. It is involved in standards for medical drug production and marketing among its many vital areas of productivity. Finally, it is always an interesting study to take one output of an organization and trace it back to how the assembly and secretariat developed the output through legislation and administration, how this process stemmed back to the delegation and the mission of states and then to the states themselves. It is this kind of linkage study that makes future research and study so important and exciting in the better understanding of the nature and potential of international organizations.

Utilization of Organization Productivity by States

The term "utilization" basically means how states incorporate outputs of international organizations into their national policies as means toward their goals of security and well-being. For the most part, organizations' productivity enhances security and well-being for states such as the outcomes of human rights assemblies and administration to advance shared and progressive well-being by people in the enjoyment of their rights. States are expected to comply with their commitments under the constitutions and the treaties of international organizations and thus incorporate in their national policy the outputs emanating from constitutions and treaties as we have observed in the field of human rights.

Clearly there is tremendous variety between and among states on what we might also term consumption of outputs. Developing states have far greater need for outputs of financial aid and technical assistance for their progressive well-being than states generously endowed with resources for advancing this goal. High state authority may resist extensive utilization of outputs as we have noted in human rights outputs and compliance, while high organization authority means high level national consumption of outputs. There is the spectrum from high state to high organization and even supra-organization authority on how states stake out positions on outputs consumption, which directly relates to how they view international organizations in their own determination of security and well-being. We thus return to the state and Chapter 7 in the correlation of state utilization of outputs to completing our cycle of state-organization-state relations and thus to the correlation of state goals of security and well-being and organization goals of shared and progressive well-being. In appraising state consumption of outputs, we thus turn to state organization for utilization, some dimensions of policy on output consumption, and the role of the international civil servants.

Organization of Government for Productivity Utilization

Utilization of organization outputs in the democracies will generally be along functional lines in connecting the organization and its goals and policy with the appropriate bureaucracy in the government. For the United States, the ILO outputs are administered by the Department of Labor—such as recommendations for adoption of labor treaties. The WHO outputs in AIDS research will be directed to the Department of Health and Human Welfare, and UNESCO will be wired into the Department of Education, scientific agencies, and cultural institutions such as the National Endowment for the Humanities. The same is true for more centralized governments, which will also have more centralized control over productivity consumption. In many developing nations with strong top leadership and not very strong bureaucracies, the top leader often has a commanding say in the allocations of organization outputs.

The World Health Assembly each May passes resolutions and makes decisions about its productivity and its intentions on how such outputs should be utilized by and in member states. International civil servants at the WHO, working with the executive board, have considerable responsibilities in implementing the utilization of outputs, such as financial resources for expanding hospital care in Sebago, a developing nation. The top leader of Sebago, however, has his own ideas about hospitals and wants the state-of-the-art hospital located in Obego, the capital of Sebago. WHO officials may say the intent of the output was to provide for decentralized hospital services in the rural areas of the nation, but the top leader sees the urban hospital as an institution to provide health care for his friends, political allies, government workers, and elites in Obego, which are the foundation of his political power and security of office. This is not a fictional case study, but a fairly accurate appraisal of how top leaders in many nations may seek to channel the organization output toward their own interpretation of security and well-being for the nation, which may well be their own security and well-being.

A more public case is that of financial aid and policy as an output of the World Bank and the IMF. Both require specific conditions to be met by the state seeking financial aid and both make certain that if the conditions are not met by the receiving state shaping its policy to incorporate those conditions, then aid may be leveled off or cut off until the conditions match the utilization of funding. It is easier for the financial organization to control the utilization because it has authority to turn that aid on and off. It is more difficult for other organizations, especially in the service realm such as the WHO, to impose conditions for utilization. Further, bureaucracies in many developing nations in the area of health, food, education, labor, and development are generally not strong and are often politically obedient and subservient to top leadership, which is much more authoritative than government agencies to control organization productivity. In brief, government organization for output consumption varies tremendously, but it should always be kept in mind the close relation between government agencies shaping organization policy we studied in Chapter 6 and government organization in consuming organization outputs.

Government Policy

The same relation holds between policy on outputs and policy on inputs into organizations. A major policy consideration is the relevance of and relation to what organizations offer states and state goals of security and well-being. How far does the state want to go in channeling its goals of security and well-being into the organizations' intended goals of shared security and shared and progressive well-being? What kinds of supports would top leadership need to move in that direction, given the dimensions of high state authority we studied in Chapter 5? A brief look backward would see the pulls of high state authority on President Wilson when he saw in 1919 the concept of shared security, or "concert of power" as he put it, as essential to U.S. security. High state authority power defeated the United States joining the shared security organization of the league. Winston Churchill preached shared security against his government's leadership in the late 1930s, which who saw no such need for the security of Great Britain. Take outputs of any organization and explore how those outputs relate to how any one state defines its goals and requirements for those goals.

Related to this policy issue is how the state then seeks to influence the organization to produce outputs that correlate well with its own goals, or how its participation in the organization makes it realize that organization outputs are vital to the pursuit of goals. What is the time frame for utilization of outputs? Is Sebago in such dire condition that it must have immediate food resources to fight off famine and thus it seeks to maximize world food organizations as well as having other nations blessed with food resources send it immediate aid? Or, over the years, had Sebago considered utilizing world food organizations' outputs of assistance and development training to improve Sebago's food production capability? Did the government consider the venerable saying: Feed the hungry man to satisfy him for the day or give him seeds to satisfy him for life.

Any government must appraise the outputs of international organizations and make determinations as to how to incorporate the productivity available to the government into the policy machinery and toward its goals. The developing nations' security and especially well-being depend on organizations' productivity and this is increasingly the case for all nations given the patterns of interdependence we studied in Chapter 2. Here we are talking about outputs of hundreds of intergovernmental organizations and their suborgans, such as the Commission on Human Rights, and also goals and policies of over 160 sovereign states. This is a vast subject that must also include the work and goals of thousands of nongovernmental organizations as well. It is an essential part of our total study because how organization outputs are utilized, and toward what ends, is the bottom line of the entire cycle of state-organization-state.

The International Civil Servants

The secretariat members of organization, often working with experts who themselves serve in a personal and nongovernment capacity, are the people charged with the responsibility for linking outputs to utilization. The majority are in the field or in regional offices such as the six of the WHO. These utilization specialists often have to exercise extraordinary diplomacy to link the objective of an output—such as hospital services—with the government organization official who may have much to say about the utilization of the output. These officials are responsible and accountable to the top leadership in their own organization and eventually to the secretary-general of the United Nations or the director-general of the WHO. On the other hand, they must be sensitive to and emphathize with officials of receiving governments in their mission of incorporating outputs into the policy machinery of those governments and toward the goals of shared security and shared and progressive well-being of the organization.

If we turn back to the categories of organization outputs in this section, we have some idea of the many kinds of organizations and thus outputs and also some idea of the variety of logistics necessary by international civil servants to implement organization productivity. We can only review these many and varied approaches to effective utilization in our study and trust that we may have significant case studies to enlighten us better on the relation between outputs, utilization, and then evaluation of their impact on the goals and policies of receiving states.

Thus the cycle continues. States use outputs of organizations and then prepare for the next cycle of development of policy, work of the missions, shaping and instructing the delegations, participation in the member state assembly, and the diplomacy and politicking for assembly outputs that are significant for states' goals. The chemistry of this annual cycle over the period since 1945, however, has brought states far more together in goals of shared security and shared and progressive well-being than states that are loose cannons in their unilateral pursuit of security and well-being goals that are far from the goals of the organizations. We have tried to demonstrate in this study that there has been a steady progression through incremental international constitutional law of shared goals while, at the same time, states may enjoy their own unique existence, history, values, and vision. The reality of the world in the early 1990s is still one of enormous problems, human distress for hundreds of millions, violence unwanted but still the option of those who shun peaceful settlement of disputes, and continued degradation of human rights. However, the international constitutional system is in place, the law is there, and what remains is the political will and support by domestic sources of policy to give genuine meaning to shared security and shared and progressive well-being.

NOTES

1. *United Nations Action in the Field of Human Rights* (New York: United Nations, 1988), pp. 15–18.

2. *United Nations Action in the Field of Human Rights* (New York: United Nations, 1983), p. 283.

3. AGENDA, 47TH SESSION, UNITED NATIONS COMMISSION ON HUMAN RIGHTS, January 28–March 8, 1991

1. Election of officers.
2. Adoption of agenda.
3. Organization of the work of the session.
4. Question of the violation of human rights in the occupied Arab territories, including Palestine.
5. Violations of human rights in southern Africa.
6. Adverse consequences for the enjoyment of human rights given to the colonial and racist regime in southern Africa.
7. Question of realization in all countries (of all rights in the Declaration and Covenants on Human Rights) and study of special problems which developing countries face.

8. Question of the realization of the right to development.
9. Right of peoples to self-determination (including report of Special Rapporteur on mercenaries).
10. Rights of persons subjected to any form of detention or imprisonment including reports on torture, enforced or involuntary disappearances, hostage taking, etc.
11. Further promotion and encouragement of human rights and fundamental freedoms (including program and methods of work of the Commission and Centre for Human Rights).
12. Question of violation of human rights in any part of the world (country and theme reports and action of the Sub-Commission at its 42nd session).
13. Measures to improve rights of migrant workers.
14. Human rights and scientific and technological developments.

Agenda items 15–26 deal with a wide variety of other items including status of the international covenants on human rights, effective functioning of bodies and organs dealing human rights, advisory services, draft provisional agenda for the 48th session of the Commission, and report to the Economic and Social Council on the Commission's 47th session.

4. See *United Nations Action* for this group's membership, methods of work relationship with the Organization of African Unity and also with African national liberation movements, nongovernmental organizations, and individuals.

5. For an official appraisal of the subcommission, see *United Nations Action*, 1988, ibid., p. 18.

6. Johan Kaufmann, *Conference Diplomacy*, 2d ed. (Boston: Martinus Nijhoff, 1988), p. 18. See also Kaufmann's *Effective Negotiation: Case Studies on Conference Diplomacy* (Boston: Martinus Nijhoff, 1989).

7. *Commission on Human Rights, Report on 43rd Session, Economic and Social Council Official Records 1987*, p. 111.

8. Ibid., pp. 160–183.

9. See William J. Dixon, "The Evaluation of Weighted Voting Schemes for the United Nations General Assembly," in Paul F. Diehl, *The Politics of International Organizations* (Chicago: Dorsey Press, 1989), p. 134, as well as the excellent bibliography on bloc voting, pp. 151–52.

10. NON-GOVERNMENTAL ORGANIZATIONS, 47th SESSION, U.N. COMMISSION ON HUMAN RIGHTS, February, March, 1991

The official roster of the 47th session of the U.N. Commission on Human Rights lists 120 non-governmental organizations officially accredited to the United Nations and in attendance at the session. A random listing of eleven of the NGOs participating in the session is as follows: Amnesty International, Baha'i International Community, Coordinating Board of Jewish Organizations, Human Rights Internet, International Association Against Torture, International Commission of Jurists, International Council of Women, International Human Rights Law Group, Muslim World League, Pax Romana, and World Federation of UN Associations.

11. See *United Nations Action in the Field of Human Rights*, 1983 p. 288, for a catalog of these important studies.

12. Quantitative analysis of the annual reports of the Economic and Social Council to the General Assembly that contains the report of the Commission on Human Rights and records the bulging content of international procedural law in the area of human rights.

See also the annual publications of *Issues Before the General Assembly*, published by the United Nations Association/U.S.A. for appraisal of the growth of human rights procedural law.

13. For the 1959 Declaration, see Ian Brownlie, *Basic Documents on Human Rights* (Oxford: Clarendon Press, 1981), pp. 108–10. The annual publication, *The State of the World's Children* (New York: Oxford University Press, 1989), with an introduction by James P. Grant, Executive Director of UNICEF, surveys the achievement and obstacles to child health and well-being. It has comprehensive data on health indicators, nutrition, education, and other measures of well-being, plus and minus. The tragic statistics remain: More than 40,000 children die daily from lack of food, shelter, or primary health care. About 100 million children work under hazardous conditions, 80 million are homeless, and there are about 10 million child refugees.

14. 1979 was also the International Year of the Child under a General Assembly resolution. Top leaders from 72 nations met at a summit conference on the rights of the child at the United Nations early in October 1990 to reaffirm childrens' rights and to accelerate national and international policy for enhanced child well-being.

15. A number of delegates at the commission also represent their nations on the council, on assembly committees, and in the assembly itself. However, more senior diplomats will be in attendance at plenary assembly sessions.

16. Legislative history is vitally important because it is the prime source for appraising intent of member states' inputs and thus for interpretation of the convention or treaty. *Human Rights: A Compilation of International Instruments* (New York: United Nations Centre for Human Rights, 1988) is a late collection of all human rights covenants. *Human Rights: Status of International Instruments* (New York: Centre for Human Rights, 1987) lists the signatories, date of signature and ratification, and the terms of the declarations and reservations of states committing themselves to the international law of human rights.

17. See the Declaration on the Right to Development that flowed up from the commission and was adopted by the General Assembly on December 4, 1986, which is a collective right of the developing nations to "enjoy economic, social, cultural and political development." United States and others are concerned about the impact and possible collision between the collective right and individual rights. See "The Right to Development," *United Nations Action in the Field of Human Rights*, 1988, pp. 179–80 and other entries under the right to development in the Index of this volume.

18. As a prime case study for the United States on this key issue, see Philip Alston, "U.S. Ratification of the Covenant on Economic, Social, and Cultural Rights: The Need for an Entirely New Strategy," *American Journal of International Law* (April 1990), p. 365 ff.

19. International administrative law is comparable to administrative law exercised by U.N. administrative agencies, such as the Federal Communications Commission, that are not in the formal structure of the three branches of the federal government. See Christopher D. Cooker, *International Administrative Law and Practices in International Organizations* (Boston: Martinus Nijhoff, 1990) as well as "Administrative Law, Part IV," in Hartley, *The Foundations of European Community Law*.

20. An excellent study of some problems and issues of international administration and its rules and laws is David Pitt and Thomas G. Weiss (eds.), *The Nature of United Nations Bureaucracies* (Boulder, Colo.: Westview Press, 1986).

21. *United Nations Action in the Field of Human Rights*, 1983, p. 297.

22. *Human Rights Machinery: Fact Sheet Number One*, Centre for Human Rights, 1988.

23. *United Nations Action in the Field of Human Rights*, 1983, p. 297.

24. The formal address is Centre for Human Rights, United Nations Office in Geneva, 8–14 avenue de la Paix, 1211 Geneva 10, Switzerland.

25. See Philip Alston and Maria Rodriguez-Bustelo, *Taking Stock of United Nations Human Rights Procedures* (Medford, Mass.: Tufts University, 1988), p. 10. Also, see H. Tolley, *The U.N. Commission on Human Rights* (Boulder: Westview Press, 1987), for a fine discussion of Resolution 1503; Tom Zuijdwijk, *Petitioning the United Nations: A Study of Human Rights* (New York: St. Martin's Press, 1982); *United Nations Action in the Field of Human Rights*, 1988, p. 1503; U.N. Centre for Human Rights Fact Sheet 7, *Communications Procedures: Human Rights*, May 1989.

26. For a splendid review of problems and issues of this treaty committee, see Philip Alston and Bruno Simma, "First Session of the Economic, Social and Cultural Committee," *American Journal of International Law* (July 1987): 747; "Second Sessions," *AJIL* (July 1988):603.

27. See J. Hermann Burgers and Hans Daneius, *The United Nations Convention Against Torture: A Handbook on the Crime of Torture and Other Cruel, Inhuman or Degrading Treatment or Punishment* (Boston: Martinus Nijhoff, 1988).

28. Alston and Rodriguez-Bustelo, *Taking Stock*, p. 31.

29. See Chapters 6 and 7, Theodor Meron, *Human Rights in International Law* (Oxford: Clarendon Press), for ILO procedures, as well as *United Nations Action*, 1988, "Handling of Communications by the Specialized Agencies," pp. 326–331 for the ILO and pp. 331–334 for UNESCO. See also Hurst Hannum, *Guide to International Human Rights Practice*, edited for the International Human Rights Law Group, University of Pennsylvania Press, Philadelphia, 1984, and especially Part 2 on Resolution 1503, Optional Protocol procedures and those of many other conventions, as well as a model communication, pp. 291–294. Appendix D has addresses for organizations and treaty bodies receiving complaints.

30. *Yearbook of the Human Rights Committee*, United Nations, New York, 1989. See also *United Nations Action in the Field of Human Rights*, 1988. See charter for Human Rights Committee due process at end of chapter.

31. Alston and Rodriguez-Bustelo, *Taking Stock*, p. 30.

32. *Human Rights: Status of International Instruments* (New York: United Nations, 1987).

33. See the commission's annual report and Israeli state papers that include Israel's response to the annual report as presented on the floor of the annual meeting of the Human Rights Commission.

34. See *Issues Before the General Assembly* for 1988, 1989, 1990, and 1991 for a careful analysis of the chemistry between working group and rapporteur experts and the countries and themes to which they are assigned.

35. Annual reports are available at the Centre for Human Rights in Geneva and in libraries that are depositories for U.N. documents. See also the annual review of extra-convention procedures in *Issues Before the General Assembly*; *United Nations in Action in the Field of Human Rights*, 1988, pp. 264–282; Alston and Rodriguez-Bustelo, *Taking Stock*, for a critical analysis.

36. Hans Thoolen and Berth Verstappen, *Human Rights Missions: A Study of Fact-Finding Practice of Non-Governmental Organizations* (Boston: Martinus Nijhoff Publishers, 1986). The authors examined some 340 human rights reports and presented

significant conclusions. See also B. G. Ramcharan, *International Law and Fact-Finding in the Field of Human Rights* (Boston: Martinus Nijhoff Publishers, 1982).

37. See *Issues Before the 44th General Assembly of the United Nations*, 1989, pp. 139–158.

38. Gerhard von Glahn, *Law Among Nations*, 5th ed. (New York: Macmillan, 1986), p. 7.

39. See B. G. Ramcharan, "The Good Offices of the United Nations Secretary General in the Field of Human Rights," *American Journal of International Law* (January 1982): 130; *Humanitarian Good Offices in International Law* (Boston: Martinus Nijhoff, 1983); *United Nations in Action*, 1983, p. 297.

40. The 1985 commission condemnation of violations of human rights in Soviet-controlled Afghanistan, backed by solid evidence presented by Special Rapporteur, Professor Felix Ermacora, left no doubt of Soviet culpability with respect to those violations.

41. See von Glahn, *Law Among Nations*, pp. 10, 11. See also *New York Times*, November 13, 1988, for an extensive analysis of the sanctions squeeze on the Republic of South Africa.

42. Margaret Doxey's *International Sanctions in Contemporary Perspective* (New York: St. Martin's Press, 1987) is an excellent study of the coercive, demonstrative, and cultural effects of sanctions, but she cautions on expectations of results. She urges cooperative problem solving, conflict avoidance, and assessment of costs of sanctions, in addition to a careful tailoring of sanctions if and when they are considered necessary. See also Gary Clyde Hufbauer and Jeffrey J. Schoot, *Economic Sanctions Reconsidered: History and Current Policy* (Washington, D.C.: Institute for International Economics, 1985).

43. Jerome Shestack, "Sisyphus Endures: The International Human Rights NGO," *New York Law School Law Review* (1978): 89. See also the roles of the NGOs in Hurst Hannum's *Guide to International Human Rights Practice* (Philadelphia: University of Pennsylvania Press, 1989), edited by the International Human Rights Law Group of Washington, D.C. Human Rights Internet, works with over 2,000 organizations and individuals. Its *Human Rights Internet Reporter* is a comprehensive reference work covering both governmental and nongovernmental activities.

44. In addition to citations above on compliance, see Louis Sohn, "Human Rights: Their Implementation and Supervision by the United Nations," in Meron, *Human Rights in International Law* (Oxford: Clarendon Press, 1984); "Realization of Economic, Social and Cultural Rights" and "Realization of Civil and Political Rights," Parts 7 and 8, *United Nations Action in the Field of Human Rights*, 1988. See also Christine Gray, *Judicial Remedies in International Law* (Oxford: Clarendon Press, 1987).

45. "Advisory Services" in *United Nations Action in the Field of Human Rights*, 1988 p. 341; *Advisory Services and Technical Assistance in the Field of Human Rights*, U.N. Centre for Human Rights, Fact Sheet (monograph) 3, 1988; and *U.N. Assistance for Human Rights*, International Commission of Jurists, Swedish Section, 1988. This is an analysis of present programs and proposals for future development of U.N. advisory services, technical assistance, and information activities in the field of human rights.

APPENDIX: THE CHARTER OF THE UNITED NATIONS

We the peoples of the United Nations determined

to save succeeding generations from the scourge of war, which twice in our lifetime has brought untold sorrow to mankind, and

to reaffirm faith in fundamental human rights, in the dignity and worth of the human person, in the equal rights of men and women and of nations large and small, and

to establish conditions under which justice and respect for the obligations arising from treaties and other sources of international law can be maintained, and

to promote social progress and better standards of life in larger freedom,

and for these ends

to practice tolerance and live together in peace with one another as good neighbors, and

to unite our strength to maintain international peace and security, and

to ensure, by the acceptance of principles and the institution of methods, that armed force shall not be used, save in the common interest, and

to employ international machinery for the promotion of the economic and social advancement to combine our efforts to accomplish these aims.

Accordingly, our respective Governments, through representatives assembled in the city of San Francisco, who have exhibited their full powers found to be in good and due form, have agreed to the present Charter of the United Nations and do hereby establish an international organization to be known as the United Nations.

CHAPTER ONE

Purposes and Principles

Article 1

The purposes of the United Nations are:

1. To maintain international peace and security, and to that end: to take effective collective measure for the prevention and removal of threats to the peace, and for the suppression of acts of aggression or other breaches of the peace, and to bring about by peaceful means, and in conformity with the principles of justice and international law, adjustment or settlement of international disputes or situations which might lead to a breach of the peace;

2. To develop friendly relations among nations based on respect for the principle of equal rights and self-determination of peoples, and to take other appropriate measures to strengthen universal peace;

3. To achieve international cooperation in solving international problems of an economic, social, cultural, or humanitarian character, and in promoting and encouraging respect for human rights and for fundamental freedoms for all without distinction as to race, sex, language, or religion; and

4. To be a center for harmonizing the actions of nations in the attainment of these common ends.

Article 2

The Organization and its Members in pursuit of the Purposes stated in Article 1, shall act in accordance with the following Principles:

1. The Organization is based on the principle of the sovereign equality of all its Members.

2. All Members, in order to ensure to all of them the rights and benefits resulting from membership, shall fulfill in good faith the obligations assumed by them in accordance with the present Charter.

3. All Members shall settle their international disputes by peaceful means in such a manner that international peace and security, and justice, are not endangered.

4. All Members shall refrain in their international relations from the threat or use of force against the territorial integrity or political independence of any state, or in any other manner inconsistent with the Purposes of the United Nations.

5. All Members shall give the United Nations every assistance in any action it takes in accordance with the present Charter, and shall refrain from giving assistance to any state against which the United Nations is taking preventive or enforcement action.

6. The Organization shall ensure that states which are not Members of the United Nations act in accordance with these Principles so far as may be necessary for the maintenance of international peace and security.

7. Nothing contained in the present Charter shall authorize the United Nations to intervene in matters which are essentially within the domestic jurisdiction of any state or shall require the Members to submit such matters to settlement under the present Charter;

but this principle shall not prejudice the application of enforcement measures under Chapter 7.

CHAPTER 2

Membership

Article 3

The original Members of the United Nations shall be the states which, having participated in the United Nations Conference on International Organization at San Francisco, or having previously signed the Declaration by United Nations of January 1, 1942, sign the present Charter and ratify it in accordance with Article 110.

Article 4

1. Membership in the United Nations is open to all other peace-loving states which accept the obligations contained in the present Charter and, in the judgment of the Organization, are able and willing to carry out these obligations.

2. The admission of any such state to membership in the United Nations will be affected by a decision of the General Assembly upon the recommendation of the Security Council.

Article 5

A Member of the United Nations against which preventive or enforcement action has been taken by the Security Council may be suspended from the exercise of the rights and privileges of membership by the General Assembly upon the recommendation of the Security Council. The exercise of these rights and privileges may be restored by the Security Council.

Article 6

A Member of the United Nations which has persistently violated the Principles contained in the present Charter may be expelled from the Organization by the General Assembly upon the recommendation of the Security Council.

CHAPTER 3

Organs

Article 7

1. There are established as the principal organs of the United Nations: a General Assembly, a Security Council, an Economic and Social Council, a Trusteeship Council, an International Court of Justice, and a Secretariat.

2. Such subsidiary organs as may be found necessary may be established in accordance with the present Charter.

Article 8

The United Nations shall place no restriction on the eligibility of men and women to participate in any capacity and under conditions of equality in its principal and subsidiary organs.

CHAPTER 4

The General Assembly
Composition

Article 9

1. The General Assembly shall consist of all the Members of the United Nations.

2. Each Member shall have not more than five representations in the General Assembly.

Functions and Powers

Article 10

The General Assembly may discuss any questions or any matters within the scope of the present Charter or relating to the powers and functions of any organs provided for in the present Charter, and, except as provided in Article 12, may make recommendations to the Members of the United Nations or to the Security Council or to both on any such questions or matters.

Article 11

1. The General Assembly may consider the general principles of cooperation in the maintenance of international peace and security, including the principles governing disarmament and the regulation of armaments, and may make recommendations with regard to such principles to the Members or to the Security Council or to both.

2. The General Assembly may discuss any questions relating to the maintenance of international peace and security brought before it by any Member of the United Nations, or by the Security Council, or by a state which is not a Member of the United Nations in accordance with Article 35, paragraph 2, and, except as provided in Article 12, may make recommendations with regard to any such questions to the state or states concerned or to the Security Council or to both. Any such question on which action is necessary shall be referred to the Security Council by the General Assembly either before or after discussion.

3. The General Assembly may call the attention of the Security Council to situations which are likely to endanger international peace and security.

4. The powers of the General Assembly set forth in this Article shall not limit the general scope of Article 10.

Article 12

1. While the Security Council is exercising in respect of any dispute or situation the functions assigned to it in the present Charter, the General Assembly shall not make any recommendations with regard to that dispute or situation unless the Security Council so requests.

2. The Secretary-General, with the consent of the Security Council, shall notify the General Assembly at each session of any matters relative to the maintenance of international peace and security which are being dealt with by the Security Council and shall similarly notify the General Assembly, or the Members of the United Nations if the General Assembly is not in session, immediately the Security Council ceases to deal with such matters.

Article 13

1. The General Assembly shall initiate studies and make recommendations for the purpose of:

a. promoting international cooperation in the political field and encouraging the progressive development of international law and its codification;

b. promoting international cooperation in the economic, social, cultural, educational, and health fields, and assisting in the realization of human rights and fundamental freedoms for all without distinction as to race, sex, language, or religion.

2. The further responsibilities, functions, and powers of the General Assembly with respect to matters mentioned in paragraph 1(b) above are set forth in Chapters 9 and 10.

Article 14

Subject to the provisions of Article 12, the General Assembly may recommend measures for the peaceful adjustment of any situation, regardless of origin, which it deems likely to impair the general welfare or friendly relations among nations, including situations resulting from a violation of the provisions of the present Charter setting forth the Purposes and Principles of the United Nations.

Article 15

1. The General Assembly shall receive and consider annual and special reports from the Security Council; these reports shall include an account of the measures that the Security Council has decided upon or taken to maintain international peace and security.

2. The General Assembly shall receive and consider reports from the other organs of the United Nations.

Article 16

The General Assembly shall perform such functions with respect to the international trusteeship system as are assigned to it under Chapters 12 and 13, including the approval of the trusteeship agreements for areas not designated as strategic.

Article 17

1. The General Assembly shall consider and approve the budget of the Organization.

2. The expenses of the Organization shall be borne by the Members as apportioned by the General Assembly.

3. The General Assembly shall consider and approve any financial and budgetary arrangements with specialized agencies referred to in Article 57 and shall examine the administrative budgets of such specialized agencies with a view to making recommendations to the agencies concerned.

Voting

Article 18

1. Each member of the General Assembly shall have one vote.

2. Decisions of the General Assembly on important questions shall be made by a two-thirds majority of the members present and voting. These questions shall include: recommendations with respect to the maintenance of international peace and security, the election of the non-permanent members of the Security Council, the election of members of the Trusteeship Council in accordance with paragraph 1 (c) of Article 86, the admission of new Members to the United Nations, the suspension of the rights and privileges of membership, the expulsion of Members, questions relating to the operation of the trusteeship system, and budgetary questions.

3. Decisions on other questions, including the determination of additional categories of questions to be decided by a two-thirds majority, shall be made by a majority of the members present and voting.

Article 19

A Member of the United Nations which is in arrears in the payment of its financial contributions to the Organization shall have no vote in the General Assembly if the amount of its arrears equals or exceeds the amount of the contributions due from it for the preceding two full years. The General Assembly may, nevertheless, permit such a Member to vote if it is satisfied that the failure to pay is due to conditions beyond the control of the Member.

Procedure

Article 20

The General Assembly shall meet in regular annual sessions and in such special sessions as occasion may require. Special sessions shall be convoked by the Secretary-General at the request of the Security Council or of a majority of the Members of the United Nations.

Article 21

The General Assembly shall adopt its own rules of procedure.

It shall elect its president for each session.

Article 22

The General Assembly may establish such subsidiary organs as it deems necessary for the performance of its functions.

CHAPTER 5

The Security Council
Composition

Article 23

1. The Security Council shall consist of fifteen Members of the United Nations. The Republic of China, France, the Union of Soviet Socialist Republics, the United Kingdom of Great Britain and Northern Ireland, and the United States of America shall be permanent members of the Security Council. The General Assembly shall elect ten other Members of the United Nations to be non-permanent members of the Security Council, due regard being specially paid, in the first instance to the contribution of Members of the United Nations to the maintenance of international peace and security and to the other purposes of the Organization, and also to equitable geographical distribution.

2. The non-permanent members of the Security Council shall be elected for a term of two years. In the first election of the non-permanent members after the increase of the membership of the Security Council from eleven to fifteen, two of the four additional members shall be chosen for a term of one year. A retiring member shall not be eligible for immediate reelection.

3. Each member of the Security Council shall have one representative.

Functions and Powers

Article 24

1. In order to ensure prompt and effective action by the United Nations, its Members confer on the Security Council primary responsibility for the maintenance of international peace and security, and agree that in carrying out its duties under this responsibility the Security Council acts on their behalf.

2. In discharging these duties the Security Council shall act in accordance with the Purposes and Principles of the United Nations. The specific powers granted to the Security Council for the discharge of these duties are laid down in Chapters 6, 7, 8, and 12.

3. The Security Council shall submit annual and, when necessary, special reports to the General Assembly for its consideration.

Article 25

The Members of the United Nations agree to accept and carry out the decisions of the Security Council in accordance with the present Charter.

Article 26.

In order to promote the establishment and maintenance of international peace and security with the least diversion for armaments of the world's human and economic resources, the Security Council shall be responsible for formulating, with the assistance of the Military Staff Committee referred to in Article 47, plans to be submitted to the Members of the United Nations for the establishment of a system for the regulation of armaments.

Voting

Article 27

1. Each member of the Security Council shall have one vote.

2. Decisions of the Security Council on procedural matters shall be made by an affirmative vote of nine members.

3. Decisions of the Security Council on all other matters shall be made by an affirmative vote of nine members including the concurring votes of the permanent members, provided that, in decisions under Chapter 6, and under paragraph 3 of Article 52, a party to a dispute shall abstain from voting.

Procedure

Article 28

1. The Security Council shall be so organized as to be able to function continuously. Each member of the Security Council shall for this purpose be represented at all times at the seat of the Organization.

2. The Security Council shall hold periodic meetings at which each of its members may, if it so desires, be represented by a member of the government or by some other specially designated representative.

3. The Security Council may hold meetings at such places other than the seat of the Organization as in its judgment will best facilitate its work.

Article 29

The Security Council may establish such subsidiary organs as it deems necessary for the performance of its functions.

Article 30

The Security Council shall adopt its own rules of procedure, including the method of selecting its President.

Article 31

Any Member of the United Nations which is not a member of the Security Council may participate, without vote, in the discussion of any question brought before the Security Council whenever the latter considers that the interests of that Member are specially affected.

Article 32

Any Member of the United Nations which is not a member of the Security Council or any state which is not a Member of the United Nations, if it is a party to a dispute under consideration by the Security Council, shall be invited to participate, without vote, in the discussion relating to the dispute. The Security Council shall lay down such conditions as it deems just for the participation of a state which is not a Member of the United Nations.

CHAPTER 6

Pacific Settlement of Disputes

Article 33

1. The parties to any dispute, the continuance of which is likely to endanger the maintenance of international peace and security, shall, first of all, seek a solution of negotiation, enquiry, mediation, conciliation, arbitration, judicial settlement, resort to regional agencies or arrangements, or other peaceful means of their own choice.

2. The Security Council shall, when it deems necessary, call upon the parties to settle their dispute by such means.

Article 34

The Security Council may investigate any dispute, or any situation which might lead to international friction or give rise to a dispute, in order to determine whether the continuance of the dispute or situation is likely to endanger the maintenance of international peace and security.

Article 35

1. Any Member of the United Nations may bring any dispute, or any situation of the nature referred to in Article 34, to the attention of the Security Council or of the General Assembly.

2. A state which is not a Member of the United Nations may bring to the attention of the Security Council or of the General Assembly any dispute to which it is a party if it accepts in advance, for the purposes of the dispute, the obligations of pacific settlement provided in the present Charter.

3. The proceedings of the General Assembly in respect of matters brought to its attention under this Article will be subject to the provisions of Articles 11 and 12.

Article 36

1. The Security Council may, at any state of a dispute of the nature referred to in Article 33 or of a situation of like nature, recommend appropriate procedures of methods of adjustment.

2. The Security Council shall take into consideration any procedures for the settlement of the dispute which have already been adopted by the parties.

3. In making recommendations under this Article the Security Council should also take into consideration that legal disputes should as a general rule be referred by the parties to the International Court of Justice in accordance with the provisions of the Statute of the Court.

Article 37

1. Should the parties to a dispute of the nature referred to in Article 33 fail to settle it by the means indicated in that Article, they shall refer it to the Security Council.

2. If the Security Council deems that the continuance of the dispute is in fact likely to endanger the maintenance of international peace and security, it shall decide whether

to take action under Article 36 or to recommend such terms of settlement as it may consider appropriate.

Article 38

Without prejudice to the provisions of Articles 33 to 37, the Security Council may, if all the parties to any dispute so request, make recommendations to the parties with a view to a pacific settlement of the dispute.

CHAPTER 7

Action with Respect to Threats to the Peace, Breaches of the Peace, and Acts of Aggression

Article 39

The Security Council shall determine the existence of any threat to the peace, breach of the peace, or act of aggression and shall make recommendations, or decide what measures shall be taken in accordance with Articles 41 and 42, to maintain or restore international peace and security.

Article 40

In order to prevent an aggravation of the situation, the Security Council may, before making the recommendations or deciding upon the measures provided for in Article 39, call upon the parties concerned to comply with such provisional measures as it deems necessary or desirable. Such provisional measures shall be without prejudice to the rights, claims, or position of the parties concerned. The Security Council shall duly take account of failure to comply with such provisional measures.

Article 41

The Security Council may decide what measures not involving the use of armed force are to be employed to give effect of its decisions, and it may call upon the Members of the United Nations to apply such measures. These may include complete or partial interruption of economic relations and of rail, sea, air, postal, telegraphic, radio, and other means of communication, and the severance of diplomatic relations.

Article 42

Should the Security Council consider that measures provided for in Article 41 would be inadequate or have proved to be inadequate, it may take such action by air, sea, or land forces as may be necessary to maintain or restore international peace and security. Such action may include demonstrations, blockades, and other operations by air, sea, or land forces of Members of the United Nations.

Article 43

1. All Members of the United Nations, in order to contribute to the maintenance of international peace and security, undertake to make available to the Security Council, on its call and in accordance with a special agreement or agreements, armed forces, assistance, and facilities, including rights of passage, necessary for the purpose of maintaining international peace and security.

2. Such agreement or agreements shall govern the numbers and types of forces, their degree of readiness and general location, and the nature of the facilities and assistance to be provided.

3. The agreement or agreements shall be negotiated as soon as possible on the initiative of the Security Council. They shall be concluded between the Security Council and Members or between the Security Council and groups of Members and shall be subject to ratification by the signatory states in accordance with their respective constitutional processes.

Article 44

When the Security Council has decided to use force it shall, before calling upon a Member not represented on it to provide armed forces in fulfillment of the obligations assumed under Article 43, invite the Member, if the Member so desires, to participate in the decisions of the Security Council concerning the employment of contingents of that Member's armed forces.

Article 45

In order to enable the United Nations to take urgent military measures, Members shall hold immediately available national air-force contingents for combined international enforcement action. The strength and degree of readiness of these contingents and plans for their combined action shall be determined, within the limits laid down in the special agreement or agreements referred to in Article 43, by the Security Council with the assistance of the Military Staff Committee.

Article 46

Plans for the application of armed force shall be made by the Security Council with the assistance of the Military Staff Committee.

Article 47

1. There shall be established a Military Staff Committee to advise and assist the Security Council on all questions relating to the Security Council's military requirements for the maintenance of international peace and security, the employment and command of forces placed at its disposal, the regulation of armaments, and possible disarmament.

2. The Military Staff Committee shall consist of the Chiefs of Staff of the permanent members of the Security Council or their representatives. Any Member of the United Nations not permanently represented on the Committee shall be invited by the Committee to be associated with it when the efficient discharge of the Committee's responsibilities requires the participation of that Member in its work.

3. The Military Staff Committee shall be responsible under the Security Council for the strategic direction of any armed forces placed at the disposal of the Security Council. Questions relating to the command of such forces shall be worked out subsequently.

4. The Military Staff Committee, with the authorization of the Security Council and after consultation with appropriate regional agencies, may establish regional subcommittees.

Article 48

1. The action required to carry out the decisions of the Security Council for the maintenance of international peace and security shall be taken by all the Members of the United Nations or by some of them, as the Security Council may determine.

2. Such decisions shall be carried out by the Members of the United Nations directly and through their action in the appropriate international agencies of which they are members.

Article 49

The Members of the United Nations shall join in affording mutual assistance in carrying out the measures decided upon by the Security Council.

Article 50

If preventive or enforcement measures against any state are taken by the Security Council, any other state, whether a Member of the United Nations or not, which finds itself confronted with special economic problems arising from the carrying out of those measures shall have the right to consult the Security Council with regard to a solution of those problems.

Article 51

Nothing in the present Charter shall impair the inherent right of individual or collective self-defense if an armed attack occurs against a Member of the United Nations, until the Security Council has taken the measures necessary to maintain international peace and security. Measures taken by Members in the exercise of this right of self-defense shall be immediately reported to the Security Council and shall not in any way affect the authority and responsibility of the Security Council under the present Charter to take at any time such action as it deems necessary in order to maintain or restore international peace and security.

CHAPTER 8

Regional Arrangements

Article 52

1. Nothing in the present Charter precludes the existence of regional arrangements or agencies for dealing with such matters relating to the maintenance of international peace and security as are appropriate for regional action, provided that such arrangements or agencies and their activities are consistent with the Purposes and Principles of the United Nations.

2. The Members of the United Nations entering into such arrangements or constituting such agencies shall make every effort to achieve pacific settlement on local disputes through such regional arrangements or by such regional agencies before referring them to the Security Council.

3. The Security Council shall encourage the development of pacific settlement of local

disputes through such regional arrangements or by such regional agencies either on the initiative of the states concerned or by reference from the Security Council.

4. This Article in no way impairs the application of Articles 34 and 35.

Article 53

1. The Security Council shall, where appropriate, utilize such regional arrangements or agencies for enforcement action under its authority. But no enforcement action shall be taken under regional arrangements or by regional agencies without the authorization of the Security Council, with the exception of measures against any enemy state, as defined in paragraph 2 of this Article, provided for pursuant to Article 107 or in regional arrangements directed against renewal of aggressive policy on the part of any such state, until such time as the Organization may, on request of the Governments concerned, be charged with the responsibility for preventing further aggression by such a state.

2. The term enemy state as used in paragraph 1 of this Article applies to any state which during the Second World War has been an enemy of any signatory of the present Charter.

Article 54

The Security Council shall at all times be kept fully informed of activities undertaken or in contemplation under regional arrangements or by regional agencies for the maintenance of international peace and security.

CHAPTER 9

International Economic and Social Cooperation

Article 55

With a view of the creation of conditions of stability and well-being which are necessary for peaceful and friendly relations among nations based on respect for the principle of equal rights and self-determination of peoples, the United Nations shall promote:

a. higher standards of living, full employment, and conditions of economic and social progress and development;

b. solutions of international economic, social, health, and related problems; and international cultural and educational cooperation; and

c. universal respect for, and observance of, human rights and fundamental freedoms for all without distinction as to race, sex, language, or religion.

Article 56

All Members pledge themselves to take joint and separate action in cooperation with the Organization for the achievement of the purposes set forth in Article 55.

Article 57

1. The various agencies, established by intergovernmental agreement and having wide international responsibilities, as defined in their basic instruments, in economic, social,

cultural, educational, health, and related fields, shall be brought into relationship with the United Nations in accordance with the provisions of Article 63.

2. Such agencies thus brought into relationship with the United Nations are hereinafter referred to as specialized agencies.

Article 58

The Organization shall make recommendations for the coordination of the policies and activities of the specialized agencies.

Article 59

The Organization shall, where appropriate, initiate negotiations among the states concerned for the creation of any new specialized agencies required for the accomplishment of the purposes set forth in Article 55.

Article 60

Responsibility for the discharge of the functions of the Organization set forth in this Chapter shall be vested in the General Assembly and, under the authority of the General Assembly, in the Economic and Social Council, which shall have for this purpose the powers set forth in Chapter 10.

CHAPTER 10

The Economic and Social Council
Composition

Article 61

1. The Economic and Social Council shall consist of fifty-four members of the United Nations elected by the General Assembly.

2. Subject to the provisions of paragraph 3, eighteen members of the Economic and Social Council shall be elected each year for a term of three years. A retiring member shall be eligible for immediate re-election.

3. At the first election after the increase in the membership of the Economic and Social Council from twenty-seven to fifty-four members, in addition to the members elected in place of the nine members whose term of office expires at the end of that year, twenty-seven additional members shall be elected. Of these twenty-seven additional members, the term of office of nine members so elected shall expire at the end of one year, and of nine other members at the end of two years, in accordance with arrangements made by the General Assembly.

4. Each member of the Economic and Social Council shall have one representative.

Functions and Powers

Article 62

1. The Economic and Social Council may make or initiate studies and reports with respect to international economic, social, cultural, educational, health, and related matters

and may make recommendations with respect to any such matters to the General Assembly, to the Members of the United Nations, and to the specialized agencies concerned.

2. It may make recommendations for the purpose of promoting respect for, and observance of, human rights and fundamental freedoms for all.

3. It may prepare draft conventions for submission to the General Assembly, with respect to matters falling within its competence.

4. It may call, in accordance with the rules prescribed by the United Nations, international conferences on matters falling within its competence.

Article 63

1. The Economic and Social Council may enter into agreements with any of the agencies referred to in Article 57, defining the term on which the agency concerned shall be brought into relationship with the United Nations. Such agreements shall be subject to approval by the General Assembly and to the Members of the United Nations.

Article 64

1. The Economic and Social Council may take appropriate steps to obtain regular reports from the specialized agencies. It may make arrangements with the Members of the United Nations and with the specialized agencies to obtain reports on the steps taken to give effect to its own recommendations and to recommendations on matters falling within its competence made by the General Assembly.

Article 65

The Economic and Social Council may furnish information to the Security Council and shall assist the Security Council upon its request.

Article 66

1. The Economic and Social Council shall perform such functions as fall within its competence in connection with the carrying out of the recommendations of the General Assembly.

Voting

Article 67

1. Each member of the Economic and Social Council shall have one vote.

2. Decisions of the Economic and Social Council shall be made by a majority of the members present and voting.

Procedure

Article 68

The Economic and Social Council shall set up commissions in economic and social fields and for the promotion of human rights, and such other commissions as may be required for the performance of its functions.

Article 69

The Economic and Social Council shall invite any Member of the United Nations to participate, without vote, in its deliberations on any matter of particular concern to that Member.

Article 70

The Economic and Social Council may make arrangements for representatives of the specialized agencies to participate, without vote, in its deliberations and in those of the commissions established by it, and for its representatives to participate in the deliberations of the specialized agencies.

Article 71

The Economic and Social Council may make suitable arrangements for consultation with non-governmental organizations which are concerned with matters within its competence. Such arrangements may be made with international organizations and, where appropriate, with national organizations after consultation with the Member of the United Nations concerned.

Article 72

1. The Economic and Social Council shall adopt its own rules and procedure, including the method of selecting its President.

2. The Economic and Social Council shall meet as required in accordance with its rules, which shall include provision for the convening of meetings on the request of a majority of its members.

CHAPTER 11

Declaration Regarding Non–Self-Governing Territories

Article 73

Members of the United Nations which have or assume responsibilities for the administration of territories whose people have not yet attained a full measure of self-government recognize the principle that the interests of the inhabitants of these territories are paramount, and accept as a sacred trust the obligation to promote to the utmost, within the system of international peace and security established by the present Charter, the well-being of the inhabitants of these territories, and, to this end:

a. to ensure with due respect for the culture of the peoples concerned, their political, economic, social, and educational advancement, their just treatment, and their protection against abuses;

b. to develop self-government, to take due account of the political aspirations of the peoples, and to assist them in the progressive development of their free political institutions, according to the particular circumstances of each territory and its peoples and their varying stages of advancement;

c. to further international peace and security;

d. to promote constructive measures of development, to encourage research, and to cooperate with one another, and, when and where appropriate, with specialized international bodies with a view to the practical achievement of the social, economic, and scientific purposes set forth in this Article; and

e. to transmit regularly to the Secretary-General for information purposes, subject to such limitation as security and constitutional considerations may require, statistical and other information of a technical nature relating to economic, social, and educational conditions in the territories for which they are respectively responsible other than those territories to which Chapters 12 and 13 apply.

Article 74

Members of the United Nations also agree that their policy in respect of the territories to which this Chapter applies, no less than in respect of their metropolitan areas, must be based on the general principle of good-neighborliness, due account being taken of the interests and well-being of the rest of the world, in social, economic, and commercial matters.

CHAPTER 12

International Trusteeship System

Article 75

The United Nations shall establish under its authority an international trusteeship system for the administration and supervision of such territories as may be placed thereunder by subsequent individual agreements. These territories are hereinafter referred to as trust territories.

The basic objectives of the trusteeship system, in accordance with the Purposes of the United Nations laid down in Article 1 of the present Charter, shall be:

Article 76

a. to further international peace and security;

b. to promote the political, economic, social, and educational advancement of the in-habitants of the trust territories, and their progressive development towards self-government or independence as may be appropriate to the particular circumstances of each territory and its peoples and the freely expressed wishes of the people concerned, and as may be provided by the terms of each trusteeship agreement;

c. to encourage respect for human rights and for fundamental freedoms for all without distinction as to race, sex, language, or religion, and to encourage recognition of the interdependence of the peoples of the world; and

d. to ensure equal treatment in social, economic, and commercial matters for all Members of the United Nations and their nationals, and also equal treatment for the latter in the administration of justice, without prejudice to the attainment of the foregoing objectives and subject to the provision of Article 80.

Article 77

1. The trusteeship system shall apply to such territories in the following categories as may be placed thereunder by means of trusteeship agreements:

a. territories now held under mandate;

b. territories which may be detached from enemy states as a result of the Second World War; and

c. territories voluntarily placed under the system by states responsible for their administration.

2. It will be a matter for subsequent agreement as to which territories in the foregoing categories will be brought under the trusteeship system and upon what terms.

Article 78

The trusteeship system shall not apply to territories which have become Members of the United Nations, relationship among which shall be based on respect for the principle of sovereign equality.

Article 79

The terms of trusteeship for each territory to be placed under the trusteeship system, including any alteration or amendments, shall be agreed upon by the states directly concerned, including the mandatory power in the case of territories held under mandate by a Member of the United Nations, and shall be approved as provided for in Articles 83 and 85.

Article 80

1. Except as may be agreed upon in individual trusteeship agreements, made under Articles 77, 79, and 81, placing each territory under the trusteeship system, and until such agreements have been concluded, nothing in this Chapter shall be construed in or of itself to alter in any manner the rights whatsoever of any states or any peoples or the terms of existing international instruments to which Members of the United Nations may respectively be parties.

2. Paragraph 1 of this Article shall not be interpreted as giving grounds for delay or postponement of the negotiation and conclusion of agreements for placing mandated and other territories under the trusteeship system as provided for in Article 77.

Article 81

The trusteeship agreement shall in each case include the terms under which the trust territory will be administered and designate the authority which will exercise the administration of the trust territory. Such authority, hereinafter called the administering authority, may be one or more states or the Organization itself.

Article 82

There may be designated, in any trusteeship agreement, a strategic area or areas which may include part or all of the trust territory to which the agreement applies, without prejudice to any special agreement or agreements made under Article 43.

Article 83

1. All functions of the United Nations relating to strategic areas, including the approval of the terms of the trusteeship agreement and of their alteration or amendment, shall be exercised by the Security Council.

2. The basic objectives set forth in Article 76 shall be applicable to the people of each strategic area.

3. The Security Council shall, subject to the provisions of the trusteeship agreements and without prejudice to security considerations, avail itself of the assistance of the trusteeship Council to perform those functions of the United Nations under the trusteeship system relating to political, economic, social, and educational matters in the strategic areas.

Article 84

It shall be the duty of the administering authority to ensure that the trust territory shall play its part in the maintenance of international peace and security. To this end the administering authority may make use of volunteer forces, facilities, and assistance from the trust territory in carrying out the obligations towards the Security Council undertaken in this regard by the administering authority, as well as for local defense and the maintenance of law and order within the trust territory.

Article 85

1. The functions of the United Nations with regard to trusteeship agreements for all areas not designated as strategic, including the approval of the terms of the trusteeship agreements and of their alteration or amendment, shall be exercised by the General Assembly.

2. The Trusteeship Council, operating under the authority of the General Assembly, shall assist the General Assembly in carrying out these functions.

CHAPTER 13

The Trusteeship Council
Composition

Article 86

1. The Trusteeship Council shall consist of the following Members of the United Nations:

a. those Members administering trust territories;

b. such of those Members mentioned by name in Article 23 as are not administering trust territories; and

c. as many other Members elected for three-year terms by the General Assembly as may be necessary to ensure that the total number of members of the Trusteeship Council is equally divided between those Members of the United Nations which administer trust territories and those which do not.

2. Each member of the Trusteeship Council shall designate one specially qualified person to represent it therein.

Functions and Powers

Article 87

The General Assembly and, under its authority, the Trusteeship Council, in carrying out their functions, may:

a. consider reports submitted by the administering authority;

b. accept petitions and examine them in consultation with the administering authority;

c. provide for periodic visits to the respective trust territories at times agreed upon with the administering authority; and

d. take these and other actions in conformity with the terms of the trusteeship agreements.

Article 88

The Trusteeship Council shall formulate a questionnaire on the political, economic, social, and educational advancement of the inhabitants of each trust territory, and the administering authority for each trust territory within the competence of the General Assembly shall make an annual report to the General Assembly upon the basis of such questionnaire.

Voting

Article 89

1. Each member of the Trusteeship Council shall have one vote.

2. Decisions of the Trusteeship Council shall be made by a majority of the members present and voting.

Procedure

Article 90

1. The Trusteeship Council shall adopt its own rules of procedure, including the method of selecting its President.

2. The Trusteeship Council shall meet as required in accordance with its rules, which shall include provision for the convening of meetings on the request of a majority of its members.

Article 91

The Trusteeship Council shall, when appropriate, avail itself of the assistance of the Economic and Social Council and of the specialized agencies in regard to matters with which they are respectively concerned.

CHAPTER 14

The International Court of Justice

Article 92

The International Court of Justice shall be the principal judicial organ of the United Nations. It shall function in accordance with the annexed Statute, which is based upon the statute of the Permanent Court of International Justice and forms an integral part of the present Charter.

Article 93

1. All Members of the United Nations are ipso facto parties to the Statute of the International Court of Justice.

2. A state which is not a Member of the United Nations may become a party to the Statute of the International Court of Justice on conditions to be determined in each case by the General Assembly upon the recommendation of the Security Council.

Article 94

1. Each member of the United Nations undertakes to comply with the decision of the International Court of Justice in any case to which it is a party.

2. If any party to a case fails to perform the obligations incumbent upon it under a judgment rendered by the Court, the other party may have recourse to the Security Council, which may, if it deems necessary, make recommendations or decide upon measures to be taken to give effect to the judgment.

Article 95

Nothing in the present Charter shall prevent Members of the United Nations from entrusting the solution of their differences to other tribunals by virtue of agreements already in existence or which may be concluded in the future.

Article 96

1. The General Assembly or the Security Council may request the International Court of Justice to give an advisory opinion on any legal question.

2. Other organs of the United Nations and specialized agencies, which may at any time be so authorized by the General Assembly, may also request advisory opinions of the Court on legal questions arising within the scope of their activities.

CHAPTER 15

The Secretariat

Article 97

The Secretariat shall comprise a Secretary-General and such staff as the Organization may require. The Secretary-General shall be appointed by the General Assembly upon the recommendation of the Security Council. He shall be the chief administrative officer of the Organization.

Article 98

The Secretary-General shall act in that capacity in all meetings of the General Assembly, of the Security Council, of the Economic and Social Council and of the Trusteeship Council, and shall perform such other functions as are entrusted to him by these organs. The Secretary-General shall make an annual report to the General Assembly on the work of the Organization.

Article 99

The Secretary-General may bring to the attention of the Security Council any matter which in his opinion may threaten the maintenance of international peace and security.

Article 100

1. In the performance of their duties the Secretary-General and the staff shall not seek or receive instructions from any government or from any other authority external to the Organization. They shall refrain from any action which might reflect on their position as international officials responsible only to the Organization.

2. Each Member of the United Nations undertakes to respect the exclusively international character of the responsibilities of the Secretary-General and the staff and not to seek to influence them in the discharge of their responsibilities.

Article 101

1. The staff shall be appointed by the Secretary-General under regulations established by the General Assembly.

2. Appropriate staffs shall be permanently assigned to the Economic and Social Council, the Trusteeship Council, and, as required, to other organs of the United Nations. These staffs shall form a part of the Secretariat.

3. The paramount consideration in the employment of the staff and in the determination of the conditions of service shall be the necessity of securing the highest standards of efficiency, competence, and integrity. Due regard shall be paid to the importance of recruiting the staff on as wide a geographical basis as possible.

CHAPTER 16

Miscellaneous Provisions

Article 102

1. Every treaty and every international agreement entered into by any Member of the United Nations after the present Charter comes into force shall as soon as possible be registered with the Secretariat and published by it.

2. No party to any such treaty or international agreement which has not been registered in accordance with the provisions of paragraph 1 of this Article may invoke that treaty or agreement before any organ of the United Nations.

Article 103

In the event of a conflict between the obligations of the Members of the United Nations under the present Charter and their obligations under any other international agreement, their obligations under the present Charter shall prevail.

Article 104

The Organization shall enjoy in the territory of each of its Members such legal capacity as may be necessary for the exercise of its functions and the fulfillment of its purposes.

Article 105

1. The Organization shall enjoy in the territory of each of its Members such privileges and immunities as are necessary for the fulfillment of its purposes.

2. Representatives of the Members of the United Nations and officials of the Orga-

nization shall similarly enjoy such privileges and immunities as are necessary for the independent exercise of their functions in connection with the Organization.

3. The General Assembly may make recommendations with a view to determining the details of the application of paragraphs 1 and 2 of this Article or may propose conventions to the Members of the United Nations for this purpose.

CHAPTER 17

Transitional Security Arrangements

Article 106

Pending the coming into force of such special agreements referred to in Article 43 as in the opinion of the Security Council enable it to begin the exercise of its responsibilities under Article 42, the parties to the Four-Nation Declaration, signed at Moscow, October 30, 1943, and France, shall in accordance with the provisions of paragraph 5 of that Declaration, consult with one another and as occasion requires with other Members of the United Nations with a view to such joint action on behalf of the Organization as may be necessary for the purpose of maintaining international peace and security.

Article 107

Nothing in the present Charter shall invalidate or preclude action, in relation to any state which during the Second World War has been an enemy of any signatory to the present Charter, taken or authorized as a result of that war by the Governments having responsibility for such action.

CHAPTER 18

Amendments

Article 108

Amendments to the present Charter shall come into force for all Members of the United Nations when they have been adopted by a vote of two-thirds of the members of the General Assembly and ratified in accordance with their respective constitutional processes by two-thirds of the Members of the United Nations, including all the permanent members of the Security Council.

Article 109

1. A General Conference of the Members of the United Nations for the purpose of reviewing the present Charter may be held at a date and place to be fixed by a two-thirds vote of the members of the General Assembly and by a vote of any nine members of the Security Council. Each Member of the United Nations shall have one vote in the conference.

2. Any alteration of the present Charter recommended by a two-thirds vote of the conference shall take effect when ratified in accordance with their respective constitutional processes by two-thirds of the Members of the United Nations including all the permanent members of the Security Council.

3. If such a conference has not been held before the tenth annual session of the General Assembly following the coming into force of the present Charter, the proposal to call such a conference shall be placed on the agenda of that session of the General Assembly, and the conference shall be held if so decided by a majority vote of the members of the General Assembly and by a vote of any seven members of the Security Council.

CHAPTER 19

Ratification and Signature

Article 110

1. The present Charter shall be ratified by the signatory states in accordance with their respective constitutional processes.

2. The ratifications shall be deposited with the Government of the United States of America, which shall notify all the signatory states of each deposit as well as the Secretary-General of the Organization when he has been appointed.

3. The present Charter shall come into force upon the deposit of ratifications by the Republic of China, France, the Union of Soviet Socialist Republics, the United Kingdom of Great Britain and Northern Ireland, and the United States of America, and by a majority of the other signatory states. A protocol of the ratifications deposited shall thereupon be drawn up by the Government of the United States of America which shall communicate copies thereof to all the signatory states.

4. The states signatory to the present Charter which ratify it after it has come into force will become original Members of the United Nations on the date of the deposit of their respective ratifications.

Article 111

The present Charter, of which the Chinese, French, Russian, English, and Spanish texts are equally authentic, shall remain deposited in the archives of the Government of the United States of America. Duly certified copies thereof shall be transmitted by that Government to the Governments of the other signatory states.

IN FAITH WHEREOF the representatives of the Governments of the United Nations have signed the present Charter.

DONE at the city of San Francisco the twenty-sixth day of June, one thousand nine hundred and forty-five.

ANNOTATED BIBLIOGRAPHY

International Organizations, Constitutional Law, and Human Rights lends itself to a three-fold division of the bibliography—international organizations, international constitutional law, and human rights. Many of the titles speak for themselves while we have added a sentence or two to listings that require a brief description. Although the studies cited bring us into the early 1990s, many more are constantly being published in addition to the constant flow of primary and secondary resources on many dimensions of international organizations and especially U.N. activities in the domain of international human rights law.

There is no claim to a comprehensive bibliography in three interrelated fields. Undoubtedly there are more primary and secondary resources not included here. Outstanding professional quarterlies such as *The American Journal of International Law* and *International Organization* are only two of many other scholarly publications that are required reading for the serious student.

The author is most grateful to the professional staff of the Ginn Library of the Tufts Fletcher School of Law and Diplomacy and especially to Ms. Ellen McDonald for excellence in guiding the author through the maze of references and the mysteries of computer retrieval. Clearly the scope of references in this bibliography suggests the breadth of the subject matter at hand.

INTERNATIONAL ORGANIZATIONS

Some basic reference works include:

Edmund Jan Osmanczyk, *Encyclopedia of the United Nations and International Agreements* (New York: Taylor and Francis, 1990) for an indispensable collection of references and resources on all dimensions of international organizations.

Louis Sohn, ed., *International Organization and Integration* (Boston: Martinus Nijhoff, 1986), for well over 100 international organization constitutions, conventions, and resolutions.

Union of International Associations, Brussels, *Yearbook of International Organiza-tions*, 27th ed. (Munich and New York: K.G. Saur, 1990–1991). Three volumes with listing of hundreds of international organizations and their addresses.

Sources of primary and secondary resources include:

Academic Council of the United Nations System (ACUNS), 207 Baker Library, Dart-mouth College, Hanover, NH, 03755, (603) 646–2023, for current studies of the U.N. system. A recent and valuable ACUNS study is Johan Kaufmann and Nico Schrijver, *Changing Global Needs: Expanding Roles for the United Na-tions System* (Hanover, NH: Academic Council on the United Nations System, 1990).

United Nations Publications, Department of Public Information, United Nations, New York, NY 10017, for catalogues of publications as well as publications on all aspects of organizations in the U.N. system. United Nations Association of the United States of America, 485 Fifth Avenue, New York, NY 10017 (212) 547–3232 for important U.N. studies as well as U.N. Associations in major U.S. cities.

Some leading studies on the United Nations and international organizations include:

David Armstrong, *The Rise of International Organizations: A Short History* (London: Macmillan, 1982).

Leland M. Goodrich, Edward Hambro, and Anne Patricia Simons, *Charter of the United Nations: Commentary and Documents* (New York: Columbia University Press, 1969), for origins and analysis of each Charter article to 1969.

Issues before the 46th General Assembly of the United Nations (Lexington, MA: Lexington Books, 1992).

Evan Luard, *The United Nations: How It Works and What It Does* (New York: St. Martin's Press, 1989).

Resolutions and Decisions Adopted by the General Assembly of the United Nations for its annual sessions (U.N. Department of Public Information, United Nations, New York, NY 10017).

Paul Taylor and A.J.R. Groom, eds., *Global Issues in the United Nations Framework* (New York: St. Martin's Press, 1989).

United Nations Handbook (Wellington, New Zealand: New Zealand Ministry of Foreign Affairs, 1988). This handbook is on the desks of international civil servants as it has a complete listing of state members of all organizations in the U.N. system.

F.P. Walters, *A History of the League of Nations* (New York: Oxford University Press, 1969/reprint), the best single volume on organization and policies of the League.

Douglas Williams, *The Specialized Agencies and the United Nations: The System in Crisis* (New York: St. Martin's Press, 1987) for an informative appraisal of the other organizations in the total U.N. system.

Some important textbooks on international organizations include:

A. Leroy Bennett, *International Organizations: Principles and Issues,* 5th ed. (En-glewood Cliffs, NJ: Prentice-Hall, 1991).

Paul F. Diehl, ed., *The Politics of International Organizations: Patterns and Insights* (Chicago: Dorsey Press, 1989).

Werner Feld and Robert Jordan, *International Organizations: A Comparative Approach* (New York: Praeger, 1988).

Lawrence S. Finklestein, *Politics in the United Nations System* (Durham, NC: Duke University Press, 1988).

Robert E. Riggs and Jack Plano, *The United Nations: International Organizations and World Politics* (Chicago: The Dorsey Press, 1988).

Current studies for issues in the early 1990s include:

G. R. Berridge, *Return to the UN: UN Diplomacy in Regional Conflicts* (New York: St. Martin's Press, 1991). Focus is on increased efficacy of the United Nations with new superpower cooperation and top level diplomacy by Secretary General Perez de Cuellar.

Arthur A. Stein, *Why Nations Cooperate: Circumstance and Choice in International Relations* (Ithaca: Cornell University Press, 1990). A study of modes and structures for international cooperation for the 1990s.

The United Nations in the Gulf Crisis: Options for U.S. Policy and *Roles for the United Nations After the Gulf War* (New York: United Nations Association of the United States, 1991).

INTERNATIONAL LAW

Treaties are basic to international law. Key sources include the United Nations Treaty Series, United Nations, New York, NY, and on deposit in many university libraries for the most comprehensive collection of international treaty law. Sohn's *International Organization and Integration* cited often in this study contains the best collection of founding constitutions of international organizations—the principal source of international constitutional law. See also collections by states such as the United States Treaty Series, Department of State, Washington, DC, and at other libraries, especially at law schools.

Some basic primary and secondary resources in international law include:

Antonio Cassese, *International Law in a Divided World* (Oxford: Clarendon Press, 1986), for a penetrating study by a leading European scholar (University of Florence).

Anthony D'Amato, *International Law: Process and Prospect* (Dobbs Ferry, NY: Transnational Publishers, 1987), for human rights as entitlements and norms of customary international law.

Richard Falk, Friedrich Kratochwil, and Saul Mendlovitz, eds., *International Law: A Contemporary Perspective* (Boulder, CO: Westview Press, 1985).

Thomas Franck, *The Power of Legitimacy Among Nations* (New York: Oxford University Press, 1990) for nations holding international law as legitimate and essential for their many and varied interests.

A.J.R. Groom and Paul Taylor, eds., *Frameworks for International Cooperation* (New York: St. Martin's Press, 1990), for a sound appraisal of theoretical foundations of international organization and integration, especially in functionalism and neofunctionalism.

M. Hamalengwa, C. Flinterman, and E.V.O. Dankwa, *The International Law of Human Rights in Africa* (Boston: Martinus Nijhoff, 1988), for treaties and arrangements annotated by African scholars.

Louis Henkin, Richard C. Pugh, Oscar Schachter, and Hans Smit, *International Law: Cases and Materials* (St. Paul: West Publishing Company, 1980).

Mark W. Janis, *An Introduction to International Law* (Boston: Little, Brown & Co., 1988).

Frits Kalshoven, *Constraints on the Waging of War* (Geneva: International Committee of the Red Cross, 1987), for substance and application of the Hague and Geneva conventions on international humanitarian law.

Frederic L. Kirgis, Jr., *International Organizations in Their Legal Setting: Documents, Comments, and Questions* (St. Paul: West Publishing Co., 1977).

Jessica Tuchman Mathews, ed., *Preserving the Global Environment: The Challenge of Shared Leadership* (New York: W.W. Norton & Co., 1991), co-sponsored by the American Assembly and the World Resources Institute, is a pioneering collection of papers on the international legal response to transnational environmental villains.

Theodore Meron, ed., *Human Rights in International Law: Legal and Policy Issues* (Oxford: Clarendon Press, 1984), for one of the best collection by outstanding scholars of the basic categories of human rights and human rights law.

Daniel Patrick Moynihan, *On the Law of Nations* (Cambridge: Harvard University Press, 1990), for the imperative for nations to base their foreign relations on international law.

Adam Roberts and Richard Guelff, *Documents on the Laws of War* (Oxford: Clarendon Press, 1982). This collection includes the four Geneva Conventions of 1949 and the two Geneva Protocols of 1977 which comprise the modern body of international humanitarian law.

Paul Sieghart, *The International Law of Human Rights* (Oxford: Clarendon Press, 1983), for historic development and domestic effect of international human rights conventions as well as an excellent bibliography.

Waldemar A. Solf and J. Ashley Roach, eds., *Index of International Humanitarian Law* (Geneva: International Committee of the Red Cross, 1987).

Gerhard von Glahn, *Law Among Nations,* 5th ed. (New York: Macmillan Publishing Co., 1986).

Burns H. Weston, Richard A. Falk, and Anthony A. D'Amato, *International Law and World Order,* 2d ed. (St. Paul: West Publishing Co. 1990).

HUMAN RIGHTS

A prime source for authoritative publications is the United Nations Centre for Human Rights at 8–14, Avenue de la Paix, Geneva, and at the United Nations, New York. The Centre's Division of External Relations and its Publication and Documentation Section have been cited for important human rights resources as well as such periodic publications as the Human Rights Newsletter.

United Nations Action in the Field of Human Rights (New York: United Nations, 1988) is the most recent publication of this indispensable volume of official U.N. documents and developments in human rights.

Yearbook on Human Rights (New York: United Nations, 1989) is another basic source for official U.N. action in human rights from the first volume in 1946 through the most recent in 1984.

Two important collections are *Human Rights: A Compilation of International Instruments* (New York: United Nations, 1988), which includes 67 human rights conventions adopted through 1987, and *Human Rights: Status of International Instruments* (New York: United Nations, 1987) for the status and reservations of 22 major human rights conventions.

Two important studies which have extensive bibliographical references to publications, resources, organizations, human rights procedures, national governments, and other important information are Albert Blaustein, Roger S. Clark, and Jay Sigler, *Human Rights Sourcebook* (New York: Paragon House Publishers, 1987) and Julian Friedman and Marc Sherman, *Human Rights: An International and Comparative Law Bibliography* (Westport, Conn.: Greenwood Press, 1985). *The Human Rights Library: Amnesty International, 1990* (New York: Amnesty International, 322 8th Avenue, New York, NY 10001) is the basic catalogue for Amnesty publications, including listings for its authoritative country reports.

Human Rights Internet, Human Rights Centre, University of Ottawa, 57 Louis Pasteur, Ottawa, Ontario, K1N6N5, Canada, (613) 564–3492 is the location of the best global collection of human rights information. Its principal publication is the quarterly *Human Rights Internet Reporter* with complete listings of publications, research, conferences, nongovernmental organizations, and other developments. It also has published directories for all regions of the world. The *Human Rights Internet Reporter MasterList of Human Rights Organizations and Serial Publications*, Spring 1989, is indispensible to student and scholar alike. *Human Rights Documents* is a major research collection on microfiche with inputs from over 200 nongovernmental organizations.

Some leading studies include:

J.A. Andrews and W.D. Hines, *International Protection of Human Rights* (New York: Facts on File, 460 Park Avenue South, 10016), for extensive information and bibliographical sources including lists of nongovernmental organizations and their addresses.

Abdullahi A. An-Na'im and Francis M. Deng, *Human Rights in Africa* (Washington: The Brookings Institution, 1990).

Jan Beating et al., eds., *Human Rights in a Pluralistic World: Individuals and Collectivities* (Westport & London: Meckler Corporation, 1990). Published in cooperation with UNESCO, this volume is basic to the concept of cultural relativism in human rights.

Thomas Buergenthal, *International Human Rights in a Nutshell* (St. Paul: West Publishing Co., 1988), for a most readable and concise reference work.

David Louis Cingranelli, ed., *Human Rights Theory and Measurement* (New York: St. Martin's Press, 1988), for a modest quantitative approach to human rights policy and law.

Richard Pierre Claude and Burns H. Weston, eds., *Human Rights in the World Community: Issues and Action* (Philadelphia: University of Pennsylvania Press, 1989), for a comprehensive appraisal of contemporary human rights law and especially law implementation.

Country Reports on Human Rights Practices for 1990 (Washington, DC: Department of State, 1991) is the fourteenth annual report by the Department to Congress on human rights practices in most other nations with extensive commentary.

Jack Donnelly and Rhoda E. Howard, *International Handbook of Human Rights* (New York: Greenwood Press, 1987), for a review of human rights in selected nations from the United States to Uganda and a fourteen-page bibliography.

Hurst Hannum, *Guide to International Human Rights Practice* (Philadelphia: University of Philadelphia Press, 1986), is a key source book for students and practitioners at all levels.

Hurst Hannum, with Ellen Lutz and Kathryn Burke, *New Directions in Human Rights* (Philadelphia: University of Pennsylvania Press, 1989).

Charles Humana, *World Human Rights Guide* (New York: Facts on File/Economist, 1986), for specific country protection of personal and legal rights.

Rhoda B. Howard, *Human Rights in Commonwealth Africa* (Totawa, NJ: Rowman & Littlefield, 1986).

John Humphrey, *No Distant Millennium: The International Law of Human Rights* (Paris: UNESCO, 1989), for a very authentic history of human rights law by the first director of the U.N. Division of Human Rights. A companion volume to Professor Humphrey's *Human Rights and the United Nations,* cited in Chapter 6.

International Commission of Jurists, P.O. Box 120, Ch1224, Geneva, Switzerland. Also the American Association International Commission of Jurists (AAICJ), 777 United Nations Plaza, New York, NY 10017, for many valuable primary and secondary resources and publications on all dimensions of human rights.

Richard B. Lillich, *International Human Rights: Problems of Law, Policy and Process* (Cincinnati: Anderson Publishing Co., 1990), for a study by one of the most authoritative scholars of international law.

Frank Newman and David Weissbrodt, *International Human Rights: Law, Policy and Process* (Cincinnati: Anderson Publishing Co., 1990), for the most thorough volume on international human rights available as well as a thirty-page bibliography and reference section.

A.H. Robertson, as revised by J.G. Merrills, *Human Rights in the World: An Introduction to the Study of the International Protection of Human Rights* (Manchester: Manchester University Press, 1989).

Eric Sottas, *The Least Developed Countries: Development and Human Rights* (Geneva: World Organization Against Torture, 1990), for perhaps the best review of obstacles to enhancement of human rights in the most disadvantaged nations, including infliction of torture.

ON TEACHING AND DIPLOMACY

Asbjorn Eide and Marek Thee, eds., *Frontiers of Human Rights Education* (Oslo: Universiteforglaget, 1983); *The Teaching of Human Rights: Report of an International Seminar* (Geneva: U.N. Centre for Human Rights, 1989) and *United Nations Action in the Field of Human Rights* (New York: United Nations, 1988), Section K, "Teaching about Human Rights." The U.N. Centre for Human Rights Divisions of External Relations has specific responsibilities for global education on all dimensions of human rights.

Finally, *Negotiating World Order: The Artisanship and Architecture of Global Diplomacy* edited by Alan K. Henrikson of the Fletcher School of Law and Diplomacy (Wilmington, DE: Scholarly Resources Inc., 1986) is a collection of papers by leading scholars which provides exciting insights into the construction of world order. The protection and enhancement of human rights are an indispensable component of any genuine world order but diplomacy and dedication, woven into the chapters of this book, are likewise indispensable for the reality of the dignity and value of all humans everywhere.

INDEX

About the Author

JOHN S. GIBSON is Professor of Political Science at Tufts University, and Director of Tufts Program in International Relations. A graduate of Oberlin College, he received his Ph.D. in international law and comparative jurisprudence at Columbia University, where he served as research assistant in international organizations to Professor Leland Goodrich. His internship at the United Nations in 1951 led to his career involvement in international organizations in academia, scholarship, and the United Nations Commission on Human Rights. Dr. Gibson has been at Tufts since 1963 as Professor, Director of the Lincoln Filene Center, and the author and first Director of the International Relations Program. He gave annual seminars on international organizations at the United Nations in Geneva in the 1980s and continues to serve as official observer and consultant to the Commission on Human Rights.